THE
GOOD BEER
BOOK

Brewing and Drinking
Quality Ales and Lagers

Timothy Harper and Garrett Oliver

BERKLEY BOOKS, NEW YORK

Contents

Acknowledgments

THE AUTHORS WOULD LIKE TO ACKNOWLEDGE the help of more people than could possibly be listed in this limited space, including literally hundreds of folks from the craft brewing industry: brewers, entrepreneurs, investors, salespeople, distributors, administrators, clerical help, bartenders, servers, event organizers and many more. We'd say you all know who you are, but in truth we had considerable help from many people who probably didn't even realize their significance to this project.

We'd specifically like to thank Jessica Faust, who came up with the idea for this book, recruited us to do it and then showed great patience and skill in guiding us through the editorial process in much the same way a master brewer shepherds a special beer through the brewing process. If you appreciate the balance and complexity, the fizz and the bite of the book we have brewed together, Jessica deserves much of the credit.

We'd also like to thank Steve Hindy, the president of the Brooklyn Brewery and a not-quite-reformed journalist who encouraged us when we needed it and gave us solid editorial advice when we needed that, too. Michael Jackson provided his usual gracious support from both far and near. For further reading on beer, we enthusiastically recommend any and all of his books.

Garrett Oliver would also like to thank the crew at the Brooklyn Brewery, all the folks from the New York City Beer Guide (*http://www.nycbeer.org*), and his many friends at the Campaign for Real Ale in Britain, particularly Roger Protz and Mark Dorber. He'd like to thank friends and family for putting up with his stressed-out demeanor during the weeks when he was trying to renovate an apartment, build a brewery and write a book—all at the same time. Finally, he'd like to thank Eamonn Hahessy for listening to him whine, Larry Lustig for buying him a homebrewing kit a long, long time ago, and Joyce Oliver for putting up with the permanent malt crust on her stove.

Tim Harper would also like to thank the Beer Travelers, Stan Hieronymus and Daria Labinsky, and encourage anyone who likes beer to check out their newsletter, guidebook and Website. And thanks to his wife, Nancy Bobrowitz, and their children Lizzie and Jonathan, for once again cheerfully putting up with the sometimes untidy process of brewing up a book.

Finally, we'd like to thank each other for making what can be a stressful experience a little less stressful and a lot more enjoyable, and for everything that we learned from each other while researching and writing this book.

—Brooklyn, 1997

Foreword

EVEN THE LEAST SOPHISTICATED DRINKER tends to know more about wine than about beer. That is why I, and the authors of this book, so often use wine comparisons to illuminate our explanations of beer.

Can you imagine a world of wine in which every bottle (or jug) contained a generic chablis? Until a decade or two ago, the chablis jug wines of the beer world were everywhere. In America, scarcely anything else existed. A few discerning souls criticized the big American brewers for making bland beer, but the most famous imports were not, in truth, much different, despite the respect they received. Except in a handful of countries, pretty much all beer tasted the same. It tasted of nothing very much. In many places, it still does.

That is why, as the authors observe, few people drank beer for its taste. There scarcely was any, so it would have been an impossible feat.

In the intervening period, the American scene has changed beyond recognition. Today, no other country can match the range of beers available in the United States.

By this, I do not mean the hundreds of nearly identical beers that are still around. I mean brews that range in style from rye beer to oatmeal stout, from stone beer to smoked beer, from the hoppiest beers in the world to the spiciest.

Yes, the hoppiest or spiciest on the planet. Not only does the United States have a wider selection of beers than any other country, it also has many of the most intense-tasting. An India pale ale made in, say, Eugene, Oregon, is likely to be far hoppier than its counterpart in Britain, whose empire gave birth to the style. An Irish red ale born in Florida may be bigger in palate than one made in Kilkenny. A Belgian abbey-style beer brewed in, for example, Fort Collins, Colorado, may have more coriander than one produced in Flanders or Wallonia. A German-style wheat beer produced in Chicago might be as clovey as

anything in Bavaria. A Pilsner brewed in Pittsburgh, Pennsylvania, may
be more aromatic than one made in Bohemia.

The new generation of small brewers in the United States, and some
of the big guys who are now beginning to imitate them, have exceeded
the imagination and daring of their original inspiration, the consumerist
"real ale" movement in Britain of the mid to late 1970s.

The United States has created its own new styles of brew, notably
the almost piney-tasting ales of Northern California and the Northwest,
while also making almost every European style and continuing to im-
port many of the originals.

The United States' one thousand–plus breweries today make far more
styles of beer than were produced by the country's immigrant Irish,
British, Belgian, German and Czech brewers before Prohibition. They
certainly produce more styles than the nine or ten breweries operating
today in Ireland, the three hundred-plus in Britain, the one hundred-
plus in Belgium, or even the twelve hundred in Germany, let alone the
diminishing number in the Czech Republic. Nor are imported beers
nearly as widely available in those countries.

You may be tempted to say, "But it's only beer." Would you say
the same about wine? These are staples, a part of our heritage of food
and drink and, for those of us who enjoy them, central to the quality
of life. Enormous pleasure can come from exploring and understanding
the new beers of America. Today, millions of Americans do, indeed,
drink beer for its taste. I think more people do so in America than
anywhere, even perhaps Britain and Belgium. Certainly more than in
Germany. There, people are apt to like a beer "because it is German."
I do not find that reasoning very logical, though I have a sneaking
admiration for the loyalty to local brews. In the United States, that
pride is slow in developing, except perhaps in Seattle and Portland,
Oregon.

Is every microbrew wonderful? No, but a surprising number are. Do
all have the subtlety of some European beers? No, but there is also a
case for bold flavors. Do I wish it were easier to find some of the best
American beers? Certainly. How better to understand the beer movement? Read on. . . .

This book, combining clarity of narrative and passion of commitment, will enhance that understanding for novice and devotee alike. I
have spent many hours enjoying beer with both authors. In the earliest
days of Brooklyn Lager, Tim Harper personally brought a sample to
my home in London. At my dining table, Garrett Oliver unashamedly

asked if I had anything unusual in my wine rack. I did, and thus was opened my rarest bottle of barley wine.

They'll have you open one, too, if you're not careful.

—MICHAEL JACKSON

Michael Jackson's writing introduced many classic styles of beer to American drinkers. Among his most recent works are *Michael Jackson's Beer Companion* (Running Press), *The Simon and Schuster Pocket Guide to Beer* and *The Beer Hunter* CD-ROMs (Discovery Channel).

ONE
An Introduction to Good Beer

THE ROOTS OF the good beer revolution go back to the 1960s, when today's aging baby boomers were young and impressionable and first became suspicious of large corporations and mass marketing. They began looking for ways to be different. Different jobs. Different entertainment and sports. Different food and drink. Some people moved to small towns in Vermont and made fine wood stoves. Some became legal aid lawyers or ski instructors or social workers or inner-city special education teachers. On the other hand, most of us ended up in traditional careers and jobs. But we still yearned for something different, for some tangible representation of quality in our lives. We wanted better pasta, better TV shows, better clothes. Life was too short to eat cardboard spaghetti, watch *Brady Bunch* reruns or wear polyester leisure suits. Life was also too short to drink cheap beer.

The problem was, there just wasn't a lot of choice beer-wise. When we went to Europe, either lugging a backpack on the grand tour or a briefcase on business trips, we found lots of new and different beers in England, Belgium, France and Germany. Moving around America, we found the occasional regional beer: Rolling Rock, Yuengling, Straub, Stegmaier and Iron City in Pennsylvania; Christian Moerlein and Little Kings in Ohio; Genesee in New York; Point, Huber and Leinenkugel in Wisconsin; Schell in Minnesota; Coors in Colorado; Dixie in Louisiana; Lone Star, Pearl and Jax in Texas; Anchor Steam in California; Olympia in Washington; Weinhard's in Oregon. These regional beers may or may not have tasted better to us. The important thing was that they tasted a little different, that they had different labels, that they were made locally and that they didn't advertise on national television with singing frogs and Swedish bikini teams.

One of the important foundations of the good beer revolution was laid down by the classy resurrection of a regional brewery: Anchor Steam out of San Francisco. Fritz Maytag, an heir to the washing-machine fortune, bought the decrepit Anchor brewery in 1965, and slowly began building it up by reviving the all-but-forgotten style of "steam" brewing. In Chicago, newspaper columnist Mike Royko be-gan writing favorably about imported beers and local beers, and created a run on Point beer in Stevens Point, Wisconsin—Chicagoans were driving up to the brewery and loading up their cars—by saying how it tasted like real beer. In response to negative reaction when he praised foreign beers and said most mass-market American beers tasted as if the brewing process included passing through a horse, Royko wrote: "This offended many people in the American beer industry, as well as patriots who thought I was being subversive in praising foreign beers. Now I must apologize. I have just read a little-known study of Amer-ican beers. So I must apologize to the horse. At least with the horse, we know what we're getting."

Many of the 80 million Americans who drink beer remember the first time they tasted the stuff. A few of us knew immediately that this was nature's nectar. For many of us, however, it took a while to learn to appreciate beer. It was an acquired taste. For some, drinking beer was a rite of passage, of acceptance into a certain crowd when we were young, a very public signal that we were eager to have fun. For years, we drank beers that were sold to us through mass marketing. We bought a certain brand of beer because it was cheap, or because it was a little more expensive, or because it had good TV commercials, or because it was lower in calories or alcohol content. Few of us, until relatively recently, drank beer for its taste.

Now, however, the virtual explosion in the labels and styles of small breweries making distinctive, flavorful beers has opened up new worlds of taste to us. We find ourselves drinking flavorful beer with the dis-tinctive tastes produced only through the natural ingredients: malt, hops and yeast. We're interested more in taste, less in having our thirsts quenched or our senses dulled (though certainly the relaxing, social-izing aspects of beer are as important as ever). We're drinking better beer, but less of it.

We're talking about beer the same way wine aficionados talk about different vintages; indeed, many of the people drinking craft beer—good American microbrews and gourmet imported beers—are also wine lovers, especially those over forty. We're cooking with beer, and matching beer and foods with considerably more flexibility than al-lowed by wine. As Michael Jackson points out in his books (all of which we recommend heartily, by the way), many foods are difficult to match with wine—asparagus, for example—but can be nicely teamed with certain styles of beer. Small wonder that studies have shown a person ordering a good beer has more influence over fellow diners than the person ordering good wine.

For many people, wine is intimidating. There's too much to know about it to even begin learning. Beer, on the other hand, is more accessible, less snobbish, something we can all talk about simply by taking a sip and saying what we think. That's not to say the beer world doesn't have its own snobs. (Beer geeks, some call themselves, proudly.) But beer remains the world's favorite—and we think best—grown-up drink. And you probably think so, too.

This book aims to be an introduction to the world of good beer. We're going to describe how beer is made, and why the brewing process is considerably more sophisticated than winemaking. We're going to discuss the different styles of brewing and beer, and define many common beer terms. We'll profile a range of "beer people," including professional and homebrewers, brewpub owners, online beer forum hosts, a beer lawyer, a brewspaper editor, a festival organizer, a retailer and the much-envied Beer Travelers, the couple with maybe the best job in the world. We'll relate a general history of beer, from ancient times to the phenomena of today's craft brewing. We'll also discuss the beer business, and specifically the investment opportunities—and risks—presented by microbreweries and brewpubs. We'll talk about how beer should be purchased, stored, poured, tasted and used in the kitchen or at the dinner table with different dishes and foods. We'll offer a long list of specific places around the United States where you can try good beer, and describe our favorite American and international breweries and some of their best beers. We encourage you to sip your way through this book, trying new craft beers as you thumb through the pages. And we hope that you'll remember the first time you tasted them.

Tod Ardoin

TOD ARDOIN IS a Louisiana deputy sheriff who began homebrewing in 1991, and finally decided to do something about his dreams of opening a brewpub. In his own words:

"At the end of the summer of 1995, I began really looking for a way to make the project work. I started by calling around to several equipment manufacturers. This brought me some response by some manufacturers. Surprisingly, the ones I thought would give me info packets on their stuff didn't even respond to my calls. Of the few that took me seriously, I chose to go with Bohemian Brewery Importers, manufacturers of the Monobloc Brewing System. I can't praise them enough. They have provided me with serious consulting when others wouldn't even talk to me.

"We are in the financing stage of the project right now. I have taken some investors on, and am still soliciting for the remaining. I have spoken with two banks, and feel sure that one or both would finance us. We are planning for a ten-barrel system, and hope to be able to do some regional sales, if we have the extra beer available. The name of our company is the Calcasieu Brewing Company, but we plan to operate the restaurant under the name Trinidad Jack's Tavern and Brewery.

"I would say the hardest part of starting the whole thing is the background research that must go into it. The banks put a lot of stock in how well you know the business. If I hadn't worked so hard, reading and researching the brewing industry, I would not be in the position that I am today. I can't state strongly enough how important knowing the industry is. Without fully knowing what is going on, you can lose your ass. If someone were to try and come into an area and rely on hired persons to advise them on the brewing end of a brewpub, they could be setting themselves up for a big loss. If you want something done right, do it yourself. No consultant can replace hard work and research.

"I plan to serve mainly ales. I am an ale freak. I really don't like lager, and consider it slumming if I have to drink one. I really prefer English ales, but will experiment around with other styles as well. I think that most people will find that ales have much richer flavor than lagers, but ultimately we will sell whatever sells! Since we are in Louisiana, we will be serving seafood, but have steak and pasta as well. We plan to hire a chef trained here in the state to help us put the full menu together.

"As far as regrets, I can say that I have none. I am not sure that I was capable of doing the project even as recently as two years ago. Failures, I think, are generally caused by substandard brewing equipment (you would be surprised how many *big* manufacturers have piss-poor equipment!) and bad food. I personally think that you can have average food and average beer, but if your atmosphere and service are bad, you will certainly fail. In a brewpub, the profit margins are so high on beer, I think that it is more likely to carry the food than the food carry the beer. That doesn't mean that a pub could make it in the long run with bad food. I just mean that good beer could possibly buy you some time to correct a bad food problem. I really feel that you have to stay aggressive, and stay on top of everything. Never become content."

T W O

History of Beer, 5000 BC–1976

IN 1946, THE Master Brewers Association of America published *The Practical Brewer: A Manual for the Brewing Industry*. It was intended to be a bible for professional beermakers. The text was dedicated to "the art of brewing," but acknowledged that the focus was on "practical problems." These practical problems, a close reading reveals, were anything that added to the cost of making beer. The quality and taste of the beer were barely mentioned, in contrast with chapter after chapter on how master brewers—or "production superintendents," as the book calls them—could produce more pilsner-style lager more cheaply.

For the next thirty-plus years, making beer acceptable to the mass market as cheaply as possible was the one and only thrust of the American beer industry. For brewers, it was a clear repudiation of the credo of their predecessors—sometimes literally their own grandfathers and great-grandfathers—who had dedicated themselves to making beer with only natural ingredients and with only brewing procedures appropriate to the classic styles of Europe. There is no mention in *The Practical Brewer* of the ancient German purity law that forbade making beer with anything other than water, yeast, malt and hops. Indeed, one of the longest and most involved sections of *The Practical Brewer* was dedicated to adjuncts such as sugar, syrups, soybeans, rice and corn, among others. "Only a few" craft-brewed, all-malt beers were produced in the United States at the time, according to *The Practical Brewer*.

Fifty-plus years later, many more "craft" beers—brewed in small batches, with the emphasis on quality and taste rather than quantity and cost—are being produced in the United States and in the rest of the world. It's a new trend, but today's craft brewing has a long and varied history, and in many ways harks back to the brewing traditions of bygone centuries. The story of beer dates to prehistory, and there is considerable historical evidence that brewing is one of the world's oldest professions. There are various theories about how beer was discovered, but it was no doubt an accident, probably when rain soaked some loaves of coarse bread and then airborne yeast was blown into the crude mash. The theory is that some passing cave man (or woman) was lured by the intoxicating aroma, tasted the crude brew and then changed the course of human history by offering it around the cave. (There is no truth to the theory that pretzels, pizza and TV channel-changers were invented within a few days.) Later, another accident showed that if the barley was dried first—malted, in other words—the fermentation process was faster and stronger, and the brew tasted better.

THE FIRST BEER

Some historians believe beer was the foundation for civilization, that humans began to live together in villages and cultivate crops not to make bread, but to make beer. Certainly bread is still made in some parts in the world—as in the *kvass* sold in street corner vats in parts of the former Soviet Union, and in the areas of Brooklyn populated by Russian immigrants—merely as an intermediate step to brewing. Archaeological digs show that six thousand years ago, in Mesopotamia, the earliest human communities raised barley, which makes poor bread but good beer. Pottery from that period depicts two brewery workers stirring a vat of beer, and there are various recipes for beer and household supply lists that include beer. The Sumerians, Babylonians and Nubians brewed beer. Sometimes known as *kash,* beer was used as currency, and was part of the payment to workers building the Pyramids. Noah may have taken some beer on the Ark, and beer is mentioned in Chinese documents dating to 2300 B.C. Ancient Romans and Greeks drank beer, and Julius Caesar supposedly developed a taste for *cerevisia,* the beer that was the national drink of Gaul when he captured it. Our word "beer" comes from the Latin *bibere,* which means "to drink." The word in old High German was *bior,* while the Vikings called their brew *öl,* the probable origin of "ale."

For centuries, beer was the drink of health and nutrition. The alcohol made it a safe alternative to water, which was often contaminated, and helped prevent typhoid and cholera. It wasn't until the eighth century A.D. that hops were added to the brewing process, first as a flavoring and later as a preservative, in the breweries of the castles and abbeys and roadside inns where early travelers could rest on their arduous journeys. Some local brews became famous, and travelers began to seek them out. Also, travelers who enjoyed the camaraderie of drinking beer around an inn's hearth sparked the creation of local taverns where a man could enjoy beer and conversation in his own hometown.

Churches were important in brewing, as in virtually every other aspect of life in the Middle Ages. Just as they raised crops and livestock for sale, bishops oversaw commercial brewing operations. Moreover, monasteries became important brewing centers, developing distinct "abbey" styles, many of them strong beers that served as "liquid bread," providing nutrition during fasting periods. One innovation by monks was storing beer in mountain caves. They discovered that cool, even temperatures made the beer last longer—the beginning of the process for making "lager" beer, the golden, crisp brew that dominates the world beer markets today. (The word *lager* comes from the German "to store.") Travelers and pilgrims spread the fame of the best abbey beers, and a few of them still exist today. In twelfth-century England, a tax on beer, the Saladin Tithe, was imposed by Henry II to finance the Crusades. In the thirteenth century, Henry III established quality controls, and set the price of beer at a penny a gallon. By the year 1300, London was a metropolis with more than one thousand pubs, many of which made their own beer.

Into medieval times, brewing was a domestic duty, undertaken by wives while their menfolk were out hunting, farming, serfing, slaying dragons, whatever. In fact, the word "bridal" comes from "bride ale," in reference to the wedding feast that featured a special batch of beer brewed up by the village's women. This is one English luminary's description of the perfect wife, circa 1632: "Her ale, if new, looks like a misty morning, all thick; well, if her ale be strong, her reckoning right, her house clean, her fire good, her face fair, and the town great or rich, she shall seldom or never sit without chirping birds to bear her company."

Brewers laid the foundation for today's labor movement and trade associations, founding the first craft guilds in the fourteenth century. In the fifteenth century, William IV of Bavaria laid down the first rules for *reinheitsgebot,* the German purity law. That rule—beer may be made only of malt, water, yeast and hops, with no preservatives, no chemicals, nothing else—remains the self-imposed law for many of the world's best brewers, including today's leading American microbrewers. These craft brewers produce their beer in small, hand-crafted batches according to recipes that are far too costly and time-intensive for the huge commercial breweries that advertise on national television. At the same time, many good, traditional brewers do not follow the strict letter of the old German purity law. Belgian brewers, for example, use fruit or candy sugar in some specialty brews, and some British brewers add full-flavored or raw sugars.

Beer became an ingrained part of the English national character and language. In Olde England, for example, beer was often carried in a heavy, waxed leather jug known as a "black jack." Shakespeare was a homebrewer, and sneered at "small beer," the relatively weak brew that was made for servants while their masters upstairs drank the strong, good stuff. That ever-popular quotation from *Henry VI,* "First thing we do, let's kill all the lawyers," comes right after another quote: "I will make it a felony to drink small beer." Samuel Johnson, in his famous dictionary, noted the longtime distinction between ale, made with malt only, and beer, which was made with malt and hops. Today, of course, "beer" is the overall term for fermented grain beverages, and the two great families of beer are "ale," made with top-fermenting yeast, and "lager," made with bottom-fermenting yeast.

BEER IN THE NEW WORLD

During the era of exploration, ships relied on beer to keep crew and passengers healthy. But bad beer, according to some sources, was indirectly to blame for the deaths of hundreds of sailors and passengers crossing the Atlantic from England to the New World in the seventeenth century. Apparently some London breweries were selling spoiled beer to would-be colonists, figuring—rightly so, as it turned out—that they would never see them again. When the beer went bad, the sailors and passengers were forced to drink water—often contaminated—which is what really killed them.

In America, Spanish explorers found the Indians of what is now Mexico and the Southwestern United States brewing a maize-based beer. The Native Americans of the Northeast apparently made no beer, but early Dutch and English settlers quickly remedied that. The first evidence of brewing in what became the Colonies was in 1587, two decades before the first permanent settlement would be established at Jamestown. The earliest colonists got off their ships and started building shelter and making beer, not necessarily in that order. A journal from one of the first Virginia settlers, Thomas Heriot, noted: "We made of the same in the country some Mault, whereof was brewed as good

Ale as was to be desired. So, likewise by the helpe of Hops, thereof may be made as good Beere.'' In the early years of Jamestown, the epidemics that periodically seized the community were inevitably blamed on the shortage of good beer.

In 1620, the Pilgrims were put ashore, reluctantly, on the forbidding Cape Cod shore near Plymouth Rock, instead of where they were aiming—Hudson's River, the more habitable land to the south. But the *Mayflower* was running low on beer, and the sailors wanted to turn around and head back to England as soon as possible, to make sure they could get home before running out. According to a 1622 journal entitled *The Beginnings and Proceedings of the English Plantation Settled at Plymouth*: ''. . . for we could not now take time for further search or consideration: our victuals being much spent, especially our beer . . .'' If the *Mayflower* had sailed with more beer, or if the crew and passengers had not drunk so much of it on the voyage to the New World, the Pilgrims might well have landed in what is now New York. In that case, the Pilgrims might not have needed as much help from the Indians, and they might never have had that first Thanksgiving.

The first commercial brewery in America apparently was built in lower Manhattan in 1623 by the Dutch West India Company. But homebrewing remained common throughout the colonies in the eighteenth century, particularly on large farms and plantations and among the wealthy. Most important men brewed their own beer, among them colonists such as William Penn. Even the Puritans liked beer, at least at first, because it was a relatively sober alternative to hard liquor. Writings from New Amsterdam report that the first White Horse Tavern, located near what is now the Battery in Manhattan, was crowded every night in 1646, often with drunks. The Dutch tried to tax beer, but the brewers refused to pay, and that led to a civic backlash that was seen as one of the reasons Peter Stuyvesant lost authority as governor. By the time the English took over New Amsterdam from the Dutch in 1664, the Manhattan colony had a population of 1,600 and at least ten breweries.

In America, as in England, beer was brewed and consumed according to class or social standing: The wealthy landowners and their guests drank strong beer, tradesmen and craftsmen drank medium-strength ''table'' beer and servants drank small beer. The colonists brewed with barley when and where they could find it or grow it, but they also used maize, wheat, oats, even pumpkins and Jerusalem artichokes. In Virginia, where tobacco quickly became such a dominant cash crop that there was little land left for growing barley or anything else, malted barley imported from England became so cherished that one colonist's will specified that his twenty bushels of malt go to his wife.

When Harvard College was established in Cambridge in 1636, students could pay their tuition with malt. Harvard's first president lasted only three years; then he was forced out by students' complaints about mismanagement. One complaint was that the president's wife, who was in charge of providing their meals, did not make very good beer. An even bigger complaint was that she sometimes ran out of beer altogether, and the students were forced to drink water with the two meals a day provided by the college. Drunkenness first became a social issue in America in the mid-1600s, when the Puritans began cracking down on beer as well as hard liquor. In Connecticut, men who got drunk in public were tied to a post in the town square and horsewhipped. After Georgia became a royal province in 1753, the governor tried to ban rum and encouraged settlers to drink beer only.

BREWING AS INDUSTRY

In England, which was generally regarded as being about fifty years ahead of America in terms of economic development, the Industrial Revolution brought huge changes in brewing. The steam engine replaced men and horses as the primary source of power, and large commercial breweries began to replace small home- and tavernbrewing operations. Commercial brewing also brought a new beer style—porter, created from a mixture of the malts used for dark and pale ales. It became wildly popular, and London breweries began trying to outdo each other in creating bigger and bigger commercial operations to produce porter. *The Times* of London on April 7, 1785, reported: "There is a cask now building at Messers. Meaux and Co.'s brewery in Lickapond Street, Grays Inn Lane, the size of which exceeds all credibility, being designed to hold 20,000 barrels of porter." Twenty-nine years later, this vast cask's metal hoops gave way, flooding the neighboring tenements with porter. In all, eight people were killed by drowning, by the falling debris, by the fumes from the beer, or by drinking too much of it. Accidental deaths, the coroner's jury ruled. Another important new beer style, pale ale, was created in the late eighteenth century by London brewer Geoffrey Hodgson. A later innovation, India pale ale, was brewed to satisfy soldiers serving in India, the "Jewel in the Crown" of the burgeoning British Empire. The soldiers needed beer, and shiploads of it were being sent, but arriving stale after the long, hot journey. Knowing that hops and alcohol are preservatives, London brewers created a strong, highly hopped beer that would stand up to months in the hold of a ship and arrive fresh and tasty—East India pale ale, later shortened to India pale ale and abbreviated to IPA.

Meanwhile, in the American colonies, beer was the typical beverage served with meals, even to children. Many of the fathers (and mothers) of the American Revolution were brewers. George Washington was a beer guy, with a particular taste for porter—ordering it by the gross from his favorite breweries in Philadelphia, one on Callowhill and the other at the corner of Pear and Dock streets. Washington even had a favorite bar in New York, Fraunces Tavern, which is still a good place to have Tavernkeeper's Ale and raw oysters in front of the hearth, much as the Sons of Liberty did. Thomas Jefferson, a wine connoisseur, became enamored of beer relatively late in life. As a gentleman farmer, he saw beer as a healthy alternative to hard liquor. Jefferson was widely hailed for the careful, scientific approach he took to brewing, but in truth it was his wife, Martha, who actually made most of the beer at Monticello. A note from Jefferson's records, on Sept. 3, 1814, read: "Began to malt wheat. A bushel will make 8 or 10 gallons of strong beer such as will keep for years, taking ¾ lb. of hops for every bushel of wheat." (Philadelphia's Dock Street brewpub does a modern-day version of Jefferson's recipe.)

Samuel Adams, despite the words "patriot" and "brewer" on the bottles bearing his name today, was not really a brewer, according to historians. Adams did inherit a malt house from his father, and ran it for several years with little success. He finally gave it up to pursue revolution full-time, but not before making beer a political issue. Adams' newspaper advertisements for his "Old Malt" were a not-so-subtle slap at the English, and discouraged Americans from buying English malt or drinking imported English beer. As the independence movement grew, Patrick Henry and other prominent patriots organized boycotts of English beer, and homebrewing was seen as an act of defiance toward George III. On at least one occasion, a shipload of malt from England was refused. Imagine: The Boston Tea Party just as easily could have been the Philadelphia Malt Party.

Speaking of Boston, some historians believe that many volunteers joined the Minutemen primarily because they knew they could stumble their way through a few quick drills and then get free beer afterward at one of the local taverns. Once independence was declared, the soldiers in the ragtag American militias were promised a ration of a quart of beer a day, but they often didn't get it. On the other hand, the British overconfidence was underscored by the fact that the Redcoats, supposedly brought in to mop up a small insurrection, did not bring enough beer with them. Meeting more resistance from armed colonists than they anticipated, the English generals had to send for emergency beer supplies. That was the first indication to the military leadership back in London that they had a real fight on their hands.

When the Revolution ended, "Home Brew'd Is Best" was on the banners that American brewers carried in victory parades, wearing garlands of hops and carrying their malt shovels and mashing oars over their shoulders like muskets. One of the first bills passed by the new House of Representatives in 1789 set a ceiling on beer taxes at eight cents a barrel. James Madison, who sponsored the proposal, said, "This low rate will be such an encouragement as to induce the manufacture of beer in every State in the Union." The states, meanwhile, did their part to foster good brewing. The Massachusetts Act of 1789 held that "the wholesome qualities of malt liquors greatly recommend them to general use, as an important means of preserving the health of the citizens of this commonwealth, and of preventing the pernicious effect of spirituous liquors." Furthermore, the act exempted the real and personal property of brewers from all taxes. By 1810, the United States had 7 million people and 132 breweries, 90 of them in New York and Pennsylvania. In 1790, the average American over the age of fifteen drank thirty-four gallons of beer per year, about two-thirds more than today's per capita consumption.

As the young country grew, brewers played a prominent role, ranking in business and society alongside bankers and railroad barons. In some cities, all that is left of the early brewing kings are streets, parks and other landmarks named after them, like Van Cortlandt in New York or Diversey in Chicago. Vassar College was built with money from the Vassar family brewing operation. In Brooklyn, some of Evergreen Cemetery's largest mausoleums mark the burial sites of brewers. In some cities, breweries lived on after their founders: Hamm in St. Paul, Stroh in Detroit, Weinhard in Portland, Ballantine in Newark. Family dynasties were established, such as Coors in Golden, Colo., and Pabst in Milwaukee. Sometimes the dynasties were founded by aggressive young men who married into a brewing family. For example, Adolphus Busch married Eberhard Anheuser's daughter in St. Louis. Joseph Schlitz, a Milwaukee bookkeeper, married the brewer's widow, took over the brewery and renamed it after himself.

MODERN BREWING

Until the mid-1800s, American brewers typically stopped making beer in spring, when it got too warm for adequate refrigeration, and the ale made with top-fermenting yeast, in the English style, would spoil quickly. Around 1840, however, a wave of immigrants came to America from Germany, seeking to avoid political unrest and economic hard times. They brought with them the bottom-fermenting yeast used in brewing lager, which had a cleaner appearance and taste. And its golden color looked especially appealing in the new clear-glass mugs and steins that were coming into use. Lager became the American style of beer, and beer halls reminiscent of old Munich sprang up not only in cities with big German populations, such as Milwaukee, St. Louis and Brooklyn, but everywhere. A derisive *New York Times* comment on Manhattan beer halls concluded: ''The object is to drink just as much beer as you can hold, smoke just as many cigars as you can bite the ends off of, and see who can sit in his chair the longest. It is an institution worthy of the gods.'' Beer, after being everyone's everyday beverage in the colonial period, became a working-class drink, partly because it was cheap, and partly because it was favored by Germans, who as new immigrants often had to settle for the worst jobs in factories and slaughterhouses. The most popular beers of the time no doubt were similar to the best lagers made by microbreweries a hundred years later: dry and crisp, but darker, with more taste and body than today's relatively bland mass-market lagers.

Several developments in the late nineteenth century combined to have a huge impact on beer and brewing. Pasteurization killed the bacteria in finished beer. Sterilization of bottles and kegs meant that beer would last longer without spoiling. For the first time, beer could be safely bottled. Icemaking machines meant that brewers no longer had to harvest huge chunks of ice from frozen lakes and cart them to caves or cellars where beer could be lagered over the summer. (Sometimes the ice was moved on ''plank'' roads of boards laid end to end over city streets.) Freight cars could be refrigerated and factories cooled. For the first time, brewing could be a national, year-round business. As a result, the turn of the century was a time of competition and consolidation. There were expositions, shows and fairs where breweries from different cities, able to compete head to head for the first time, boasted of their gold medals and blue ribbons. In the first part of the twentieth century, many smaller breweries either folded or sold out to big breweries that came into their markets with expensive advertising campaigns and cheaper prices. Pabst and Schlitz took over a railroad, the better to ship their beer. Brewers grew enormously wealthy. For example, Yankee Stadium is called the House that Ruth Built, but a more apt nickname might be the House that Ruppert Beer Built, given that Jacob Ruppert used the profits from his brewery to buy Babe Ruth from the Boston Red Sox.

PROHIBITION AND BEYOND

Beer consumption rose steadily until the outbreak of World War I, when a backlash against everything and anything associated with Germans and Germany—including beer—sent per capita consumption down from nearly thirty gallons in 1910 to barely twenty-one gallons in 1917. During and after the war, the Anti-Saloon League and the Women's Christian Temperance Union trumpeted their message of fundamentalist morality and family values. On Jan. 16, 1920, the Volstead Act, implementing the Eighteenth Amendment to the U.S. Constitution, prohibited the sale of any beverage with more than 0.5 percent alcohol. Some brewers switched to brewing near beer, or root beer and birch beer. Many of them stayed in business by selling malt and hops, ostensibly for homebrewing, which wasn't illegal as long as the homebrewer didn't transport or sell the beer. "Every second household has become a homebrewer," H. L. Mencken wrote from Baltimore. "In one American city of 750,000 inhabitants there are now 100 shops devoted exclusively to the sale of beer-making supplies, and lately the proprietor of one of them, by no means the largest, told me that he sold 2,000 pounds of malt syrup a day." In truth, it was the bootleggers who kept the commercial breweries alive during Prohibition, relying on them as unofficial supply houses. On Dec. 5, 1933, Utah—in many respects the driest state, then and now—became the necessary thirty-sixth state to ratify the Twenty-first Amendment, repealing Prohibition, though only 3.2 percent beer was legal at first. Of the 1,600 breweries in the United States before Prohibition, 750 were back in business within a year.

But it was the Depression. In 1914, American beer consumption was 66 million barrels. By 1940, it had recovered to only 53 million barrels. Then came World War II, and more anti-German backlash. Some small breweries with German names never recovered; some changed their names, some changed their names and still never recovered. There was also grain rationing: Malt was needed to make alcohol for munitions. Brewers turned to corn, rice and other ingredients that led to lighter, less hearty-tasting beer. In addition, the use of adjuncts usually made beer cheaper to brew. Figuring that women prefer thinner, paler beers, the big breweries shifted marketing strategies to target Rosie the Riveter. Many women, working in jobs that ordinarily would have gone to men, became beer drinkers. At the same time, the breweries did their part for the war effort—and their own cause—by shipping their beer overseas to GIs. Young men far from home, eager for any diversion from war, particularly if it was a reminder of home, became committed beer drinkers. Many remained loyal to the national brand that had supplied their battalions overseas. American beer consumption grew at an incredible rate during World War II—from 53 million barrels in 1940 to 80 million barrels in 1945.

The postwar boom time for America was also a boom time for brewing. There were still many small breweries in the United States after World War II, many of them local operations on a scale not much beyond today's brewpubs. But few of the small operations could compete with the growth of the big breweries that expanded by brewing their own beer in different cities across North America. Pabst, Schlitz, Budweiser, Hamm's, Falstaff and Carling (from Canada) became national brands by opening breweries in different regions—producing beer that tasted the same in Peoria as in Pittsburgh, but delivering it without the high cost of cross-country shipping. After World War II, several different labels, including Pabst Blue Ribbon and Schlitz, took turns as America's No. 1 beer before Budweiser finally gained the stranglehold it has not relinquished. Television threw the power of national advertising into the mix, and few local breweries could match the mass-market breweries' economy of scale.

By 1961, the number of breweries in the United States had dwindled to a mere 230. The beer market was dominated by the big national brands, but a few good regional and local breweries hung on through the 1960s and '70s. Sometimes word spread about a beer that was "good," if for no reason other than it tasted a little different from the mass-market national brands. Some of those regional breweries, such as Coors from Colorado and Rolling Rock from Pennsylvania, built on their local loyalty to break out of their regional markets. At the time, beer drinkers were craving taste and quality, but having a hard time finding it. The growth of international travel was also a major factor. A couple of generations of Americans, after growing up with modern advertising and getting enough education to be suspect of big business and high-powered marketing, strapped on backpacks, took cheap flights to Europe and discovered a new world of beer taste in the Old World. After drinking the beers of England, Belgium and Germany, they weren't satisfied with America's mass-market beers. By the mid-1970s, the seeds of a beer revolution were in place.

Carol Stoudt

CAROL STOUDT IS a former kindergarten teacher who decided she didn't want to go back to teaching when the youngest of her five kids started school. She wanted to do something with flexible hours. She wanted to work with her husband, Ed Stoudt, who runs Stoudt's Black Angus, a steakhouse in Adamstown, Pa., on the edge of Lancaster County's Pennsylvania Dutch country. They both were students of their German heritage, and had always come home from their trips to Germany wishing there was a reliable, reasonably priced source of good German-style beer in their area. So Carol decided to start a brewery, and Ed promised to be her first customer. During her first two years, 1987–88, Ed bought probably 85 percent of the beer Carol made in the little brewery next door. Today, Ed still has first call on Carol's beer, but he's just one of many customers who wish they could get more.

Since 1989, Carol Stoudt has won more prestigious awards for her beer than any other microbrewer. She is America's best-known woman brewer, and is quick to dispel the notion that brewing is man's work. Historically, women were the brewers. Making beer was a domestic duty, part of hearth and home; the name Brewster came from women who were the best brewers. Carol Stoudt, who can rattle off the names of several other women who are commercial microbrewers in America, is more like an executive brewer nowadays. She is in charge of Stoudt's brewhouse in the same way that an executive chef runs a gourmet kitchen. Her work is in educating people and building new business relationships, and she is one of America's most sought-after speakers on beer and brewing. With teenagers still at home and in school, she tries to limit herself to two nights a week on the road giving speeches and presiding over beer dinners and tastings.

Stoudt's Brewing Co. hosts three beer festivals each year, specializing in a mix of far-ranging microbrews that would be hard to find in any one shop, let alone poured fresh. Ed's restaurant has been expanded to include a beer garden and a beer hall, and a regular feature is the pig roast, when the pig is hung on a pole and paraded through the beer hall, led by an oom-pah band. Here's a recipe for a great weekend: cruising the Amish sites of Lancaster County, touring the Stoudt's brewery, checking out the antiques market and village behind the brewery, and then drinking and eating at the Black Angus. For more information, call 717-484-4385 or 717-484-4387.

THREE

What Is Beer?

THOUGH IT IS one of the most ubiquitous and popular consumables found in the American household, beer stands alone in its mystery. The average American does not know what beer actually is; where it comes from, what it's made of and the techniques used in its production remain unknown to most of us.

People are sometimes shocked, their sensibilities tweaked, when it is suggested that brewing is a far more complicated art than winemaking. They shouldn't be so surprised. After all, at its simplest, winemaking requires only grapes. Brewing, on the other hand, requires at least barley malt, yeast, hops and water. True, the vintner must choose the grapes carefully and then oversee a long and involved process. The brewer, however, must choose among a dizzying array of malts, roasted grains and unmalted grains, dozens of varieties of hops and hundreds of strains of yeast, and be familiar with water chemistry. This is before the brewer even turns an eye to technique. And after the brewer is finished, any protestations about a "bad year" for the raw materials will fall on unsympathetic ears.

Brewing is hard work—there are no easy days of dancing on grapes around the brewhouse. Barley starts out with no juice to yield up, and the brewer must work to loosen its grip on the goods. This process starts with the mash, where starches are converted into a sweet liquid called the wort. The wort (pronounced "wert") is collected in a kettle, where the bitterness, flavor and aroma of the hops are extracted by boiling. Then the cooled wort is sent into a fermentation vessel where yeast is added and works its wonders, transforming homely sweet wort into glorious beer. Sound simple? In some ways, it is. Yet as elsewhere in life, both trouble and triumph lurk in all the tiny details.

Come now on a journey from grain to glass, and uncover the mysteries of brewing. First, let's look at the ingredients. Every journey must begin with a single step, and when it comes to beer, that first step is barley malt.

MALT

Barley *(hordeum vulgaris)* is a tall tawny-colored grass with a seeded stalk on top. A field of barley looks a lot like a wheat field. But for the brewer, barley has special gifts that other grains cannot offer. Its hard husk, low protein and high starch content all make it better suited to brewing than to breadmaking. Barley grows in temperate climates around the world. Like many grains, it comes in a number of varieties. The stalks of European varieties tend to have two rows of seed rather than the American six, but these days the varieties are becoming homogenized. There are, however, still barleys that command respect and higher prices for their rare depth of flavor, such as the old British varieties Marris Otter and Golden Promise.

Malted barley, also known simply as "malt," is barley that has been steeped in water, germinated for several days, then dried out in a kiln. The germination is traditionally carried out by spreading the barley about six inches deep over a large concrete floor specially built for the purpose. Water is sprayed onto the barley and the germination begins. During the germination the barleycorn, packed with starch, develops natural enzymes. The barley plant uses these enzymes to convert the seed starch into sugar, which the plant would use as fuel until its leaves unfurl.

The brewer has different plans for both the enzymes and the seed starch. During the brewing process, the brewer will use the barley's natural enzymes to break down the seed starch into sugar, and it is a solution of that sugar that will eventually become beer. All alcoholic beverages are the result of the consumption of sugar by a microorganism, usually yeast. In brewing, the barley malt provides the sugars, proteins, lipids and amino acids that the yeast needs in order to create beer.

Ah, but not so fast. What kind of malt? From the beginning of the malting process, subtle differences in moisture content, barley variety, processing and kilning temperatures are crucial, and result in different varieties of malt. A good brewer needs to understand malt characteristics and what any particular malt will do for the beer. This is where the brewer starts to "design" the beer, choosing the color and flavor components. Here is a basic selection of malts that are commonly used:

Lager (Pilsner) Malt. The palest malt generally available, pilsner malts are widely used in the production of pilsner and other light lagers.

A low kilning temperature results in a malt that can give a true golden color and a slightly biscuity flavor to a beer.

Pale Ale Malt. Kilned at slightly higher temperatures than pilsner malt, pale ale malt gives a somewhat deeper color and toastier, more biscuity flavors to beer, sometimes with toffee and caramel notes. This is the base malt for most English-style beers.

Mild Ale Malt. Not used much in the United States, this malt is kilned at still higher temperatures and produces toffeeish, nutty flavors.

Vienna Malt. Similar in production to the mild ale malt above, this malt is often used as a higher percentage of the grist (grain recipe). It produces caramel and toffee flavors associated with European dark lagers.

Munich Malt. Raw Munich malt is stowed and then kilned at over 200 degrees Fahrenheit. This converts some of the starches into sugars, and gives an orangy, amber color and the classic toffeeish, nutty flavor to Oktoberfest beers and other Bavarian specialties. It is often used as a high percentage of the grist. Some brewers try, generally unsuccessfully, to replace true German Munich malt with domestic versions of Munich malt or Caramel malts. The flavors in the beer are just not the same.

Carapils Malt. Raw, wet Carapils malt is heated up, causing a breakdown in some of the starches, and then it is kilned. This results in a malt with a sweetish, round flavor. Carapils malt is often added to other malts to give the beer additional body. And it is often used in small amounts to prevent lagers from having too thin a finish or aftertaste.

Wheat Malt. Used in very high proportions in wheat beers and in smaller proportions in many others. Wheat has a high protein content that can help form a nice head, and then keep the head as the beer is consumed. These same proteins, however, along with glutens and a very thin husk, make wheat difficult to work with at high proportions of the grist. It is sometimes used to lighten the body of a beer and give it a brisker mouthfeel.

Caramel/Crystal Malt. This raw wet malt is stewed until all of the starch is converted into sugars; then it is kilned to varying degrees (often noted in ''Lovibond'' color degrees: the higher the number, the darker the malt). This sweet, caramel-flavored malt imparts a reddish-amber color and rich flavor to beer, and is one of the most widely used specialty malts among both amateur homebrewers and professional microbrewers. It also enhances mouthfeel and foam stability, but if used too heavily (over 10 percent of the grist), it can cause harshness and astringency.

Chocolate Malt. This malt is prepared in a standard fashion and then roasted at over 400 degrees Fahrenheit. Used in small amounts, it can add a deep brown color and dark chocolate and coffee flavors to beer.

Roasted Barley. Unmalted barley is roasted to a deep reddish-brown hue, which adds this color to beer along with strong coffee flavors and a hard, clean edge. This malt can be very nice in dry stouts.

Black Patent Malt. The malt is roasted until it is as black as espresso beans. It provides more of a sharp "bite" than an actual flavor, and is often used in stouts both for color and for that sharp bite.

Black Barley. Unmalted barley is roasted until black. Black barley (which is not interchangeable with black malt) gives color, bite and an espresso-like flavor to beer. A dash can be used to give dark beers a firmer, drier edge. This malt is a favorite ingredient in Irish stouts.

While that might seem like quite an extensive list, it is actually only a brief, broad overview of the malt horizon. For example, a brewer can choose among many brands of Pale Ale malt as the basis for a beer. All the varieties of Pale Ale malt will have slightly different flavors and properties, and therefore make different beers. Also, with various combinations of the ingredients above, it is possible to make several different beers that might be exactly the same color but will exhibit quite different taste profiles. On top of that, there are many other types of malt available; those listed above are simply the most widely used. The ability to combine these brushstrokes into a desired flavor picture is one of the keys to successful brewing. In this regard the brewer is similar to a chef, and needs both creativity and a sharp memory for flavor.

HOPS

Most people know that beer contains hops. At the same time, many people also seem to think that hops are a grain. The hop is in fact a flower. And quite a flower it is. Not only does it lend natural preservative qualities to the finished beer, but it also provides bitterness and a variety of flavors and aromas. The hop plant *(humulus lupulus)* is a vigorous perennial vine. Botanically, it is in the order *Cannabicea* and is the nearest relative to *cannabis sativa,* the marijuana plant. (Hence the old 1950s phrase "hophead" for jazz musicians who succumbed to ''reefer madness.'') The hop flower has often been used as a folk sedative; the English even used to stuff pillows with it.

The vine can grow to twenty feet tall or even higher during a summer growing season, after which it dies back to a crown near the ground in the autumn. To accommodate their natural climbing tendencies, hop plants are grown on poles or on trellises with wire supports for the vine. Hop plants are reproduced by transplanting root stock, and only the female plant is commercially cultivated. In the late summer and early autumn the hop vine flowers, resulting in a green ''hop cone,'' shaped a little like a pinecone. Inside the hop cone, at the base of the petals, are glands that produce a bright yellow powder called lupulin. The lupulin contains all of the goodies the brewer is after, and the hops must be handled gently in order to avoid losing this delicate powder.

Hops used to be handpicked by young women, but these days hops are largely subjected to the less salubrious touch of picking machines. The cones are removed and dried for storage. From there they are packaged into bales or processed into a number of forms. The most common alternative form is to crush the cones and extrude them into pellets. The pellets are easily vacuum-packed, saving them from the ravages of oxygen, which brings on unpleasant cardboardy and cheesy aromas.

Without hops, beer would be a sweet, cloying and ultimately less satisfying drink. The bitterness of the hop gives beer its balance and its quenching qualities. Throughout history, people have added spices to their beer. Wormwood, peppers, coriander, licorice, ginger and a garden of other flavorings have all graced the juices of the barley. Hops won out because of their clean, sharp bitterness and their preservative qualities. Hops are varietal like wine grapes, and there are many dozens of varieties for the brewer to choose among. Just as various chili peppers can have different amounts and qualities of spiciness, so it is with the bitterness of hop varieties. Some are more bitter than others, or sharper, or will have different flavors and aromas. The aroma of hops runs the gamut from the hay-like qualities of the English Fuggle variety to the grapefruity blast of the popular American Cascade. In the United States, the Pacific Northwest, particularly Washington and Oregon, is hop country. The local beers reflect the local hop crop, just as they do in the famous hop-growing areas of Kent in England or Zatec in the Czech Republic. Hops are grown in temperate areas worldwide, with most production centered in the United States, England, Germany and Central Europe. Japan, China, Australia and New Zealand are busily expanding their acreage, and may become major producers in the future.

YEAST

Yeast is a single-celled organism in the fungi class of flora. Yeast is everywhere: in the air, in the soil, on our skin—everywhere. There are many species of yeast, but for brewing purposes we are principally concerned with only two: *saccharomyces cerevisiae,* the ale yeast, and *saccharomyces uvarum,* the lager yeast. Yeast ferments malt sugars into beer, giving off carbon dioxide, ethyl alcohol, flavors and aromas in the process.

Unfortunately, yeast doesn't care what kind of beer it makes, or whether it tastes good. The brewer's job is to anticipate the conditions under which the yeast will produce the desired beer, and then maintain and replicate those conditions. The brewer will ''harvest'' some yeast from each fermentation and use it to ferment the next wort. The yeast strain has been carefully chosen by the brewer within the two species— ale and lager yeast. There are hundreds of strains of yeast within the two species of brewing yeast, and each strain has its own unique characteristics. Especially for ales, the yeast strain often makes a major contribution to the flavor of the finished beer.

Besides the production of flavor characteristics, the brewer wants the yeast to have other attributes as well. Does it rise to the surface of the fermenting vessel at the end of fermentation or drop to the bottom? How long does it take to complete the fermentation? How much sugar will it consume? Is it resistant to higher levels of alcohol? The yeast must satisfy dozens of criteria before it is chosen to make beer.

In many ways, the yeast is the single most important ingredient the brewer selects. Centuries ago, before brewers learned how to use yeast, beer was allowed to ferment spontaneously. As soon as the wort cooled, wild yeast in the air and in the fermentation vessel would invade the wort and start the fermentation. This old style of brewing lives on in the Belgian lambic beers, but all other brewers choose a specific strain depending on what kind of beer they are aiming to produce.

The two species of beer yeast provide the great divide in the beer world—the divide between ale and lager. Ales are by far the older type of brewing yeast. Ale yeasts ferment at warm temperatures, typically between 62 and 72 degrees Fahrenheit. Ales ferment rapidly, and an ale fermentation can take as little as a few days. During the fermentation, most ale yeast strains will produce flavors and aromas that lend a unique stamp to the beer. The aromas are often fruity, spicy and complex, and can combine with other characteristics to produce a beer of stunning depth. At the end of the fermentation, ale yeasts tend to rise to the top of the fermentation vessel, and float there in a cake-like mass. For that reason, ale yeasts are often described as "top-fermenting" yeasts. Traditionally, brewers gather these yeasts by skimming them from the surface of the beer in open fermentation vessels. Ales may be ready to drink within a week or so of fermentation. Lagers are a different story.

Lagers are relative newcomers to the beer world, but have made a dramatic impact. Various forms of pilsner, a hoppy, golden lager style, are the most popular beers in the world. The lager yeast was only discovered in the mid-1800s, but in Czech Bohemia brewers had probably been brewing with it many years before. Before refrigeration, the Bohemian brewers carried out their fermentations in deep, cool caves and tunnels to keep them from the spoiling ravages of heat. Eventually they ended up with yeasts that preferred cool temperatures. Lager yeasts ferment best at temperatures between 45 and 54 degrees Fahrenheit, and the fermentation is slower and less tumultuous than an ale fermentation. After the lager fermentation is finished, the beer is left with many rough edges, in terms of taste. It needs smoothing out. The German word *lager* means "to store," and beer fermented with lager yeasts are aged for weeks or even months, at temperatures as low as 32 degrees Fahrenheit, until the flavors and aromas soften. Lager yeasts tend to stand aside and let the other ingredients do the talking, giving the beer clean, straightforward flavors.

WATER

A brewer may take the best of care to select the finest malt, hops and yeast, but without a supply of good water it will all come to naught. Most beers are at least 90 percent water, so it should come as no surprise that water is a critical element in the flavor of beer.

In the last two centuries, various European cities became renowned for their unique brewing water, and for the beers brewed with them. For example, Burton-on-Trent, in the English Midlands, sits atop huge limestone deposits that suffuse the city water with minerals. The minerals promote a vigorous fermentation, and in a finished beer produce a dry, sharp-edged hop character that is the hallmark of Burton ales.

Great brewing dynasties such as Bass & Co. built their fortunes on the quality of Burton water and the resulting fine India pale ales. The Burton water was so admired by brewers the world over that the addition of gypsum and certain other minerals to brewing water is still widely practiced and is referred to as "Burtonizing." To this day, Burton beers retain a hard edge and a distinctive whiff of sulfur that arouses both pride and thirst in every proper Burtonite.

A thousand miles away, in the Czech Bohemian town of Pilsen (also spelled Plzn or Pilsn), the water is prized for its softness rather than its hardness. The almost complete lack of mineral salts in Pilsen's water gave rise to the pilsner style, which takes the name of the town for its own. Pilsners have a sharp crackle of bitterness, but it is followed by a soft, sweet, delicate malt flavor prized by lager brewers and drinkers alike.

Today, in an age of filters and blended water supplies, most brewers adjust the mineral content of the water they use to suit their needs. A pilsner brewer whose city has a hard water supply may filter the hardness out, while a pale ale brewer might add Burton salts to the water to bring out the dry edge. Once upon a time, the majority of breweries produced only one or two styles of beer, but these days it pays to be more flexible. "Rocky mountain spring water" is a fine thing, to be sure, but it is questionable whether anyone can taste the mountains in the beer.

Now, we've gathered our ingredients—barley malt, yeast, hops and water. It's time to brew.

BREWING THE BEER

Technically speaking, it is not the beer that is brewed, but the wort, the sweet liquid that will be fermented into beer by the yeast. So producing the wort is the brewer's first task.

The grist, the recipe of grains to go into the beer, is weighed out and blended. Then the grain is sent through a mill that cracks each kernel into several pieces, exposing the starch within. The grist is then sent into a vessel called the mash tun, where it is mixed with hot water to form the mash. The mash will yield the sugars that the brewer is going to ferment into beer. In the mash, the natural enzymes developed by the barley seed during its germination are activated by the hot water, breaking down the starches in the malt into maltose, maltotriose, dextrins and other sugars. The temperature of the mash is critically important, because the malt enzymes work differently at different temperatures. A few degrees can make all the difference; a mash at 145 degrees Fahrenheit will turn out different sugars (and therefore a different beer) than one at 150 degrees. Some brewers, particularly English ale brewers, use a single temperature mash, in which the porridge-like mixture is held at one temperature for an hour or more. Other brewers, depending on the type of malt they are using, prefer to heat the mash to several different temperatures to achieve a particular sugar profile in the wort.

The vessel holding the mash, also called the mash tun, may be equipped with a false bottom containing a set of screens. If not, then the entire mash will be pumped into another vessel, called a lauter, that is fitted with screens. The screens act as a filter, holding the empty grain husks behind as the brewer drains off the sugars. An hour or two later, the appearance of the mash has changed. The white flecks of starch are all gone, and the mash looks darker and more viscous. Now it's time for the sugar extraction, called the runoff.

Imagine that you're standing in front of a huge bowl of hot, heavily sugared oatmeal. At the bottom of the bowl is a fine stainless-steel screen. The trick is to leave all the cereal behind in the bowl, while removing all the sugar to another bowl. Easier said than done. At this point, the mash is composed largely of barley husks and concentrated wort that has the consistency of a light syrup. The wort is strained out through the screen at the bottom of the vessel and sent into the boiling vessel, called the kettle or copper. The undiluted wort that is sent into the kettle first is referred to as the "first runnings." When making barley wines (very strong ales), some brewers use only the first runnings of the mash, yielding impressively heavy beers.

Once the first runnings have drained out, it is time to start the process of rinsing the rest of the sugars out of the mash. Hot water, usually at temperatures between 160 and 170 degrees Fahrenheit, is sprayed down on top of the grain bed. This process is called sparging, and it must be done carefully lest the grain bed compact and clog up the runoff. When the runoff is finished, the kettle should be full of a wort of the concentration that the brewer intended, and the lauter tun should be full of damp grain husk. The grain husks are often sold off as cattle feed.

Now the hops are added, and the kettle is brought to a boil. The hops that are added at the beginning of the boil are largely for bitterness, since their aromatic compounds vaporize during the boil. At first the hops lie very still on the surface of the wort. Then the liquid shifts a bit under the green mass and a shard of white foam cracks through.

Finally the hops are swallowed up as the wort settles into a rolling boil. The brewhouse fills with the heady aroma of hops. In order for the bitter hop resins to be properly extracted, the boil has to be vigorous. The boil also sterilizes the wort and coagulates proteins.

After an hour or more of boiling, the brewer who is seeking a hoppy aroma may toss in a final flourish: another dose of hops, often of a different variety than the original bittering hops. These "finishing hops" are largely for aroma, since they will not be boiled long enough to remove all their aromatic oils or to provide additional bitterness to the brew. A few minutes does the trick—just long enough for the aromatics to dissolve into the wort. The heat is cut off, the boil breaks, the wort settles into a simmer and finally lies still.

FERMENTATION

Now we have a kettle full of bittersweet wort, coagulated protein and spent hops. The protein and the spent hops are removed, either by straining or by a whirlpool vessel. As the clear wort leaves the vessel, it is crash-cooled from over 200 degrees Fahrenheit to 70 degrees or below. Sterile oxygen is often added to the wort at this point to kick-start the fermentation. As the wort surges into the fermentation vessel, the raw unfinished beer reaches the moment of truth—will it be an ale or a lager? If it is to be a lager, then the wort must be chilled to 52 degrees Fahrenheit or cooler, and lager yeast added. If it is destined to be an ale, then more moderate temperatures are called for—65 to 70 degrees Fahrenheit—and an ale yeast is added.

During the next few hours, the wort lies quiet, but there's plenty going on. The single-celled yeast are furiously dividing and building their numbers in preparation for the fermentation. Several hours later, their strength gathered, they begin their real work. At first, a small wisp of foam appears, but soon the entire surface of the liquid is churned up into a foam. Ales put on the more impressive display; their higher fermentation temperatures and natural surface activity give rise to a thick yeast formation on top of the fermenting beer. On the second day of the fermentation, the activity reaches a crescendo and then begins to slow down.

When the beer has reached the gravity (sugar content) intended by the brewer, it is cooled further for a day or two, causing the yeast to settle. Then the beer is sent into conditioning tanks for a rest. If the beer is an ale, its respite may be brief—some English ales need only a few days of aging before they are ready to drink. Most ales require no more than a month of conditioning, though some very strong ales might be conditioned for up to a year. During the aging, flavors become more refined, more yeast and protein sediment out, and sometimes an additional bit of fermentation takes place. The brewer may also add raw hops at this stage, in a time-honored process called "dry hopping." The hops are left to steep like tea leaves, suffusing the beer with additional aroma, but with no added bitterness. This technique, popular for centuries among English brewers, has gained widespread adherence among American microbrewers in recent years.

When lagers emerge from primary fermentation, their flavor is still coarse and the nose—aroma—is still sulfurous. The aging process is necessary to allow the beer to mellow and develop its finely delicate flavors. Traditionally, a small amount of still-fermenting beer will be added to the lagering tank, restarting the fermentation. This process, called *krausening,* helps remove sulfurous aromas and adds natural carbonation. Then the temperature of the lagering tank is dropped further, often just above freezing, and the beer settles down for a long sleep. A proper lager enjoys a slumber of two or three months, but the average mass-market American pilsner is rudely awakened after only a few weeks. When you're not going to be very pretty anyhow, who needs a beauty rest?

FILTRATION AND PACKAGING

At this point, some beers are ready to be packaged. Some beers, including most big-brand, mass-market beers, are pasteurized—steam-heated to the point that any bacteria in them are killed. This is done for sanitation, and to extend shelf life. Many types of more flavorful beer are not pasteurized. Instead, they continue to age and "condition" in the bottle or in the keg. Traditional cask-conditioned English ales (sometimes referred to as "real ales") will be siphoned directly into casks, sometimes with a natural clarifier and a handful of hops. The finished beer will be ready to draw through the handpumps in the pub in a few days.

Bottle-conditioned beers will usually have a dose of yeast and sugar added before bottling. The yeast consumes the sugar, producing a natural, spritzy carbonation similar to that of champagne. Many Belgian ales are bottle-conditioned, as are some English ales, American microbrewed ales, Bavarian weizenbiers and the occasional German keller-bier.

Most beer, pasteurized or not, is filtered before packaging. There is nothing wrong with filtering per se. Filtering clarifies the beer, removing unwanted yeast and proteins that may cause haziness and decrease shelf life. Like most refinements, however, filtering can be overdone, and often is. "Genuine Draft" in a can? This actually means that while the beer hasn't been pasteurized, it's been put through a filter so tight that it removes any spoilage organisms. That technique would be terrific if it didn't also filter out body, flavor and aroma. And tightly filtered beers generally don't have any body, flavor or aroma to spare in the first place. When done properly, filtration protects the beer while leaving its desirable qualities relatively undisturbed. After passing through the filter, the beer is sent into the "bright beer" tank, and some carbonation is usually added. Now the finished beer is ready for bottling, canning or kegging.

Randy Sprecher

IN HIS PANELED office, the one in the back, past where his employees play table tennis or darts on breaks, Randy Sprecher leans back in his chair, looking like a large, blond, mustachioed, checked-shirt lumberjack. He is on the phone, cajoling, begging, charming. "Well, I'd like to get those berries. I need 'em now," he says. "I want to do a new beer, but I don't want to do it without your berries. They'll really add character. How about if I come out this afternoon? I'll have a check with me. I'll bring you some beer, and a few cases of root beer for the kids for your next company picnic."

He hangs up, satisfied. He has talked the manager of a big yogurt factory into selling him a few cases of the whole raspberries it uses to make that fruit-on-the-bottom kind of yogurt. "Most people who use fruit in beers in America use extracts," he explains. "It's not the same. I want whole berries, like they do in Belgium." That kind of stubbornness has given Sprecher's beer a good name in Milwaukee, where it is brewed, and in the towns within two and a half hours where Sprecher sells it. That's also the sort of stubbornness that keeps Sprecher Brewing from growing. Randy Sprecher is reluctant to distribute his strong (up to 9 percent alcohol), unpasteurized beer more widely because he's afraid it won't be served as fresh, and therefore won't taste as good. "Controlling sales and distribution is really hard," he says. "Getting people trained to keep beer cold, and fresh, is the biggest problem."

Sprecher, originally from Oregon, came to Milwaukee as a brewer for Pabst. He started his own brewery in 1985, and remains one of the few people in American microbrewing who is the founder of the brewery, the sole owner and the chief executive officer, and still pulls on the coveralls to actually brew every batch of beer himself. "I'm just trying to keep ahead of the big guys muddying the waters with all those pseudo-beers," he says. "There's a sea of colorful labels out there. I call them Fruit Loops and Hula Hoops. You can buy what's supposed to be a nut brown ale, but some of these brewers could care less about how they make it, and whether it's really a nut brown ale. People buy it, but don't even know what it should taste like. Everybody's making a Weisse beer now, but hardly anybody is making it right."

continued . . .

Sprecher is perhaps better known for his root beer, which he also makes in the brewery, than for his beer—which is saying something, since his beer is almost invariably very good. He will probably distribute the root beer nationally before the beer, and he is making some new lines of soft drinks, such as an orange soda made with real oranges.

Sprecher gives a brisk tour of his forty-barrel brewery. He's proud of it. At the end, he pauses by a small bar set up next to some taps. He fills some tasting glasses with Sprecher beer: a lager, a wheat, an ale, a Belgian brown, a stout. He smiles as he sips. He looks like he'd like to sit and drink all afternoon, but he can't. He's got to load up that beer and root beer, grab his checkbook and drive off into the Wisconsin countryside in search of whole raspberries for his next brew.

FOUR

Great Beer Styles of the World

W HEN IT COMES to wine, "style" is often determined by the grape being fermented or the region in which the wine is produced. This gives the wine drinker a basic idea of what's in the bottle, at least within certain parameters. Where a wine is from, or what grapes it is made from, leads to certain expectations on the part of the wine drinker.

With beer, however, it's not so easy. With beer, "style" carries a deeper meaning. It encompasses all of the brewer's many choices, from the malt and hops to the mashing techniques, through the yeast strain, fermentation temperatures and packaging. Little or nothing is left to chance in the brewhouse. Everything that happens to a beer, everything you taste in a beer, is the result of a myriad of choices made by the brewer. Beer styles also tell histories, conjure up the past and fly the flags of nations. Within any beer style, there are many variations, sometimes large ones. This is fortunate, of course. Otherwise, beer would be pretty boring. Each style has at least a few characteristics that recognizably identify it. The more you know about beer styles, the better you'll be at finding beers that suit your palate, your mood and your food.

Remember, beer is divided into two great families: ale and lager. Let's explore both of them, and the most popular styles within each family.

LAGERS

Lager is the junior branch of the beer family, a relative newcomer with bottom-fermenting yeast, a storage period called lagering, and a taste profile that is often—though not always—cleaner, lighter, drier and less fruity than ales. Here are some of the more common styles of lager.

Pilsner. Pilsner is, broadly speaking, the world's most popular beer style. Originated in the town of Pilsen (also spelled Pilsn and Plzn) in the Czech region of Bohemia, developed in Denmark, and brought to full flower in Germany, pilsners burst onto the European palate only about 150 years ago. The newfound ability to make very pale malts, the isolation of lager yeast and the availability of inexpensive machine-made glassware all helped make pilsner beers the brewing sensation of the late 1800s.

Genuine pilsners are all-malt beers—which means they contain no corn, rice, wheat or any grain other than malted barley. Pilsners range from pale gold to deep gold in color, and are dry and refreshing. Hop bitterness is sharp, clean and well-focused, but not overwhelming. A pleasant floral aroma and soft, bready malt center round out the taste. The alcohol content should be moderate, at about 5 percent by volume.

Even among the true pilsners there are regional variations. In southern Germany, the Bavarian pilsners are round and full-bodied, while in northern Germany the preferred version of pilsner is drier and hoppier. In the Czech Republic, Pilsner Urquell, the originator of the style, remains the flagship brand. Bohemian pilsners tend to be a deeper gold hue than their German counterparts, and feature a full-bodied, almost buttery malt character. The classic Czech hop, the Saaz, leaps from the glass and gives the beer an appetizing nose.

Once off its home turf, the pilsner style is less steady. There is an "international" pilsner style that is brewed around the world, but its pedigree is less impressive than the German-Czech style. These beers tend to be lighter in color and less bracingly hopped, both in the bitterness and aroma. Sometimes adjuncts—rice, corn and other cheap grains excluded from German brewhouses—make their way into these beers, lightening their character to achieve mass-market ambitions. Heineken (an all-malt beer) and Carlsberg (which uses adjuncts) are well-known examples of the international pilsner style.

American Pilsner. It is a long, depressing slide to mass-market American pilsner, a style that includes some of the world's best-selling brands. Many of these beers are marvels of technology and quality control that, combined with successful mass marketing, have allowed big American brewers to make beers with virtually no taste at all. Gone is the all-malt flavor, the sharp fragrant hops and the smoothness achieved through months of aging. In its place, American pilsner presents a watery beer that is quickly produced out of a half-malt mash—

with virtually no hops (some big U.S. brewers simply use a hop extract). The beer is then filtered within an inch of its already pallid life. The result bears the same relationship to true pilsner that mass-market white bread does to a loaf fresh out of an oven in Tuscany. That is to say, virtually none.

Helles. It is also known as *hell,* which means "pale," rather than a quick ticket to perdition. Popular in Bavaria, hellesbier is a straw-colored lager with a lighter touch than pilsner. Rather than a sharp crackle of bitterness, helles shows a soft, balanced character with malt dominating slightly. Fairly light, at a touch over 4 percent alcohol by volume, hellesbier is the favorite everyday beer of Munich. Several American microbreweries, including Stoudt's, make an excellent hellesbier.

Dortmunder Export. Slightly stronger, sweeter and more full-bodied than pilsners, perhaps Dortmunder export beers were originally designed to travel. These golden lagers are easily found in the region near Dortmund, but apparently do not get around as much anymore, at least as exports. However, the past popularity of the style is reflected by the fact that brewers are still producing them from Denmark to the United States to Japan.

Vienna Lager. Vienna malts are kilned at higher temperatures than pilsner malts, resulting in a deeper color and a caramelized flavor. The Vienna lager style obviously has its origins in Austria, but has made its way around the world. Vienna lagers are light to medium amber in color and have a soft malt sweetness on the palate, balanced by a crisp snap of hops. They have a moderate alcohol content, generally around 5 percent by volume.

Vienna lagers are very versatile beers for everyday enjoyment and complement a wide variety of foods. Beers based on this style were popular in the United States before Prohibition, and are enjoying a resurrection today in the form of popular beers such as Brooklyn Lager and Samuel Adams. Interestingly, the Vienna lager style is popular in Mexico as well—Dos Equis Amber, for example, is a Vienna lager. The Hapsburg dynasty of Austria ruled Mexico for only six years, but left a legacy of Vienna lager and polka music—a far better deal for beer drinkers than for music lovers, we think.

Oktoberfest-Marzen. A close Bavarian cousin to the Vienna lager, Oktoberfest or Marzenbier is brewed largely from Munich malt. Once again, a high kilning temperature brings out both color and flavor in the malt and in the beer. Oktoberfest beers are full of caramelish, bready malt aroma and flavor, and have just enough bitterness to keep the beer balanced and refreshing. The palate is full-bodied and soft. These beers usually have an alcoholic strength of 5.5 percent by volume, sometimes a tad higher. Many American microbreweries produce their own version of Oktoberfest beer, which tend to be hoppier and less malty than their German counterparts.

The word *Marzenbier* means "March beer," though the style is no longer brewed only in March. Before refrigeration made year-round brewing possible, stronger beer was made in the early spring to last until the following harvest in September and October, when it would be greatly enjoyed at festivals. These days, Oktoberfest beers are brewed and enjoyed year-round, though the Munich Oktoberfest remains the world's largest beer festival.

Dark Lager. Long before golden beers poured onto the scene, dark beer flowed in Germany, Bohemia and parts of Poland. The German dark lager style, called *dunkel,* is still prevalent in Bavaria. Darker malts produce a spicy, sweetish palate, redolent of caramel and coffee, while the hops take a back seat. Though not particularly strong at 5 percent or so by volume, the best of them achieve complexity without being overly heavy or cloying. The clean character of lager yeast lets the flavors of the raw ingredients come through.

In the Czech Republic, similar beers are known simply as *cerny pivo,* which means simply "dark beer," and tend to have more pronounced roast flavors. For this style, it is best to stick with the southern German breweries—too many others simply add a dash of food coloring to their other recipes. That said, Heineken turns out a respectable example, as do some American microbrewers. Should you be lucky enough to find yourself in Prague, you'll find that U Fleku's house-brewed cerny pivo is still a revelation.

Bock. Since the fourteenth century, the German town of Einbeck has been famous for its beer. The "Einbecker" style of beer is known today as *bock.* In bock beers, German malt flavors really come into their own. Moderate hopping balances a slightly sweet, malty, full-bodied palate, packed with caramelish, toasty, bready flavors. The malt comes forward partly because there's plenty of it. Bock beers are fairly strong, at 6.5 to 7.5 alcohol by volume. No doubt they have always nicely fueled the fun at the various holidays and festivals where they traditionally are served.

Most bock beers are deep copper to brown in color, but there are now a fair number of pale bocks, which range from the golden hellesbocks to the light amber maibocks. All of them retain their strength and malty flavors, while generally being somewhat lighter in body.

Doppelbock. The word *doppel* means "double," and while doppelbocks do not literally have twice the goods of bock beers, they sometimes seem to make good on that promise. Abandoning all pretense of moderation, doppelbocks revel in the deep toasty flavors of German malts. They are often aged for many months to achieve a silky smoothness, with just enough hop bitterness to keep the sweet malt character from becoming cloying. At 8 percent alcohol by volume and up, these are beers to warm the soul in winter or ward off an early spring chill.

Originally, doppelbocks were brewed and enjoyed by monks. Paulaner, the Munich brewery that originated today's doppelbock style, recalled that heritage by naming its doppelbock "Salvator" (Savior). Soon after Salvator doppelbock became famous, other breweries started to produce their own versions, and began tacking on the "-ator" suffix to their brand names. Today, we can grace our palates with Celebrator, Maximator, Optimator and Bajuvator, among others. Besides the "-ator" suffix, doppelbocks have embraced the billy goat as their mascot; if you encounter a beer with a goat on the label and/or an "-ator" name, it's no doubt designed to be a doppelbock.

Doppelbocks range in color from a deep garnet to virtually black, though the malt flavors are only slightly roasty.

ALES

Ales are the older, original version of beer, brewed with top-fermenting yeast at higher temperatures. Ales usually do not require as much conditioning as lagers, and often—but not always—carry more fruity, earthy flavors. Here are some of the most popular styles of ales.

Golden Ale. When pilsners became popular in the late 1800s, many ale breweries were hard-pressed to compete with the new "golden boy" of the beer world. They started to produce ales that mimicked pilsner's bright gold color, and a new beer style was born. Many microbrewers produce golden ales today, perhaps to lure people who normally drink mass-market beers. Well-made golden ales, however, offer their own pleasures. They are often light to medium in body, lightly hopped and pleasantly fruity, with a faint hop aroma and a clean finish. They are nice beers for warm weather and light foods.

Pale Ale. Even before pilsner made its dash across Europe, the British had learned to produce pale malts. Breweries in London, dedicated to the production of popular dark porter in the 1700s, started to brew pale ales as that century drew to a close. Pale ales, despite the name, are often not particularly pale. They range in color from a very deep gold to a deep reddish amber. "Pale" in this case means "paler than porter."

Pale ale built British towns such as Burton-on-Trent, still one of the brewing hotbeds of England. Today, pale ale has become one of the flagship styles of the American microbrewing movement. British pale ales are medium-bodied beers traditionally brewed largely from pale barley malt, with some crystal (caramel) malt and the occasional dash of dark sugar or wheat. They have a clean, sharp snap of bitterness up front, followed by a nutty malt palate with caramel notes. The aroma should be fresh, fruity and full of earthy English hops. Sometimes a faint whiff of sulfur gives away the use of hard water (for which all the Burton breweries, particularly Bass, became famous). The hard water gives the beer a crisp, dry finish. An alcohol content of 5 percent by volume is typical for pale ales.

American pale ales are similar to their British cousins, but the American exuberance and verve tend to take the place of British reserve and balance. American hops, especially the grapefruity Cascade variety, are used liberally, giving the beer a citrusy aroma and a sharp hop crackle on the palate.

Bitter. Bitter, a close relative of pale ale, is the everyday beer of the English pub. While pale ale is usually bottled, bitter is usually served on draft, often through the hydraulic handpumps that have become a revered feature of old English pubs. Bitters are brewed similarly to pale ales, but when the fermentation finishes they are placed unfiltered into casks. There, the yeast drops out and the beer builds a light natural carbonation with sublime subtleties of flavor. Considerable care and skill are required to do this properly, but the rewards are great. Bitter arrives in the glass full of complex, delicate, earthy, fruity flavors that filtered pale ales strain to match.

Bitters are usually light-to-medium-bodied, and range in alcohol content from 3.5 percent (ordinary) to 5.5 percent (extra special bitter). While bitter is the English beer that many Americans mistakenly believe should be served "warm," it in fact should be served at cellar temperature. A nice cool 55 degrees Fahrenheit will allow a bitter to show off its flair.

India Pale Ale. In the late 1700s, British brewers started sending porters and newly popular pale ales to the colonies in India, where soldiers and a growing middle class eagerly awaited beer. The colonials, from viceroy to private, were often disappointed. The voyage from London to Calcutta was a rough six-month sail, and the beers often were spoiled by the time they arrived. A London brewer named Geoffrey Hodgson solved the problem by producing a beer specially designed to travel to India. To withstand the journey this beer had to be strong in alcohol content, and the addition of nearly twice the normal hops afforded additional protection since hops are a natural preservative. When his "East India Pale Ale" reached Calcutta in perfect condition, it became an instant sensation. Hodgson earned piles of money and the eternal gratitude of beer drinkers who love the taste of hops. Eventually India pale ale (IPA) became a popular style in England, too, but over time it declined to the point that it was not much different in taste from ordinary bitter. However, American microbrewers, eager for flavor, have picked up the banner of the original IPA style and are carrying it to new heights.

India pale ale should be honey to light amber in color, with a massive hop aroma and sharp, bracing bitterness backing up a full-bodied, nutty palate and a snappy dry finish. Though refreshing in hot weather, true IPAs are rather strong at 6.5 percent to 7.5 percent alcohol by volume. British brewers are starting to pick up on the revival of the IPA style, returning it to its rightful place at the pinnacle of British brewing.

Brown Ale. Brown ales, once the favorite drink of the British working class, are getting harder to find in England, apparently having migrated to American microbreweries at the same time that American mass-market pilsners are gaining a toehold in British neighborhood pubs. Brown ales range from a deep reddish amber-brown to a nearly opaque deep chocolate brown. In England, there are regional differences. For example, in the north, such beers as the famous Newcastle Brown Ale are the norm. At the lighter end of the color spectrum, northern brown ales typically sport a malty aroma, a crisp hop edge, a nutty caramel palate and a dryish finish. In southern England, in contrast, brown ales tend to hew closer to the traditional style, with fruity aromas and subdued bitterness balancing sweet palates full of caramel and chocolate malt flavors. A darkly colored but subtly flavored variant called "mild" is worth seeking out in English pubs. It's hard to believe that a beer as low in alcohol content as mild—often 3.5 percent by volume or lower—can taste so good.

As with pale ales, American microbrewers sacrifice some subtlety for flavor. American brown ales tend to be stronger, hoppier and roastier than their English counterparts. Palates tend toward more chocolate and caramel flavors, sometimes even with a dash of coffeeish black malt for accent. Those citrusy American hops make an appearance in the aroma. Typically, brown ales range from 4 percent to 6 percent alcohol by volume, and make a fine accompaniment to dark meats and stews.

Scottish Ale. Hops do not grow in the cold windy northern climate of Scotland. So in the days before modern transportation, hops were imported from southern England. This meant that hops were pretty expensive and—not to reinforce any ethnic stereotypes here—Scottish brewers tended to use them lightly. Probably due more to their brewing heritage than to their supposed national tightfistedness, Scottish brewers today continue to use hops lightly. What Scottish beers may lack in hop character, however, they make up for with their warm, rich maltiness.

While they range from moderate to quite strong in alcohol content, Scottish ales are usually tawny to deep reddish-brown, with a nutty caramel and vanilla-like quality to the malt flavor. Buttery overtones in the nose and on the palate are common, as well as a faint smokiness. Most Scottish ales (often called scotch ales, particularly in stronger versions, though they have nothing to do with scotch whisky) are full-bodied and slightly sweet, with just enough hops to hold the flavor in balance.

Old Ale. There's no telling whether this name originally referred to beers that had been nicely aged or to those brewed in an old-fashioned style. These days, old ales are deeply colored beers, ranging from deep red to dark brown, with wide malty shoulders. Strength and rich fruity complexity are the hallmarks of old ales. Hop bitterness tends to be moderate but rarely assertive, letting the malt flavors and fruit aromas come to the fore. Even in the darker old ales, roast malt flavor is restrained to chocolate notes. While the alcohol content usually ranges from 6.5 percent to 8 percent by volume, it sometimes drifts higher, taking on aspects of barley wine.

Porter. All the rage in both Britain and America during the 1700s, porter was George Washington's favorite beer. He even brewed it himself, as did many early Americans. Originating in London as a blend of various beers, porter evolved into a deep brown to black ale with a medium-bodied palate and distinct coffeeish, roasted malt flavors. Porter died out for a time in its native England, but once again American microbrewers have refocused everyone's attention. American porters tend to have a dry edge, while the reborn English ones tend toward more sweetness. The hopping is moderate to somewhat assertive, with the roasted malt and caramel malt contributing more aroma and flavor than bite. Porters are usually moderate in strength, between 5 percent and 6 percent alcohol by volume.

Stout. Stout and porter used to be the same thing, but the two terms are rarely used interchangeably anymore because the styles have diverged. Guinness, the Irish brewery now inseparable from the stout style, actually started as a porter producer. After Arthur Guinness had built his fortune on porter, he introduced a heavier "Stout Porter," which soon took plain porter's place in many people's affections. Stout has since fragmented into several variations, but they all have several things in common. Fairly large amounts of highly roasted malts are used in brewing stout, giving the beer a coffee-chocolate roasted flavor and often an espresso-like bite. The color is invariably a dark reddish-brown so deep as to appear black.

The border between stout and porter remains a fuzzy one, but stouts are generally fuller-bodied and roastier. Hop bitterness is at least moderate and sometimes fairly assertive. Irish stouts tend to have a sharpish edge and a very dry finish. While Guinness is the standard-bearer for the dry Irish stout style, there are other excellent examples, most notably Beamish, with its beautiful hop nose. Contrary to their appearance and big flavor, when it comes to alcohol content, Irish stouts are rather light beers. Draught Guinness, at about 4 percent alcohol by volume, is slightly weaker than Budweiser. When the style evolved, the Irish were traditionally a working-class people, and a flavorful beer you could drink all evening without ill effect was a wonderful thing. It still is.

English stouts tend to be sweeter, some of them to the point of being a bit cloying. Oatmeal stout is another variation, and tends to have a silky smooth quality lent by the addition of oatmeal to the mash. Microbrewed American stouts are usually medium-dry and big on roasted character. The American stouts also tend to be a bit stronger than Irish or English stouts.

Imperial Stout. Tsarina Catherine the Great was a woman of strong appetites who usually got what she wanted. And among the things she wanted was delicious stout from England. Unfortunately, by the time barrels of stout reached the Baltic ports from London, they usually had spoiled. British brewers solved the problem by brewing a very strong stout, braced against the long journey by high alcohol content and a generous dose of hops. The style became known as Imperial Russian Stout. Courage, the British brewery that was Catherine's main supplier, is still producing its Imperial Russian Stout today.

Imperial stouts are typified by a strength of over 7.5 percent alcohol by volume, and an intense roasted flavor with powerful fruity aromas. The palate is full-bodied and warming. Imperial stouts make great rich-chocolate dessert beers and great fireplace beers—the perfect thing to help you face up to a long winter, even if it only seems like you're in Siberia.

Barley Wine. In the early 1700s, the emergence of a wealthy merchant class, advances in malting technology and a more scientific approach to the brewing process gave rise to ales that rivaled the finest wines in their complexity and strength. These were originally called October beers (October was considered the best month to brew them), malt liquors or malt wines. By the early 1800s, the term ''barley wine'' had been coined. A barley wine is a very strong top-fermented ale, with an alcohol content ranging from 7.5 percent to 14 percent by volume, giving the beer a warming quality usually associated with wine, or even sherry. Even the most unassuming of ale yeasts often reacts with voluptuous passion to the strong wort, resulting in a beer with great depth of flavor, unparalleled richness and a fruity, heady aroma. A beer cannot be a true barley wine without taking on the mantle of alcoholic warmth, but it should eschew the hotter character of Belgian triples and Trappist beers. A great barley wine has all the depth, complexity, smoothness, body and power of a fat Burgundy wine.

Barley wines are usually bottled unfiltered, and they often improve with age for many years. Thomas Hardy's Ale from the Pope brewery in England is among the most famous, and the original 1968 ''vintage'' is reported to be steadily improving. We once mentioned to a Pope brewer that we had heard Thomas Hardy's Ale is best after being laid down for several years. When did he think it was best? ''After ten,'' he said. ''Ten in the morning.''

Belgian Pale Ale. Similar in many ways to English and American pale ales, Belgian pale ales, like most Belgian beers, have their own distinctive twists. While they are moderate in alcohol at around 5 percent by volume, they often have spicy aromas of the sort associated with heavier styles. Sometimes this spiciness is the result of the house yeast strain, but Belgian brewers are not averse to adding a dash of actual spice to their worts. Belgian pale ales tend to be light amber to deep copper in color, with nice head formation and toasty malt palates that bring forth notes of the fruit and a caramel sweetness reminiscent of dark candy sugar. Speciale Palm, a classic of the style, is the top-selling ale in Belgium.

Flemish Red Ale. The sharply refreshing sweet and sour ales of West Flanders are in many ways a throwback to an earlier era of brewing. Tartness is not a characteristic most brewers wish to find in their beer, but it is a central feature of the palate of these beers. The sour character comes partly from the blend of yeasts employed in the fermentation, but also from long aging in uncoated oak vats. Resins, tannins and bacterial strains migrate during the aging from the oak into the beer, lending it not only its trademark sharpness, but also a remarkable range of funky, fruity and earthy notes. Hops take a back seat and let the acidity do the work, bringing the beer to a close with a dry finish. At 4.5 percent to 5.5 percent alcohol by volume, Flemish red ales are light enough to be enjoyed every day, and are terrific with salads. Rodenbach is the reigning king of this style. Its startlingly deep red color is derived from specialty malts and from the raw wood.

Flemish Brown Ale. Flemish brown ales and red ales, identified and defined as distinct styles by Michael Jackson, share many characteristics, though browns are known for an even greater depth and complexity of flavor. Less dry than Flemish red ales, the brown ales retain the sweet and sour balance while adding deep flavors reminiscent of raisins, chocolate and sherry. Unlike the red ales, these beers are bottle-conditioned, and can age nicely for several years. Generally matured in steel rather than oak, these beers draw earthy tones from roasted malts and idiosyncratic yeast strains. Alcohol by volume is usually between 5 percent and 6 percent, but occasionally drifts higher.

Trappist Ale. Monastic brewing within the walls of abbeys has been a tradition for many centuries. The Trappist order of monks, among the most austere, still carries on brewing to this day. There are six Trappist breweries in the world. Five are in Belgium: Chimay, Orval, Westmalle, Westvleteren and Rochefort. One, Schaapskooi, is in the Netherlands. The term "Trappist," when applied to beer, is similar to an *appellation d'origine controlee* in wine—only these six breweries may use it.

Technically speaking, Trappist ales do not comprise a single style, but a family of styles that has had a profound influence on brewing in Belgium and beyond. Since life has scarcely changed inside the walls of these monasteries for centuries, the beers reflect styles of brewing that no doubt otherwise would have been lost. Trappist ales tend to be strong, sweetish, fruity, spicy, earthy, aromatic and bottle-conditioned. Alcohol by volume ranges from 6.5 percent to almost 12 percent.

Belgian Abbey Ale. The beers produced by the world's six Trappist breweries are much admired and imitated. When a brewery takes on the name of a saint or a non-brewing abbey for its products, the beer is referred to as an "abbey ale." Usually these beers mimic the characteristics of Trappist ales. Despite the fact that they are not divinely derived, some of these breweries produce excellent beers in their own right.

The most popular styles among abbey ales are *dobbel* (also spelled "dubbel") and *tripel*, for "double" and "triple." Dobbels are similar to Flemish brown ales, but tend to be deeper and a bit sweeter, and lack the sour edge. Plummy, raisiny and chocolaty aromas and flavors dominate, and hopping is moderate. Dobbels are usually deep brown in color.

The orangy bright gold color of tripels belie their strength, which is generally between 8 percent and 9 percent by volume. A fine tripel should have a snappy bitterness and a bright fruity aroma redolent of hops, peaches and pears. They are expansive and warming on the palate, and slightly sweet in the center with a spicy, hoppy finish.

Belgian Wheat Beer. Also known as "white beer" or *witbier* (in Flemish), Belgian wheat beers are among the most refreshing in the world. This old style declined into obscurity after World War II, but was revived in 1966 when Pierre Celis began producing the classic Hoegaarden Wit. The name "white beer" derives from its cloudy pale yellow appearance.

Like many Belgian ales, witbiers are bottle-conditioned for a brisk, naturally spritzy carbonation. A special strain of yeast produces apple-like aromas, but more importantly, these beers are also spiced. Dried curaçao orange peel and coriander seed are evident in the first sniff, blending with fruity fermentation aromas to produce a uniquely perfumey nose. Bitterness is quite light, and the palate is fruity, slightly tart and light-bodied, ranging from semi-sweet to medium dry. At a moderate 4.5 percent or so alcohol by volume, these beers are great for everyday drinking and make a perfect match for many salads.

Lambic. The Payottenland region of Belgium is home to the lambic beers, the world's oldest commercially produced beer styles. Where other modern brewers carefully ensure that wild yeast is excluded from their brews, lambic brewers take the opposite tack, flinging the windows open and inviting nature in. This is the way beer was fermented hundreds of years ago, when even the most accomplished brewers didn't know what yeast was, and all beers underwent "spontaneous fermentation" by wild yeast and bacteria. Opening the windows of the brewhouse today and letting whatever is out there float in would be a disaster in most places in the world; you'd be lucky to have a beer that was at all drinkable. But the microflora in Payottenland continue to produce some of the world's most complex beers.

Lambics are wheat beers of conventional strength, but spontaneous fermentation and aging in wooden barrels give them fruity, funky aromas and sharp sour palates. Behind the sourness is a riot of earthy, toasty flavors and aromas, comparable to the finest blue cheeses. Lambics are often aged in wood for years, becoming quite assertive in character. In the United States, we are likely to find a version called *gueuze,* which is a blend of old and young lambic beers: the blend softens the sour edge without sacrificing all the complexity of the older beer. (Though gueuze is a challenging taste even for some of the most devoted beer lovers. "A wet horse blanket" is one of the kinder descriptions from those who have tried but failed to become fans.) Traditionally, lambic beers are bottle-conditioned and flintily dry, but many brewers have caved in to the public sweet tooth and added sugar to their beers. While lambics are often used as a base for fruit beers, the term *lambic* refers to any spontaneously fermented wheat beer produced in the Payottenland in the same way that "champagne" refers only to bubbly from the Champagne region of France. "Lambic," it should be emphasized, does not refer to all fruit beers.

Fruit Beers. Adding fruit to beer is a tradition that is probably almost as old as beer itself. While hops are now the main flavoring for beer, the tradition of adding fruit lives on, particularly in Belgium. Lambic beers are most often used as the base for these beers, but some brewers, such as Liefmans, use other sour-edged beers as the basis for these beery confections. Raspberries (*frambozen* or *framboise*) and sour cherries (*kriek*) are most often used, both being locally grown and prized for their aromatic qualities. Peach (*peche*) is also popular. When the lambic method is used, the raw fruit is added directly to the wooden casks containing beer that is already well-aged. The yeast attacks the sugars in the fruit, breaking it down over weeks or months, and yielding a rosy-colored beer (or peachy-colored, in the case of peche) with a pronounced fruity character.

Black currants, strawberries, plums and bananas have started to make their appearances on the Belgian fruit beer scene, but most of these beers are mere cartoons, often made with syrups and juices rather than real fruit. American microbrewers have also started to latch onto fruit as an exciting (and commercial) direction for brewing. Though many of these American fruit beers have all the character of a can of soda pop, there are some worth trying out.

Bavarian Wheat Beer. Centuries before Germany's famous pilsners began pleasing palates around the world, there were wheat beers—the fastest-growing style in the German market today, and one of the fastest growing among American craft brewing styles. The use of a high proportion of wheat produces a beer that is light-bodied yet full-flavored, perfect for summer. *Weizen* being the word for wheat, the southern

German wheat beer style is known as either *weissbier* or *weizenbier*. Bavarian weizenbier is traditionally brewed from a grist containing not less than 50 percent wheat, and is pitched with a special top-fermenting yeast strain that produces the distinctive spicy flavors associated with this style. Bavarian weizenbier is of moderate strength at 4.5 percent to 5.5 percent alcohol by volume. These beers are highly carbonated, with a lightly hopped yet snappy palate, a huge creamy head produced by proteins in the wheat, and a fruity, spicy, clove-like aroma that is more pronounced in some versions than in others. Most of these beers are bottle-conditioned, leaving the beer robust, flavorful and cloudy with yeast, in which case it is referred to as a *hefeweizen* (*hefe* means yeast).

It is a tribute to the German beer drinker that hefeweizen far outsells *kristalweizen*, the filtered version of the style. Even more robust variants on this style include the considerably stronger *weizenbocks* (6 percent to 8 percent alcohol by volume) and the darker *dunkelweizens*. Weizenbier should be served in a foot-tall, 20-ounce glass that can handle its somewhat explosive carbonation and impressive head. Bavarian weizenbiers are becoming widely available in the United States, and the style is rapidly taking hold among American microbrewers and pub-brewers as well. Incidentally, the slice of lemon that Germans once flipped into their kristalweizens is now considered rather declassé in Germany, though many American beer bars and brewpubs automatically attach the slice to the top of the glass unless you ask the bartender to hold the fruit.

Berliner Weisse. In the north of Germany, the predominant wheat style is Berliner weisse (white), a pale, sparingly hopped, lightweight beer with a sharply tart palate that German drinkers usually offset by adding a dash of *schuss*—sweet raspberry or woodruff syrup. The startlingly acidic flavor of Berliner weisse is achieved by the addition of a lactobacillus to a top-fermenting yeast strain, a practice that connects these beers to the Belgian tradition of lactic fermentation. Even without the syrup, the beer has its own earthy, fruity aroma.

Tinted red or green by the syrups, bottle-conditioned Berliner weisse is usually enjoyed out of a bowl-shaped glass into which the beer has been carefully poured to avoid the yeast sediment at the bottom of the bottle. Quite a light beer at 3 percent alcohol by volume, and sometimes less, Berliner weisse can be a great aperitif or an accompaniment to smoked fish. And it's great for quaffing and quenching on those hot summer days.

Sara Doersam

SARA DOERSAM IS the editor and co-publisher of *Southern Draft Brew News,* which covers international, national and regional beer and brewing news. The paper has a circulation of forty thousand: 85 percent male, mostly twenty-one to thirty-three years old and married, 72 percent college graduates, and with annual household incomes of $40,000 to $75,000.

"I've been a swill beer drinker since my college days," says Sara, who grew up in Indiana, where sloshing down Hudepohl-Schoenling Little Kings helped her get through Indiana University. Working in San Francisco, she met her husband, Phil. She got him into homebrewing to save money on all the beer he was drinking, but didn't get interested herself until after they moved to Florida in 1989.

"Once we got settled into a home and secured jobs—Phil worked in computer operations at the corporate offices of General Mills Restaurants, Inc., and I was billing manager for a group of neurologists—he joined the Central Florida Home Brewers (CFHB). I tagged along, but didn't really have much interest in craft brewing. He then joined the Space Coast Associates for the Advancement of Zymurgy, the Cape Canaveral-based homebrew club. I still hadn't much interest. In fact, I remember telling him in 1991 that I would enjoy the tastings a lot more if we were tasting wine instead of beer. Still, his enthusiasm didn't diminish. So I decided I'd better try to change my attitude about craft-brewed beer."

Sara and Phil realized that the South, unlike most other areas of the country, didn't have a good brewspaper. With the help of her dad, Jerry Gengler, a retired newspaperman, they started the bimonthly *Southern Draft Brew News* in 1993. The paper took off, and Sara quit her job in mid-1994. Phil quit and joined her full-time on the paper, as advertising director and co-publisher, in early 1995.

"We love publishing the brewspaper," Sara says. "It allows us the opportunity to take road trips to beer conferences, festivals and brewpubs. We are working under a deadline for about three weeks every other month when we are busy contacting potential advertisers, receiving copy and advertisements, editing, writing stories, laying out the paper, pasting up the boards to be sent to the printer. We thought life would slow down once we became self-employed, but as we were warned, it was quite the opposite. We're busier than ever, but now we get to stop and enjoy good beer and good friends guilt-free."

Stan Hieronymus and Daria Labinsky

STAN HIERONYMUS AND Daria Labinsky are a couple who, like so many others in the good beer movement, came to it as a result of a mid-life crisis. They had good careers as journalists—she was entertainment editor, he was assistant managing editor at the *Journal Star* in Peoria, Ill.—but wanted something more. When the employee-owned newspaper was bought out, they grabbed the chance to cash out and start over.

Since 1992, they have been full-time freelancers. At first, Daria often did the writing, Stan the photos. Sometimes they switched. They roamed the country doing travel stories for various newspapers such as the *Washington Post, Newsday,* the *Boston Globe,* the *Los Angeles Times* and various magazines. Their first beer story was an assignment for Daria to write about brewpubs in Florida for *American Brewer.* They met Daniel Bradford, the publisher of another magazine, *All About Beer,* and he began giving them assignments. "Beer has gradually staked a major claim to our time," Stan said. It must be said that these two do not seem like unwilling victims. They may like writing about beer, but they love to drink it, too. Now they also write, together or separately, for *Beer the Magazine, Brew!, Brew Your Own, Great Lakes Brewing News* and *Brewpub.*

They started a good monthly newsletter called *Beer Travelers,* which includes news and reviews about bars and brewpubs across the country. Driving fifty thousand miles a year from bar to bar, and getting many letters and E-mail messages from readers who tell them about their favorite joints, Stan and Daria have built what is probably the most complete database in America for where to drink good beer. In addition to the newsletter, they have also put out a book, the *Beer Travelers Guide,* which is a must for anyone who travels to different American cities and likes to try the best local brews and most interesting local bars. If you can't find it in a bookstore, or you want to check out their newsletter, get in touch with Stan and Daria at *Beertrav@aol.com,* or at P.O. Box 187, Washington IL 61571. You can also order the book or their newsletter at 1-800-977-BEER. Their Website, "Destination Beer," is at *http://www.allaboutbeer.com/beertravelers.*

FIVE

The Good Beer Revolution, 1876—

T HERE WERE 2,700 breweries in the United States in 1876. A century later there were 40—a few giants and a scattering of regional and local breweries. The industry's emphasis was on producing a bland product. Taste mattered little, since marketing seemed to be the driving force behind the industry's perennial growth. Anheuser-Busch, with perhaps the best packaging in the world and extremely strong advertising campaigns year after year (actually, sports season after sports season), became dominant, building up a market share of more than 40 percent. One of every four beers purchased in America was—and is—a Budweiser.

Light beer, a little more watery and weak in flavor, with fewer calories and a little less alcohol content, became an industry standard. Many good brewers hated the idea of watered-down beer, of course. Pennsylvania brewer Joe Ortlieb once mischievously produced a "light" Ortlieb beer six-pack that included five bottles of regular beer and one bottle of water, for self-mixing.

In general, however, mass-market beer has changed little since World War II, except for the addition of more adjuncts aimed at producing beer more cheaply and lengthening its shelf life. Recipes were tweaked occasionally to create new products that were little more than the vehicles to carry new marketing and promotional campaigns. "Dry" beer, for example, used even less malt and more rice or corn, to produce less taste with a slightly higher alcohol content. (Dry beer's failure in the marketplace, we think, remains proof that even multimillion-dollar advertising campaigns can't make Americans drink just anything.) Best of all, for the big brewers' number-crunchers anyway, the additional adjuncts made their beer even cheaper to brew, thereby adding to the bottom line.

So-called "ice" beer was another slight variation, being brewed at lower than normal temperatures—but without the effort and expense that goes into the original German *eisbock* (pronounced "ICE-bock") style. The original German style calls for slightly freezing the beer to a slush and then straining out the ice to yield a beer with a higher alcohol content and a complex concentration of flavor.

Another example of misleading labeling, at least to beer purists, is the can or bottle that claims the beer is "draft" or "genuine draft." Only beer that is served straight from barrels or kegs is draft beer.

The power of mass marketing for beer companies such as Anheuser-Busch, Miller and Coors in recent years can be seen in the way that their advertising and labeling sometimes promoted the obvious. For example, on occasion a mass-market beer would promote its hops. "Hey," we once heard someone say. "Did you hear about that new beer brewed with hops?" The guy had to be let down gently: Virtually all beer is brewed with hops. Similarly, some beers occasionally boast that they are "cold-filtered" when there is no such thing as "warm-filtered."

One widespread misconception among beer lovers was that American beer was lower in alcohol content than the more flavorful, darker brews of Europe. Nonsense. Many European beers were and are quite strong, but the typical American mass-market beer remains stronger in alcohol content than many English and German beers. What's more, the big American breweries actually brew very strong beer every day. They just don't sell it to us, at least not until watering it down first. Much of America's mass-market beer is brewed at "high gravity"— about 8 percent alcohol by volume. Before being bottled or canned or kegged, however, the beer is blended down with water to about 4 percent ABV. The watering-down process allows a big brewery with a brewing capacity of 1 million barrels a year to produce 1.6 million barrels. At one point, Anheuser-Busch was grumping about Coors' advertising claims that its beer sold on the East Coast was made with Rocky Mountain spring water. A-B pointed out that the beer was actually being brewed in Colorado and freighted to Virginia, where it was blended with Virginia water before it was sold. Craft-brewed beer, in contrast, is brewed and sold at its original strength, and not watered down.

THE BEER REBELLION

The good beer revolution in America began in the West. One obvious reason was the new technology industries, especially computers and software. Northern California, Washington, Oregon and Colorado attracted a powerful young socioeconomic class that was not bound to the conservative business traditions of the East—such as wearing neckties to the office every day, and drinking expensive wine or hard liquor at lunch and after work. To the established business world, beer was a working-class drink. The young Western technocrats, on the other hand, liked beer. Moreover, they had the intellectual curiosity and financial resources to search out better beers, and when necessary the technical wherewithal to make good beer themselves.

In addition, the early commercial microbrewers of the West Coast had a model to follow. In many ways, the rise of microbreweries in America has been an echo of the growth of small family-run wineries, which over the past quarter century have gone from a tiny share of the U.S. market to about half the nation's wine sales. The first modern-era American microbrewery—all those 2,700 breweries in 1878 would be micros today, of course—was started in Sonoma County, north of San Francisco, an area well known for its small family wineries. The founder was Jack McAuliffe, who became acquainted with good beer while serving in the U.S. navy in Britain, and was impressed by the efforts of Britain's Campaign for Real Ale to promote quality brewing. The New Albion brewery started selling beer in 1977, and lasted six years. By then, there were a handful of other microbreweries that are still around, including Sierra Nevada, which two buddies began in a garage in Chico, Calif., in 1980. Colorado got its first microbrewery in 1980, Washington in 1982, and Oregon in 1984. By 1985, there were a grand total of 21 craft breweries in America—microbreweries, contract brewers and brewpubs. Today there are more than 1,000, and some industry analysts believe that could double in the next few years. One important historical note: Brewers such as Fritz Maytag and Jack McAuliffe anticipated the shift in public taste toward good beer, but the word about good beer was spread by Michael Jackson, who for years was a lone voice in the wilderness. His seminal *World Guide to Beer,* published in 1977, was the manifesto of the good beer movement.

While some of the West Coast microbreweries have done and continue to do very well, it was an East Coast contract brewer that did more than any other brewery to turn the masses on to microbrews and the appeal of craft beers. The Boston Beer Co. was founded by Jim Koch, an advertising and marketing man whose family had been in brewing for generations. There is little doubt that Koch could have made his millions marketing any number of products to the American people. Fortunately, he chose beer. Through his flagship label, Samuel

Adams Boston Lager, and more than a dozen other Samuel Adams styles, Koch introduced millions of Americans to good beer. Some now drink nothing else. For many, however, Sam Adams was a transition beer that showed them how beer did not need to taste like Bud, Miller or Coors, how it could have a richer, fuller taste. For many people, that first Sam Adams was a springboard into the world of good beer, and they began experimenting with different beers from other small breweries across America and around the world. They began to seek out brewpubs to try fresh beer and even more styles.

That is not to say, however, that everyone in the craft brewing business regards Jim Koch as the patron saint of microbrewing. In fact, most don't regard him as a microbrewer at all. Perhaps this is a good place to pause and define some terms. A microbrewer, according to the Institute for Brewing Studies, is any brewery that produces its own beer in its own production facility—brewery, in other words—and brews fifteen thousand barrels or less a year. (Originally the definition was ten thousand barrels or less a year, and now some people in the business are in favor of pushing the ceiling even higher, to twenty thousand or thirty thousand or even fifty thousand barrels a year.)

The Boston Beer Co. is not a microbrewery under that definition for two reasons. One is that it is far too big. Boston Beer brews more than 1 million barrels a year—not less than a big brewery spills, a comment that Koch borrowed from other microbrewers and adapted as one of his overstated advertising claims, but still a lot less than Anheuser-Busch's more than 80 million barrels a year.

Another reason Sam Adams is not a microbrew is that Koch does not make the beer himself in his own breweries. The company does have a small brewery in Boston, with a couple of small kettles that make batches of ten barrels. But that cute little brewery is used primarily to research new brews and to show to tourists. In truth, the Sam Adams you drink is probably made in a big brewery in New York or Ohio or Pennsylvania or somewhere else in huge kettles that make up to five hundred barrels of beer at a time. Sam Adams is not micro-brewed, but rather contract-brewed, and Jim Koch is principally a contract brewer. He contracts with other, larger brewers to make his beer to his recipe and specifications.

To some purists, Jim Koch and his Sam Adams beer are guilty of deception, of tricking consumers into thinking that what they are drinking is microbrewed in Boston. Koch suggests it's like Julia Childs coming to your house with bags full of groceries and whipping up dinner in your kitchen. When you sit down to eat, is it your dinner just because she made it in your kitchen, or is it Julia Childs' dinner? Koch insists it's his brewers and his recipe no matter where it's made, so it's his beer, too.

None of this matters very much to most beer drinkers. When you get right down to it, most people still think of a microbrew as anything that isn't imported and isn't Bud, Miller or Coors. Perhaps "craft beer" is a better term for good beer that is brewed with production procedures and recipes that go beyond the mass-market beers, no matter where the beer is brewed or who brews it. Craft brewers, for example, would not consider brewing extra-strong beer and then watering it down the way that big breweries do in order to increase the amount of beer they produce. When you drink a craft beer, you're drinking the original, all-natural product.

There are several dozen other contract brewers besides Boston Beer Co., some of them smaller than true microbreweries. There's nothing wrong with contract brewing, of course; many small brewing companies would never have made their first batches of craft beer had they waited to raise enough money to build or buy their own breweries. By renting the facilities of existing breweries that had extra capacity, they also were able to take advantage of the production methods and quality-control measures already in place. Still, most contract brewers are careful not to call themselves microbreweries, though Pete's bragged of being microbrewed on its various "Wicked" labels even when it was brewing more than 300,000 barrels a year in other people's breweries.

On a smaller scale than Sam Adams, Pete's was the other big craft beer success story of the 1980s and '90s, becoming the No. 2 "national" craft brewing operation despite having a staff of only seven. Pete Slosberg was the founder, but served primarily as the company's chief spokesman. During the periods of the most rapid growth and financial success for Pete's Wicked in the early to mid 1990s, he had relatively little to do with the actual making of the beer or running of the company. Pete's was able to have such a small staff because it was merely a marketing company that contracted everything else to Stroh's, including ingredient sourcing, production scheduling, brewing and packaging, quality control, invoicing, collecting payments and regulatory compliance. Rather than a microbrewery, the Institute for Brewing Studies classified Pete's as a regional brewery because it produced between 15,000 and 500,000 barrels—no matter that it was distributed nationally, not regionally. Any brewing company making more than 500,000 barrels, including Sam Adams, is considered a large commercial brewery.

HOMEBREWING

It would be difficult to over-estimate the importance of homebrewing in the good beer revolution. Homebrewing was not exactly a popular hobby in the 1970s. In fact, it was illegal under federal law. The handful of persistent beer lovers who scrounged ingredients and swapped recipes word-of-mouth were outlaws, akin to hillbilly moonshiners. However, in 1979 President Carter signed the law legalizing homebrewing in America. There are still specific restrictions in some states, but under federal law homebrewers now are allowed to produce up to one hundred gallons of beer a year for personal enjoyment, and up to two hundred gallons of beer a year for households including two or more adults. They are not allowed to sell the beer they brew. From a handful of homebrewers back in the early 1970s, there are now 25,000 members of the American Homebrewers Association. Tens of thousands more are in local clubs, or just making beer on their own. The AHA estimates that more than 1.5 million Americans have at least tried brewing their own beer at home.

Michael Jackson hasn't kept count, but he reckons that several thousand of those American brewers have come up to him at beer festivals where he is signing books and asked him to sample their beer. He used to take the bottles away with him to try at home, but lugging them in his suitcase became too cumbersome. Besides, the bottles of homebrew sometimes exploded. (That was why he was also sure to store them in the bathroom of his hotel room overnight, with the door closed.)

Eventually, Jackson began tasting proffered homebrew on the spot, as soon as it was offered. The homebrewer would hold forth his beer as if it was nectar straight from Olympus, carefully uncap it and then pour it, with great concentration, into an especially clean glass brought from home. No way did he want his beer sullied by the afterwash of some inferior brew that Jackson had had in his glass earlier. Michael would inevitably raise the glass to the light, study it for a moment or two, murmur something about the color, move the glass down in front of his goatee for a sniff and, after another moment of reflection, swirl it a tiny bit and then take a healthy sip. Michael always had something nice to say—color, nose, clarity, whatever—and the homebrewer would all but glow, beaming with pride. Jackson then usually had one or more cogent comments that could be taken as constructive criticism but that the homebrewer really didn't hear. He was still flying high on the compliment, and already envisioning how he would return triumphant to his homebrew club and announce, "Michael Jackson liked my beer!"

Some homebrewers have had other dreams come true, winning local, regional and national contests for their recipes. A few have had an even greater honor—seeing local microbrewers pick up their recipes and actually make their beer for public consumption. Brew-on-premises operations, small rent-a-breweries that allow homebrewers to come in and brew their own beer in larger quantities than they could at home on their stovetops, have become an intermediate step for some homebrewers who have visions of creating their own commercial labels in the same way that many of the little mom-and-pop wineries started in California.

Many homebrewers have graduated to become commercial brewers in microbreweries and brewpubs, sometimes starting a company themselves and sometimes being hired by start-up or existing micros or brewpubs. Some had no formal training and were entirely self-taught. Others served apprenticeships under experienced brewers, often starting as unpaid volunteers or interns. Some studied at the handful of formal training courses in brewing, such as the programs at the University of California at Davis or the U.S. Brewers' Academy's Siebel Institute in Chicago or the Microbrewers Association courses offered through the University of Wisconsin in Madison. Even when homebrewing evolves into commercial brewing, however, for the brewers themselves the process remains an intriguing combination of art and science.

LEGAL HURDLES

Shakespeare may have known what he was talking about when he suggested outlawing weak beer along with killing all the lawyers. If federal law was a headache for homebrewers, state laws from Prohibition and the immediate post–Prohibition era have been a bad hangover for many craft brewers. As a result, many states have had to change laws in recent years to allow people to brew and sell craft beer.

In Virginia, for example, it wasn't until 1995 that homebrewers could take their beer out of their homes, even to share with a friend next door. It was also illegal to hold a beer festival.

Georgia allowed brewpubs, but had a law requiring them to carry at least one beer from a major distributor. One brewpub owner joked that he was going to stock a single can of Busch and charge $20 for it.

Some states required that beer bottles must be a certain size—and the 22-ounce bottle favored by some of America's best microbrewers is usually not on the approved list.

A number of states have "franchise" laws, drafted after Prohibition to protect local beverage distributors, that make it difficult for a brewery to change distributors, even if the distributor is mishandling the beer or just plain refusing to sell it. One Virginia microbrewery had to pay an uncooperative distributor $75,000 to allow the brewery to use another distributor that was eager to sell its beer.

In some states, craft brewers have been forced to mount lobbying campaigns in hopes of persuading state legislators to change laws from the 1930s that require beer over a certain strength—6 percent alcohol by volume seems to be a magic number in many states—to be called a malt liquor or something else other than beer or ale. Some states continued to block any sales of beer stronger than 6 percent ABV (alcohol by volume), which made it illegal for their citizens to sample some of the best beers in the world, such as ales made by Trappist monks. In Ohio, anything over 6 percent was malt liquor, and anything over 8 percent could not be sold at all. Utah, with its heavy Mormon influence, prohibited sales of any beer stronger than 3.2 percent. Small wonder, then, that Utah now consumes barely thirteen gallons of beer per capita per year, the lowest in the United States.

Nevada, if you're curious, is the biggest beer-drinking state: thirty-five gallons per capita. Since Nevada is notoriously down the list of states for craft brewing and good beer bars, that means there's probably enough Budmillercoors running through the state to overspill the Hoover Dam. Compared with Utah's thirteen gallons and Nevada's thirty-five gallons, the national average for beer consumption is about twenty-one gallons per person per year, down slightly in recent years.

THE BUSINESS OF BEER

Brewing craft beer is one thing. Selling it is something entirely different. There is probably no craft brewer who has gotten into financial trouble and will admit that it was because people didn't like the beer. Virtually every craft brewer that has had financial difficulty, however, has blamed it at least in part on distribution problems. Even if you microbrewed a great beer, and there were plenty of people out there eager to drink it, there were often problems finding wholesalers to distribute it and retailers to sell it to the public.

Craft beer was a new and different product. The wholesaler or retailer didn't know much about it, couldn't describe it to customers and had no idea how to sell it. Most damning of all, it wasn't Bud, Miller or Coors, none of which required any selling. Distributors threw the mass-market brands on the truck and dumped them off at the bar or store, and the retailer stocked them in cases, twelve-packs and six-packs on shelves or in stacks on the floor. With the mass-market brands, there weren't any interruptions from customers saying, "Hey, what can you tell me about this beer? What does it taste like? How is it made? Where is it from? How strong is it? Is it dark or light?" For wholesalers and retailers, microbrewed beer was a pain in the butt to sell.

Any lesser product would have died right there, in the arms of the people whose job it was to sell it but who didn't know enough or care enough about how to sell it. In spite of the foot-dragging, though, consumers wanted to drink the stuff. They went into their local super-markets and liquor stores and asked about Sam Adams, Pete's, that beer they'd tried when skiing out in Colorado, the one they'd had in a pub in England or the one with the funny name that a buddy had recommended. Craft brewers and their salespeople learned that they had to educate wholesalers and retailers.

Gradually, most retailers and their distributors began to realize the good beer revolution was real. More and more people really did want to drink good beer. Moreover, distributors and retailers realized that the higher prices on American craft beer and gourmet imports—super-premium prices, in the beer trade—also provided higher margins for them. Many distributors finally became converts when they realized that their sales of craft beer just kept going up and up—50 percent a year was not unusual—while mass-market brands struggled to stay even.

Retailers, who were closer to the public, saw and heard the demand firsthand, and many of them harassed their distributors to bring in new microbrew labels and new imports. Restaurants and bars saw that craft beer drinkers were generally older, better dressed, better educated—the kind of crowd they wanted, in other words, at least compared to head-banging young guys only interested in drinking as much of the cheapest beer they could. "We switched over to all microbrews, and we haven't had a fight in here since," one bar owner testified. Good beer drinkers didn't drink as much, but their bar bills were just as big, and they were more likely to order food.

Good restaurants, however, still presented obstacles for microbrew-ers. One salesman for the Brooklyn Brewery developed a unique ap-proach when confronted with a restaurateur who had always believed beer was a blue-collar drink that had no place in his three-star restaurant. He carried a couple of mass-market labels, and that was it. "Look," the salesman said. "You make sure you have the freshest, best ingredients. You hire great cooks. You train your wait staff. You have a cellar full of fine wine to complement the food. You do everything to create a great dining experience for your customers. *Except you serve beer they can buy in a gas station.*" The restaurateur reluctantly agreed to stock a handful of American microbrews and gourmet imported beers, and within a few weeks was asking for new beers and begging the salesman to help him expand the offerings and develop a beer menu comparable to his wine list.

THE GOOD BEER PHENOMENON

As the craft brewing industry has grown, it has attracted people—drinkers, brewers, investors, sales staff, distributors, retailers, beer journalists—for a number of reasons. Some simply wanted to be part of the newest fad. Some liked the crazy names and labels, such as Great Lakes Brewing's Eliot Ness Vienna Lager, Yellow Rose Brewing's Bubba Dog Beer, SeaBright Brewery's Naughty Monkey Brown Ale, or anything from the Weeping Radish brewery in North Carolina. Many people saw the trend as an opportunity to make money, to change careers themselves, to breathe new life into their restaurants, to provide financial backing for a "fun" investment that just might pay off big someday. Most people really did like beer, and really did appreciate the taste of craft brews. Good brewers became a hot property, and a new class of consultants popped up, people who could tell you how to set up a microbrewery or a brewpub, and then hold your hand while you actually learned to brew beer.

Among the best-known consultants was Peter Austin, an English brewmaster who helped Terry Jones, the American member of Monty Python, set up a microbrewery in Britain more than twenty years ago. Austin later teamed up with another Englishman, Alan Pugsley, and together they helped open dozens of American microbreweries and brewpubs. Their distinctive style of brewing, including reliance on a strain of top-fermenting (ale) yeast called Ringwood that they jealously kept to themselves, became a standard style of American microbrewing. The Ringwood or Austin or Pugsley system, as it is variously known, is behind such well-known American microbreweries as Newman's,

Geary's, Gritty McDuff's, Shipyard, Kennebunkport, Wild Goose, Red Feather, Hartford, McAuslan, Ship Inn and Barley Creek.

Other well-known consultants include Jack Streich, John Mallett, Joe Owades and two retired mass-market brewmasters, Karl Strauss and William Moeller, who probably became better known to the public as microbrewing consultants than they ever were when they were presiding over huge brewery-factories.

One of the things that characterizes the American craft brewing industry is the incredible amount of innovation and experimentation. It is as if the new generation of American brewers had discovered a toy for the first time, and were using their imaginations to bend it and twist it and see just how many crazy things it could do. American micro-breweries produced all manner of styles, from alt to wheat: smoked beer, chili beer, pineapple beer, honey beer, coffee beer. Over the past twenty years, America has been the most exciting place to be a beer lover. That's not to say, of course, that all those experiments have been successful. European breweries that have been brewing for centuries, rather than a few months or a couple of years, say there is a reason they don't make cranberry beer, or put a pepper in each bottle, or mix their beer with Starbucks.

All sorts of tangential businesses popped up. People who managed to open brewpubs and microbreweries bundled up what they knew and sold business plans to wanna-be's for several hundred dollars. Several companies sold beer for home delivery, such as the Beer of the Month Club and Ale by Mail. Beer gear—mugs, glasses, hats, pins, patches, T-shirts, jackets, coasters, openers and just about anything else that you could put a beer logo on—was sold in brewery shops and by mail order through catalogues. Collectors scoured auctions and estate sales for brewphernalia: old beer signs, posters, magazine advertisements, bottles, bottle caps, wooden cases, stained-glass windows, neon displays, etc. An unopened six-pack of Billy Beer became valuable enough to remove all temptation—if there ever was any—to actually drink the stuff. Some people even collected and traded microbrewers' business cards.

Information about good beer became a mini-industry of its own. Periodicals (beeriodicals) began popping up: glossy magazines with slick ads and stories of beer hunting in faraway places, newspapers (brewspapers) that covered beer on a regional basis and newsletters (brewsletters) that looked at the business of craft beer. Several Internet newsgroups were started to focus on beer, along with forums offered by online services such as America Online and CompuServe. Cyberspace grew into a vast resource for beer people—drinkers, brewers, distributors, retailers, investors and industry suppliers—who created the sort of specialized, global "virtual" community that could be a model for the way the Internet can and should be used to bring people and ideas together.

Bar and restaurant managers, meanwhile, began promoting their establishments as good beer places. They hosted tastings, sponsored lectures and invited beer writers in to sign their books. They offered samplers of five or six different beers in short "flight" glasses. Bars and beer stores began competing to have the most microbrews on draft, or the largest selection of bottled craft beer, in their neighborhood or city or state. Books about cooking with beer began crowding out wine books on shelves even in the big chain bookstores in suburban shopping malls, and fine restaurants began offering beer dinners.

Indeed, in New York, where it took several years for the good beer revolution to take hold, restaurants such as American Festival Cafe in Rockefeller Center, Windows on the World at the World Trade Center, Oceana on East 54th Street, Cafe Centro at Grand Central Station and Cucina in Brooklyn led the way in introducing American microbrews as an acceptable complement to gourmet meals. Adventurous young chefs saw craft beer as an all-natural, high-quality regional or local product in keeping with the goals of their kitchens. When Delta found that its frequent flyers almost always chose Samuel Adams over mass-market beers, the airlines began offering other craft beers.

Entrepreneurs, many of them microbrewers or craft beer distributors, began organizing beer festivals and "beer camp" weekend events where attendees would listen to beer lectures, participate in beer tastings, eat beer dinners and lunches and even beer breakfasts, play beer games, sing beer songs and generally soak themselves, literally inside and out, in their love of beer.

Mary Samuels

MARY SAMUELS IS a native Kentuckian with a background in computer applications systems, including one for a distiller of fine Kentucky bourbon. As a homebrewer who now lives in the Northwest, she finds that the skills she's learned in planning and preparing meals for her family are also useful in brewing.

"The best point about homebrewing is that I can make the exact style of beer that suits me," Mary says. "It's a creative outlet, and is becoming increasingly so as I master the technical and mechanical aspects of the art. The worst part regarding brewing is the time required to do it. Especially with regard to full-mash brewing, which can become an all-day marathon, other things requiring attention may fall by the wayside. A mitigating factor, though, is that while I'm waiting for some aspect of the brewing process to be completed, I can give attention to small tasks around the house."

Mary tends to favor German alts, kolschs and lagers. She also brews weissbier, and the occasional English pale ale and stout, but the crisp and clean attributes of the German brews are more appealing to her. Mary serves her beer to dinner guests, and "anyone—of age—walking through my front door." She also routinely takes along a couple of liters of her beer when she's invited to someone else's house for dinner. Most of her friends, she admits, prefer her lighter brews, though she's gradually introducing them—educating them, that is—to the darker, stronger brews.

"Every homebrewing experience is a learning experience, and thus a good one," Mary says. "The worst experience I had was, when brewing a weizenbock, the mash stuck, so tightly that there was literally no run-off from the lauter-tun. I countered this by moving the mash back to the mash-tun and re-starting the mash using some supplemental six-row barley to break up some of the proteins which were gumming up the process. The beer turned out to be superb, but not before it sat in the bottle for over a year, finally generating enough carbonation to be enjoyable."

Mary, a section leader for CompuServe's beer forums, says that unlike many forums, there is little "flaming" on her homebrewing bulletin board: "I think it's because there's such an evident atmosphere of respect, friendliness and helpfulness that no one has anything to complain about. But mostly because of the respect, persons causing trouble are quickly put in their place by other forum members."

The Rise and Rise of the Brewpub

T HE MASS PRODUCTION and mass marketing of beer also meant the demise, in the United States and throughout most of the rest of the world, of the bar/restaurant that made its own beer on the premises. The brewpub, in other words. In 1982, Bert Grant, one of America's foremost experts on hops, opened America's first modern-era brewpub, the Yakima Brewing and Malting Co. (Grant seems to be just as proud of the place's claim that it was also America's first no-smoking bar.) In 1996, Atlanta became the last major U.S. city to get a brewpub, a John Harvard's Brew House in the trendy Buckhead section of town. Within a year, several more had opened in and around Atlanta. New York, which had only one brewpub for years, suddenly had a dozen by 1997, with a dozen more in the planning stages and predictions of thirty or more by the year 2000. Chicago has twenty-five brewpubs either open, under construction or well into the planning stages.

From zero in 1982, the number of brewpubs in America—bar/restaurants that make their own beer and serve it on the premises, usually with a food menu—increased to four hundred in 1994 and more than seven hundred in 1996. The total may well exceed a thousand by the end of 1997, and could approach two thousand by the year 2000. No one is exactly sure how many brewpubs there are in America at any given moment because they have been opening so fast across the country, five or six a week since 1995, according to the Institute for Brewing Studies, which tries to track brewpub openings but cannot keep up on a day-to-day basis.

Cities in the American West embraced brewpubs years before they became popular in the Midwest, and finally in the East and the South. Portland, Ore., became America's unofficial brewpub capital, opening an average of one a year through the 1980s and '90s. Seattle, Denver,

San Francisco and other Western cities soon followed. Colorado, a state of 3.6 million people, has dozens of brewpubs. John Hickenlooper, who has become one of the industry's leading authorities on brewpub financing, opened the state's first one, Wynkoop, in 1988 in Denver. Imagine how thrilled he was when he later learned that Denver was getting a major league baseball team, the Colorado Rockies, that would play its National League games at Coors Field—only two blocks from his brewpub. Now there are four brewpubs closer to Coors Field than Wynkoop, including one, the highly regarded SandLot Brewery, that Coors built inside the ballpark. (Incidentally, SandLot sold one hundred kegs of its first brew in its first two days—a brewpub owner's dream.) Wynkoop has managed to keep its unofficial title as the busiest brewpub in America even though it now competes with eleven other brewpubs within ten blocks in downtown Denver.

Most of the early brewpub owners were beer guys—professional brewers who wanted to do something on a boutique scale, like Bert Grant, or homebrewers with visions of grandeur, like Bill Owens. Buffalo Bill, as he has become known in the beer business, was a famous photographer who opened his Buffalo Bill's Brewery in Hayward, Calif., in 1983, and became famous again for his Pumpkin Ale, still a Halloween-to-Thanksgiving staple for many beer gourmets, and his Alimony Ale, originally so highly hopped that the label boasted "Bitterest Beer in America."

For those early brewpub pioneers, the venture was an adventure. Sure, they were interested in making money, but most of them were also looking for a lifestyle change. Many brewpub owners worked sixty to seventy hours a week and paid themselves very little, usually no more than $30,000 or $40,000 a year. They complained about the hours, the low pay and the hassles of being on the sharp end of both production and retail, but most of them also admitted that they felt privileged to be in the business, and they loved it.

The mom-and-pop character of most early brewpubs is still common at many brewpubs today, particularly independents—those that are not owned by a corporation or part of a chain. Increasingly, however, brewpubs are becoming big business. That's partly because corporate America has noticed the success of brewpubs, which are nearly twice as likely to succeed as most new restaurants, according to the Institute for Brewing Studies. Brewpubs have also become big business because the cost of opening a typical brewpub has risen beyond $1 million, and sometimes several times that, depending on the location, the brewing works and the kitchen.

But for most brewpub owners, it's been worth the money and time, in terms of both satisfaction and profits. Many brewpubs have been runaway successes, even in depressed downtown areas where other restaurants and bars are struggling. Think about it this way. The restaurant business is one of the toughest there is. The bar business is another of the toughest ways to make a living. Toss in brewing, an exacting process where it's very easy for a lot of things to go wrong. Many of the people getting into brewpubs in the 1980s did so with little or no experience or training in any of the three businesses: food service, alcoholic beverage service or commercial brewing. Many of them were homebrewers who left behind jobs as photographers, teachers, accountants, carpenters. Yet most of them have been successful. That says a lot about the strength of the concept behind the brewpub, and its continuing appeal to a wide range of people who could be spending their leisure and entertainment dollars in many other ways.

As in other new retail sectors, a successful formula spreads quickly. Moreover, the people who have early successes are eager to expand the formula themselves. As a result, a number of successful brewpubs have spawned chains operating under the same name. The Big River Brewing & Grille Works began with brewpubs in Chattanooga and Nashville, and then—in what must be the final stamp of mainstream, establishment approval for brewpubs—on the BoardWalk at Walt Disney World in Orlando. McMenamins Pubs and Breweries built a chain in the Northwest, and three chains came out of Boston: John Harvard, Brew Moon and Boston Hops. Other brewpubs, from Portland to New York, have started local sister brewpubs or branches that may become regional or national chains. The Rock Bottom chain, intent on going national and becoming sort of a TGI Friday's with fresh beer, has found no trouble raising money in public stock offerings—$50 million in 1994 and 1995. And 51 percent of the Gordon-Biersch northern California brewpub chain was sold for $17 million in 1995.

Part of the reason that brewpub chains are growing so rapidly is the owners' experience. After the steep learning curve when they opened that first brewpub, they figure they've made most of their mistakes and learned from them, so it always gets easier to open the next one. A related reason for the growth of chains, naturally, is money. Operating one busy brewpub not only provides a cash flow for future growth, but also presents the kind of track record that appeals to potential investors. They may like the idea of investing in a brewpub, but they're more interested in giving their money to somebody who's done it before than to an accountant, photographer, journalist, kindergarten teacher or carpenter who is trying to put together a business plan for the first time.

Perhaps that's why the early brewpubs were typically started by homebrewers, but most of the new brewpubs are being opened by people who have been in the restaurant business for years—or corporations that have been in the restaurant business for years. After all, the rule of thumb, at least in the first fifteen years of the brewpub revival, was that bad beer wouldn't necessarily do much to hurt business, but bad food would kill you. That's changing, of course, as beer drinkers become more sophisticated and more brewpubs appear. In cities where brewpubs are common, bad food will still kill the business, but now bad beer will, too.

Jack Joyce

IF YOU ASK the government to do something *for* you, Jack Joyce says, watch out: Somebody else will ask the government to do something *to* you. Joyce is president of Oregon Brewing Co., the maker of Rogue ales. He's known for producing good beer and clever names, such as Mogul Ale, Dead Guy Ale, Shakespeare Stout, Rogue 'N' Berry, Old Crustacean, Santa's Private Reserve and others. Joyce, who in his pre-brewing life was the main marketing guy for another little company out in the Northwest called Nike, is one of the sages of the good beer movement.

Of late, he has been battling back and forth with several big breweries and a handful of other microbreweries, and particularly with Boston Beer Co., which is something in between. Joyce thinks it is unfair of Jim Koch, head of Boston Beer Co., the maker of Samuel Adams brands, to market a new series of labels called Oregon. Joyce says the names cause confusion with his Oregon Brewing Co., and lead consumers to think Oregon beer is produced by a company based in Oregon. Of course, Joyce thinks it is also unfair of Koch to market Samuel Adams as a Boston beer, when much of it is made elsewhere, on contract, in big breweries.

Koch (pronounced Cook) has countered by criticizing Joyce for refusing to put freshness dates on his beers: "Best before" such and such a date, in other words. Rogue takes back any beer that a customer, whether a consumer or a distributor, doesn't think is fresh—full refund, no questions asked. Joyce doesn't want someone else telling him how to market his product. "I'm uncomfort-

continued . . .

able and lonely in opposing dating,'' he told us over coffee one morning as he tried to figure out how to put out a cigar someone had given him. "Dating is a commodity solution. We're dealing with a hand-crafted product here, not a mass-market commodity. They want us to define all ale like milk.'' Besides, Joyce pointed out, look at all the technical information he already has on his Rogue labels, including the Plato and IBU ratings and the apparent attenuation figures.

More significant, Joyce insisted, is the effort by big brewers— and by some microbrewers trying to become big brewers—to present their products as something else. They sell beers that are actually brewed thousands of miles away from the place names on the labels. They label a beer a certain style, but then make it in an entirely different way, leading unsuspecting consumers who drink it to believe that really is how the style should taste. But Joyce, unlike some microbrewers, is not interested in government regulation, or even any sort of industry standards, where a committee would set rules and screen beers to make sure they conform.

Instead, he believes the good beer movement in the United States needs an organization like Britain's CAMRA—the Campaign for Real Ale. With tens of thousands of members, CAMRA has been called the most effective grass-roots lobbying organization in Europe. Its leaders stage festivals, produce newsletters, put together guidebooks and generally educate the public as to what is good beer—and what isn't. As a result, in the last two decades CAMRA has had a remarkable influence on British beer and brewing, in effect bringing back real ales. Pubs are now better run, and some of Britain's biggest brewers admit—no, brag—that they have changed the way they make beer in order to meet CAMRA's standards.

"The odds are that without a CAMRA kind of movement in America, somebody like us will be driven out of business,'' Joyce said. "Writers need to tell the truth about beer as loudly as they can. If a whole bunch of consumers wake up and say, 'Hey, they don't really make that beer in Boston,' or, 'Hey, this isn't really a lambic,' then it could make a difference for small breweries that are trying to tell the truth. If you're just a marketer, doing things like that doesn't matter to you. If you're a brewer, then it would embarrass you.'' What the good beer movement needs, according to this reformed marketing man, is more people who focus on brewing rather than on marketing.

The Mass-Market Reaction

THROUGH THE 1980s, America's big breweries barely noticed the microbrewers. But then a funny thing happened. After decades of annual growth in beer consumption, the market became saturated. Beer sales flattened out. The population aged, and older people don't drink as much beer. New television channels, cable and satellite, took away the longtime three-network advertising avenue that the beer companies had always used to reach a majority of the population. Health and safety campaigns, particularly those against drunk driving, made beer drinkers more careful and responsible. Amid all these changes, per capita consumption of beer began dropping slightly in the United States. The automatic sales growth was no longer there for the big beer companies.

At first, still ignoring craft beer as an insignificant niche, the big U.S. breweries, particularly Anheuser-Busch, began looking to restore their growth curve by opening up new foreign markets. There were buyouts, takeovers, joint ventures and other forms of corporate alliances with big breweries in South America and Asia. Europe, with some of the best beer markets in the world, was a particular target. Anheuser-Busch seemed to think that the only reason the people of Britain, Belgium, Austria and Germany didn't drink Budweiser was that they had never tried it. However, Budweiser encountered several major problems in Europe. One was that it could not be sold in many European countries, thanks to the trademark held by the tiny Budweiser Budvar brewery in Ceske Budejovice, a town in Bohemia that is now part of the Czech Republic but was known as Budweis when it was part of Germany in the 19th century.

The story goes back to the mid-1800s, when an ambitious young brewmaster named Adolphus Busch, an immigrant from Germany, went to work for Ernest Anheuser, who owned one of the forty or so breweries in St. Louis at that time. Busch proceeded to marry the boss's daughter and take over the running of the brewery. One of his many ideas was to market Anheuser beer beyond St. Louis. One problem, however, was that Anheuser beer wasn't very good. So Adolphus Busch returned to Europe, touring the continent in search of a better beer. He found one in Budweis, where the style of beer made by various breweries over the centuries was known as Budweiser, just as the beer made in Pilsen was known as Pilsner. The town beer in Budweis was a rich, aromatic lager, with plenty of body and hop taste. Budweis has a brewing history going back to 1265, and its beer became famous as the "Beer of Kings" after King Ferdinand in 1531 declared Budweiser the official beer at his court. Adolphus Busch adapted the Budweis style, and introduced his own version of Budweiser in St. Louis in 1876. The American beer, like the Bohemian beer, had a red and white label. Instead of "The Beer of Kings," Anheuser-Busch called its American Budweiser "The King of Beers."

A few years later, the brewery now making Budweiser Budvar was started in Bohemia. Around the turn of the century, both the American Budweiser and the Bohemian Budweiser were offered at a trade exhibition, and the two companies each complained that the other was unfairly using its name. Lawyers for the two breweries negotiated for several years, and in 1911 finally reached a "gentleman's agreement" under which Anheuser-Busch would not sell its Budweiser in Europe, and Budweiser Budvar would not sell its beer in America. When the American beer market began to flatten in the 1980s, Anheuser-Busch wanted to sell its Budweiser across Europe. Budweiser Budvar objected, and A-B was forced to go to court in every country where it wanted to market its beer. A number of European countries upheld the Bohemian brewery's trademark claim, and ruled that the American Budweiser could not be sold under any circumstances. Some countries, such as France, ruled that it could be sold, but only as Bud, not Budweiser. A few countries, such as Britain, said both breweries could sell their beer as Budweiser. Anheuser-Busch made a deal to produce and sell its Budweiser in Britain through a big British brewery. The British brewery predicted that Budweiser would become the No. 1 beer in Britain within a few years, and the Americans believed it. After all, they were No. 1 in America, by a landslide.

That's when Anheuser-Busch encountered another problem common to big U.S. breweries trying to sell their beer in Europe: European beer drinkers didn't much like the taste. Many of them didn't like golden or amber lagers at all; they wanted darker, heavier, less bubbly brews. And if they did want a lager, they were more likely to go with something like Budweiser Budvar, with its prominent malt and hops flavor profile. In recent years Anheuser-Busch has made a number of overtures to the Budweiser Budvar brewery to resolve the trademark issues—including several years of ongoing negotiations for A-B to buy a minority stake in the brewery and distribute Budweiser Budvar in America while being allowed to market American Budweiser throughout Europe. As interested as the Czech government was in attracting new foreign investments and in expanding the market for Budvar Budweiser—one of the Czech Republic's best-known exports—the government and the managers of the brewery remained fearful that any involvement by Anheuser-Busch ultimately would lead to a dilution of the Budweiser Budvar brand or the beer or both. Negotiations stalled again and again.

Meanwhile, big breweries around the world have been forming new alliances, making acquisitions and expanding their export markets. Heineken, from Holland, grew fat in the 1980s from its export success around the world, and became a global brand. Britain's Bass and Ireland's Guinness also enjoyed great international success. By the way, the old saying is true: Guinness does taste better the closer you get to Dublin. Part of it no doubt has to do with the freshness of the beer, and part with the fact that Guinness uses slightly different recipes for export beer—including marginally higher alcohol content for the American market, and quite a bit higher for Africa.

Beyond the United States, microbreweries and regional or national breweries have become a favored means of spurring the economies of developing countries, while providing the kind of opportunities for capitalism that are needed to move the countries of the former Soviet Union and its sphere toward free-market democracy. The international financial community certainly agrees with the potential for breweries as an investment; the Luxembourg-registered Emerging Markets Brewery Fund, which requires a minimum investment of $50,000, is investing in the construction of new breweries large and small in twenty-seven developing countries. Microbreweries are springing up in Russia, China, Vietnam and other countries with long traditions of homebrewing and "village" beer.

Back in the United States, the big breweries began to notice in the early 1990s that the only meaningful sales growth—10 percent a year—

was among so-called superpremium beers, including microbrews and gourmet imported beers, that cost considerably more than their own premium labels. The population was becoming not only older, but better educated. College graduates were less likely to drink a lot of beer, particularly as they got older, but they were more likely to pay more for the beer they did drink. By 1985, microbreweries produced seventy-five thousand barrels of beer a year—about one one-thousandth of Anheuser-Busch's annual production. By the early 1990s the craft brewing industry was growing by 50 percent a year or more, producing 2.5 million barrels in 1994, followed by 4 million barrels in 1995 and nearly 6 million barrels in 1996. In contrast, Anheuser-Busch sales dropped 1 percent from 1994 to 1995. Growth in the craft brewing industry is expected to continue at 30 percent or more annually through the year 2000. From less than 1 percent of the fifty-billion-dollar annual American beer market in 1993, craft brewing now accounts for more than 3 percent and is on the way to 5 percent—and more than two billion dollars in sales per year—by 2000. Figures like those finally have forced the big breweries to react to the good beer revolution that they had tried to ignore for so long. The big brewing companies—some cynics sniff that they are really marketing companies whose commodity happens to be brewed semi-malt beverage alcohol—began to see the good beer trend as not only a small threat, but a large opportunity. After all, the microbrews were proving that beer drinkers would do something the big beer companies never thought they would do: pay a little more for quality. Higher prices mean higher margins, and higher margins mean more profits.

The big breweries responded to the competition from microbreweries, and the opportunities presented by the ever-expanding market for quality beers, in several ways. They tried to market their own beers as if they were craft brews. They tried to make their own versions of microbrewed beer. And they bought microbreweries lock, stock and (literally) barrel. Big-brewery beers that tried to masquerade as new and different, quirky with quality—the ads never actually said they were microbrewed—included Killian's Red from Coors, Red Wolf from Anheuser-Busch and Red Dog from Miller. The latter even claimed on its label that it was from the Plank Road Brewery, actually a facility behind a new facade designed to look old in front of part of Miller's huge and modern brewing operation in Milwaukee.

In many ways, Miller has been the most aggressive among the big breweries in responding to the threat and opportunities presented by changing tastes in beer. Miller's specialty brewing division came up with its own craft brews, Amber Special Reserve and Velvet Stout, that were generally well-received by beer critics but didn't exactly fly off the shelves. After all, industry analysts reasoned, why would anyone pay a dollar for a Miller beer? Miller tried another tack with a new mainstream, mass-market beer, called simply Miller Beer, that was brewed with more malt and aimed for "fuller flavor," yet was still "easy to drink and not bitter or filling." Over the past decade, Miller has purchased several smaller regional or microbreweries and, despite considerable teeth-gnashing and hand-wringing from would-be purists who warned that Miller would wreck them, so far the deals seem to be working out well for everyone. The big reason is that Miller appears to be keeping its promises not to meddle with the beer. Instead, the big company offers the smaller breweries broader distribution, management expertise where needed and money for expansion. In return, Miller gets good microbrews to distribute, greatly enhancing the range of products it can offer its distributors. For example, Miller acquired Leinenkugel, a small northern Wisconsin brewery, in 1988. Leinenkugel quadrupled production, and its distribution spread almost overnight from four states to forty—without any great outcry from longtime Leinie drinkers about changes in the beer. Later, Leinenkugel bought the Milwaukee Brewery, a small specialty brewery that Heileman had opened and then closed. Miller also bought controlling interests in the Shipyard Brewery in Portland, Maine, and the Celis Brewery in Austin, Texas, with the announced intention of providing marketing, distribution and finance— and not messing with the brewery management or tweaking the beer. The Celis acquisition was particularly important because it was a micro with a high profile. Pierre Celis was a milkman in his native Belgium who had always loved the wit (white) style of beer from his neighborhood brewery. In fact, he liked it so much that when the local brewery closed he decided to revive the style himself.

The Celis Brewery in Belgium became so successful that the former milkman was able to sell out a few years later to Interbrew, one of Europe's biggest brewing conglomerates. Pierre Celis was set for a rich retirement. Instead, Celis and his family decided to start over in the United States. The family pored over demographic studies and settled on Austin because of its high percentages of young, affluent, well-educated, cosmopolitan people, many of them connected to the University of Texas. Before long, Celis' white beer, made with wheat and herbs, was winning awards and receiving rave reviews from American beer lovers—professionals and amateurs alike. After Celis sold a controlling interest to Miller in 1995, its American fans fretted that Miller would immediately begin tinkering. At first it appeared their fears might be well founded, as Miller scaled back Celis distribution from thirty states to five. Miller, however, said this was done primarily to make sure that its accounts in Texas got the Celis they needed. Miller promised to rebuild the Celis distribution network through its own distributors nationwide, thereby avoiding the supply shortages that had sometimes plagued the brand, particularly in the Northeast. To back up its promise, Miller provided the money for Celis to begin the expansion necessary to double its fifteen-thousand-barrel annual capacity.

The other two brewers among America's Big Three were hardly idle. Besides marketing Killian's Red as a new national superpremium brand, Coors came with its own series of specialty beers under the Blue Moon label, and made deals to distribute several microbrews through its wholesale network. Pursuing its conviction that the beer market is becoming increasingly segmented, Coors went from a single label barely twenty years ago to more than a dozen different beers today. Perhaps even more importantly, Coors became the first megabrewer to build its own independent brewpub—the aforementioned SandLot Brewery at Coors Field, which was also the first brewpub in a major league baseball park. Coors bought some instant credibility with the good beer crowd by hiring a respected microbrewer to run SandLot, and producing beers that even the beer geeks loved. Meanwhile, Anheuser-Busch's specialty brewing division came up with Elk Mountain, an amber ale named after A-B's big hop farm in Bonners Ferry, Idaho. (A long-standing joke among good-beer geeks was based on wonderment that Anheuser-Busch would spend so much money raising and buying good hops, and then mask the hops' flavor in its beer.) Anheuser-Busch also began offering Crossroads, an unfiltered wheat beer, and three "originals," based on old Anheuser-Busch recipes: a lager, originally made in 1895, a dark lager dating back to 1893 and a porter from 1899. Early reports on all three were positive, but it remained to be seen whether they would run into the same problems as Miller's specialty beers. Anheuser-Busch also bought a 25 percent stake in Red Hook, one of the Northwest's biggest microbreweries, with an option to take its stake up to 49 percent. The A-B investment and a very successful public stock offering allowed Red Hook to renovate its Washington brewery and build another one in New Hampshire on the way to boosting production from 70,000 barrels a year to 450,000 barrels a year.

John Glendenning

WE RAN INTO John Glendenning at a beer festival. We both recognized that we were there for professional reasons. Nice work if you can get it, we agreed as we shared a beer. Glendenning is assistant brewer at the Marthasville Brewing Co., a microbrewery that was started in Atlanta (Marthasville was the original name of the city, after the daughter of an early governor). Opened in 1994, Marthasville was the first microbrewery in Atlanta after a change in Prohibition-era laws.

Glendenning, who is only twenty-seven, is one of the rising brewing stars of the South. "Good beer has come late to the South," Glendenning tells us. "Budweiser still has sixty percent of the market in our area. But we're getting a lot more name recognition." Glendenning started homebrewing back home in Chattanooga, and decided he wanted beermaking to be his career. He never had any formal education in beer studies, instead doing anything and everything he could—including selling for a beer distributor—to get into the business. He worked as a volunteer for a local brewery, and finally landed a job at a brewpub.

Now he works sixteen-hour days, six or seven days a week, to help make twelve thousand barrels of beer a year on Marthasville's ten-barrel system. He won't say how much he gets paid, but it's not much—probably a lot less than if he had gone into some other business or trade. So why does a young guy want to work so hard for so little money? Glendenning grins. "I know I'm doing the right thing with my life," he says, "when I take a six-pack of my beer home to my dad. He drinks a beer, and pats me on the back."

MICRO BREW, MACRO MONEY

The Red Hook initial public offering (IPO) was one of several microbrewery flotations to cause a stir on Wall Street in 1995, a year when the market boomed and new Internet stock offerings were all the rage. While the brewery offerings were relatively small, some of the IPOs nonetheless offered returns of 2,000 percent or more—twenty times the initial investment, in other words—to original investors, and in the long run the brewery stocks outperformed many Internet stocks, which had dramatic early runs and then sank back to more realistic levels. Rock

Bottom Brewpubs had its second public offering within a year in February 1995, raising thirty-four million dollars to go with the sixteen million dollars raised in 1994. In August 1995, Red Hook went public and raised thirty-three million dollars, followed by Pete's Brewing (fifty-one million dollars) and Boston Beer (seventy-six million dollars) in November, and Hart Brewing (forty-four million dollars) in December. Those issues were so oversubscribed that it was difficult for everyday small investors to participate in the IPOs, but Boston Beer got its drinkers involved by setting aside 1 million shares and putting applications for up to 33 shares in six-packs. Incidentally, Jim Koch, the Boston founder and president who paid himself more than a quartermillion dollars that year but still joked that he did his own radio ads so he wouldn't have to pay an announcer, personally made seven million dollars from the IPO.

While the big public offerings have been getting a lot of attention from Wall Street, most microbreweries are not in that league. They still scrape around for money on the smaller regional exchanges or through private offerings. Most startup microbreweries, who don't want big corporate investments and probably couldn't get any even if they did want them, aim strictly for small investors. Some have tried to get investors involved by appointing them unsalaried "marketing representatives" in the hopes that they will line up bars, restaurants and stores as accounts. One small brewery's innovative method of raising money will have a far-rippling effect. The Spring Street Brewing Co., which is based in New York and contract brews its Belgian-style Wit beer in Minnesota, was one of the first small firms of any kind to aggressively market its stock on the Internet. The idea was to raise capital by selling shares for $1.85 apiece to investors through Spring Street's page on the World Wide Web. The attraction was that the company could raise money without paying underwriting fees or giving up a substantial portion of its equity to venture capitalists. To make the investments more appealing, Spring Street also set up its own trading system over the Internet, matching buyers and sellers for shares that it had already sold. (The prices for the stock were up and down, and some investors who bought at $1.85 were able to make tidy profits by quickly selling at more than $2.) The Securities and Exchange Commission had doubts, however. When the SEC ordered Spring Street to stop the trading because it was not a registered broker-dealer, many Wall Street observers felt that the regulators were striking a blow against the technological innovations of the Internet. Many were surprised, then, when the SEC agreed, after several weeks of review, that Spring Street could use the

Internet to underwrite and sell shares. The SEC merely asked for some changes in Spring Street's trading system. The approval sent an unexpected but strong message not only to microbreweries, but to small businesses and the financial services industry across America: The SEC views the Internet and other new communications technology as an opportunity for new kinds of investments that should be encouraged, not discouraged. Many other small companies began scrambling to set up their own Websites, and the lawyer who had quit practicing law to start Spring Street Brewing Co. hung his shingle out again as a consultant to other companies that want to use the Internet for low-cost corporate finance.

Jack MacDonough

AS THE PRESIDENT and CEO of Miller Brewing, Jack Mac-
Donough has some definite thoughts on the macro-micro split in
the beer universe:

"My concern with some craft beer fans is when they knock
other brewers large or small. Obviously, if they are a small brewer,
it is to their advantage to suggest that their beer is unique, but
there's no reason to denigrate a large brewer's large brands on the
basis of taste or quality unless they just like being snobs. Most
beer in the world is consumed for refreshment versus 'savoring.'
To complain about the existence of 'refreshment' beers is as
wrong as to complain about beer drinkers who have a big thirst.
Let's please never denigrate our customers. We all now know that
any large brewer is able to produce very unique beers, that they
have the technical talent. On the other hand, I'm not sure all the
smaller brewers could easily produce a clean light beer.

"The real issue is not technology or brewing expertise; it's listening to the customer. Obviously, larger brewers skipped on the
chance to provide truly unique beers back in 1985 because there
didn't seem to be a market. I'd say at that time the majority of
the beer market was trending to maximum refreshment with light
beers. Perhaps if Michelob at that time had brewed a unique beer,
Sam Adams would never have gotten off the ground. Fritz Maytag
signaled the way even earlier. But what's important is that the free
enterprise system worked, and the barriers to entry for a small
brewer are few. Net, we now have more beer types in the USA
than any other country in the world.

"At Miller, we initially tried to respond to a demand for unique
tastes with the Miller Reserve line of beers and ales. Many beer
drinkers liked our offerings and had renewed respect for our brewing expertise and range. Unfortunately, many then moved on to
unique beers from much smaller breweries because they not only
wanted unique beers but also unique breweries. Our solution has
been to invest in unique breweries, like Leinenkugel, Celis and
Shipyard, to meet that demand for the very unique. Additionally,
our introduction of Miller Beer with more aroma via four times
more hops than other 'regular premium' beers is our reaction to
the possibility that unique beers may be conditioning some beer
drinkers to want more aroma in the beers they drink for 'refreshment.' So you see, the full range of consumers are listened to at
Miller, and we have respect for all our beer drinkers' desires.

"P.S. We don't spill beer."

EIGHT

The Future of Craft Beer

SOME INDUSTRY ANALYSTS expect America to have two thousand craft breweries by the year 2000. That estimate may be too conservative. Some industry analysts predict five thousand or more craft brewing operations in the United States within a few years. A few naysayers still insist that microbrewed beer is just a fad that will follow the so-called "Snapple scenario"—a fast start followed by fading fortunes. Here's what one investment newsletter said: "A long time from now investors will look back at the craze for microbreweries and wonder how they could have been sucked in by mob dynamics to such a prosaic, non-growth field." The Beer Travelers, Stan Hieronymus and Daria Labinsky, offer a good response to the skeptics: "They should tear themselves away from their stock quotes and visit a bar or two."

Here's another way to look at it: Maybe mass-market, adjunct-laden American pilsners, which have been around for barely fifty years in all the centuries of brewing, are the fad whose time is fading. We think craft beer is a fad in the same way that pizza was a fad. It's a fad that's here to stay. Certainly the growth of the market for craft beers, from zero only a few years ago to more than 2 percent in 1996, to an expected 5 percent of the market and billions in sales by 2000, is a testament to the shift in consumer tastes toward quality beer. Certainly growth cannot continue at the 50 percent annual rate of the mid-1990s. But this business has a long way to go before the beer-drinking public says it doesn't want any more good, new, hand-crafted beers.

Forget the figures for a moment. Look at yourself, and your friends. If you're reading this book, you probably know many people who always drank mass-market beers that advertise on national TV. You were probably one yourself. Your friends and relatives who started drinking craft beer probably don't drink much mass-market beer anymore. If and when they have a choice, including when they're buying in a bar or store, they go for a craft beer. You probably feel the same way yourself. After drinking good beer, are you ever going back to not-so-good beer?

That's not to say that every part of the country is going to become like Oregon, where about 30 percent of the draft beer market is microbrews. What it does mean, however, is that the big mass-market breweries are going to continue to respond to the demand for better beer, and they're going to get more aggressive both in terms of marketing their beer like craft beer, and actually brewing craft beer themselves. Competition from other craft breweries and the mass-market breweries may well lead to a shakeout in the microbrewing industry. More and more microbrewers will face some tough choices if their beer is not as good as it should be, or their marketing is lax, or their distribution is weak or their business practices, particularly financing and cash flow, are shaky.

Even microbrewers who have done everything right will face some tough choices. Should they grow by producing more and widening their markets? Should they try to do it on their own by raising money? If they want to raise their own money, should they look for private investors or try to go public? Is raising money worth the risk of losing control of the company to the new investors? Should they sell out to somebody bigger? A mass-market brewery? A distributor?

One thing is clear: A microbrewery can't just make craft-brewed beer anymore and expect to be successful. It has to be good craft beer, supported by sound business practices. This means that would-be brewers need to approach the business with considerably more money and expertise than in the past; fewer teachers or journalists or carpenters will be teaching themselves to brew at home and then starting breweries with investments from friends and relatives.

A PIECE OF THE ACTION

Certainly there will still be ample opportunities for investors large and small to risk their capital on microbreweries and brewpubs, whether in a Wall Street IPO or a small unregistered offering on the Internet. In terms of future microbrewery IPOs—and there will be more—stock analysts offer some advice for the potential investor. One of the most important things, of course, is that the beer be good—but that is often impossible to determine, particularly in start-ups where no beer will actually be brewed for months, until after the capital has been raised and largely spent. So it's important to look at what styles of beer will be brewed and who will be brewing it. Are the styles likely to find a ready audience, or will they be too sophisticated or "pure" for the expected clientele? Where have the brewers worked before? Why did they leave? How does the beer they used to make taste? Is it good, and does it sell?

Equally important is whether the company management has a viable plan for making money off the beer. A key part of the equation is what the microbrewery management intends to do with the money it is raising—especially in the case of IPOs from brewers who have been in business for a while. Some of the money may go to pay debts. Some may go to making the original investors rich. But it might be a bad sign if all the money is going to debts or investors or both. A considerable portion of the new money should also be earmarked for the growth of the business, such as building new production facilities or expanding the marketing and distribution.

Like Internet stock flotations in recent years, the IPOs for microbreweries left some of them vastly over-valued, at least in terms of the traditional wisdom of price/earnings ratios. Some of those breweries will no doubt be hard-pressed to do enough business to pay the kind of dividends that may be needed to justify such high valuations. If the market sours on those microbrewers, it could sour on future microbrewery IPOs, or the general concept of investing in microbreweries. Before putting money into a brewery or anything else, of course, it's advisable to consult with a lawyer or financial planner who specializes in such investments.

BREW(PUB)ING UP A STORM

Brewpubs are growing at a much faster rate than microbreweries or contract brewers, and small wonder. The initial investment is usually lower, and the immediate returns are usually higher. But all those new brewpubs will no doubt lead to more competition, and a shakeout in that part of the craft brewing industry, too. Some brewpub owners insist that their competition will never be other brewpubs. Instead, they say, their competition will always be TVs, VCRs and computers—the toys that keep people at home instead of out spending their money on food and drink. We disagree. The fact that there are three or four brewpubs in one neighborhood or even on the same block will mean sharper competition, and there will be winners and losers in that competition.

Some early brewpubs didn't make great beer or serve great food, and their locations were iffy, too. Yet they made money and stayed in business for years. Now some of those older brewpubs are having trouble keeping their customers, who are being lured away by neighboring brewpubs with better food, beer and locations. Chains and franchises with strong concepts and business practices will gain larger shares of the market as they spread across the country. We never expect it to be like McDonald's, where the beer in, say, a John Harvard brewpub in Atlanta tastes just like the beer at a John Harvard brewpub in Boston. But if you're familiar with the John Harvard in Boston and you like its beer, when you're on the road you may be more likely to go to the John Harvard in Atlanta than to some other neighboring brewpub you've never heard of.

The brewpubs of the future are going to become more narrowly defined. Some will go upscale, embracing the white-tablecloth look and the gourmet menu with prices to match. Many brewpubs will be developed with themes, and there will be super-brewpubs with themed rooms for different types of atmosphere and different styles of beer. The Oldenberg brewpub outside Cincinnati has the theme of a beer museum. The Stoudt brewpub in Lancaster County, Pa., is the site of a big antique fair every weekend, and the owners are building a model of a medieval Bavarian village next door where pedestrians can stroll from shop to shop. In Doswell, Va., there's a new brewpub in a Paramount amusement park; the kids go on the rides while the parents relax with a pint or two of craft beer. Following the lead of Coors Field, a brewpub was incorporated into the design of the Olympic stadium in Atlanta, and other major league sports arenas and stadiums are sure to follow. There are brewpubs going in casinos, health clubs, theme parks and airports.

THE BUSINESS OF BEER

Bert Grant, who started America's first brewpub, sold out in 1995 to Stimson Lane Vineyards and Estates, the winery that makes Chateau Ste. Michelle in Woodinville, Wash. The sale sent shudders through the craft-brewing world, which has always had a bias toward the small, self-controlled, mom-and-pop, boutique approach to brewing and selling good beer. Without Grant and his wife Sherry, skeptics warned,

Grant's beers could be subject to retinkered recipes and cost-cutting. Grant, however, made a point. He and his wife, who handled the marketing and business side of their brewery, had worked hard and deserved a chance to move toward retirement with the time and money to enjoy it. By selling to Stimson Lane, a company used to producing and handling a fragile, upscale beverage, Grant tried to guarantee that his beer would continue to be brewed and marketed the way he wanted after he and his wife aren't around to brew and market it themselves.

Even for younger microbrewers who aren't facing retirement and may still have one or two more new careers awaiting them, there is the temptation to cash in, sell out and reap the rewards of those years of long hard work for uncertain gains. The best microbreweries will find themselves in a sellers' market as big breweries, major distributors and specialty companies such as Stimson Lane look to diversify and get a toehold in the fast-growing craft beer niche.

Will selling out change the beer? Sometimes, sure. Before it sold a minority interest to Anheuser-Busch, Red Hook's top managers used to say their goal was to make the best beer they could. Afterward, they said their goal was to make the best beer they could for lots of people. Jim Koch, the founder of Boston Beer Co., said this of the takeovers by big breweries: "If it's not the beginning of the end, it's the end of the beginning."

Indeed, the maturing of any industry, even one so small and specialized as craft brewing, will mean changes. There is no doubt that some recipes will change and some beers will disappear, or remain in name and label only, as more microbreweries are taken over by big mass-market breweries or raise enough money to become big brewers themselves, the way the Boston Beer Co. has done. Will Jim Koch change his Samuel Adams recipes to make more money and keep his new shareholders happy? It's possible, of course. Or is it more likely that he will keep brewing Sam Adams the same way rather than risk changing the recipe and losing longtime customers? That could make his new shareholders far from happy. Either way, becoming big businesses will mean new pressures for craft breweries, and many of them will be faced, on a smaller scale, with the same sort of quality-versus-volume issues that led today's mass-market breweries to opt for volume because it affords greater potential profits.

Yes, some microbreweries will be swallowed up by big breweries and cease to exist as craft brewers. Yes, some microbreweries that cannot or will not sell out may find themselves squeezed out of business. But the small mom-and-pop, local boutique brewery has become a permanent part of the American cultural, consumer and commercial landscape. Many of them will not grow much beyond where they are now, and they will never distribute their beer beyond an hour or two of where it's brewed. As long as they continue to make good beer, however, they will have a loyal following.

A danger for many small breweries today and in the future is in distribution—not only in making sure their beer gets out there, but also in making sure it doesn't get too far out too fast. They are tempted to fill every order they can as quickly as they can, even if that means going into new territories and taking on new accounts that they may not be able to maintain later, when they are stretched for cash or sales people or beer supplies. Some prominent microbreweries have encountered major financial difficulties by extending their markets too quickly, and then finding their longtime local customers—bars, restaurants and stores that helped them get started—abandoning them when they can't get the beer they need because it's been sold to someone else.

CONSUMING BEER

Beer wholesalers and retailers will continue to catch up to their customers in terms of beer sophistication. Customers will prod retailers for more craft beer, and retailers will prod distributors. New distributors will specialize in craft beer, and some distributors that now concentrate on wine, water and/or soda will add craft beer to their lists. Existing distributors and retailers who now get 75 percent or more of their beer sales from mass-market beers will not become craft beer purveyors overnight, but neither will they ignore the higher margins and higher-spending customers that go with craft beer. So far there has been little discounting of microbrewed beer, but there will be more in the future as the number of new labels leads to fiercer competition. Consumers may be willing to pay more for good beer, but they aren't stupid. If one good beer is always cheaper than another, or is on sale for a special price this week only, that's going to affect sales.

The key to selling craft beer, however, will continue to be the quality of the product and the level of service provided to the consumer. Craft beer fans want to come into a beer store and browse, like they do in wine shops. (Indeed, beer stores already are starting to look and feel more like upscale wine shops.) Customers want to be able to put together a case of different micros at a per-case price for each bottle. They want the sales clerk to be able to suggest different beers to serve with different courses at a dinner party. In a bar, they want the bartender to be able to tell them a little about each craft brew—something about the brewery, something about the recipe, something about the taste. In a restaurant, they want the waiter to be able to make a recommendation for an appetizer that will go well with the beer they've chosen for an aperitif.

The demand will continue to grow for good beer, and for information about good beer. More and more information on craft beer and breweries will continue to spring up on the World Wide Web, and the Internet will further establish itself as the place to go to find out anything about beer and the beer business anywhere in the world. Mail-order companies and clubs that offer beer selections every month will probably fade away as more craft beers become available regionally and nationally. After all, why should you pay more than top dollar for a six-pack of something that you can get cheaper around the corner? Instead, the next big step in consumer service for craft beer will be selling beer electronically. The Brooklyn Brewery, and no doubt others, is working on a plan under which people in the New York area can order beer through the brewery Website. You can scroll through the descriptions of the beers that Brooklyn brews, along with the three hundred other craft beers distributed by its marketing arm, the Craft Brewers Guild, and place an order with a couple of clicks and keystrokes. The next day the beer is delivered to your door.

BREWING

It's hard to say how much homebrewing will continue to grow. If it does continue to become a more popular hobby, it may well be because more women, particularly mothers working in the home, take up brewing. A better bet for growth are the brew-on-premises operations that are springing up across the country. For as little as $100 and a few hours of time, homebrewers can expand their operations by going to these small rent-a-brewery operations and brewing up a few barrels or several dozen cases of their own beer with the assistance of professional brewers who help them with every step of the process, down to putting their own personalized labels on every bottle. In the coming years, expect to go to more and more Christmas parties in offices or homes where the brew is made by the host or the boss, and served in bottles bearing a picture of the brewmaster or his wife or his dog or his boat or whatever.

On the professional level, the shortage of qualified, experienced, competent brewers is going to get worse as the number of microbreweries and brewpubs increases across the United States. The hospitality industry is slowly realizing what it takes to be a skilled brewer, and that not everyone can learn to do it well in a week or two. Restaurant people eager to open brewpubs are finding out the hard way that saving money on a brewmaster can cost your entire business. Too many restaurateurs rush out to hire a good local homebrewer or the owner of the local homebrew shop who will work cheap but turns out to be incompetent for commercial brewing. Brewpubs are realizing they must pay brewmasters decent salaries, and provide them with the quality ingredients they need to produce the right mix of beers that satisfy yet challenge the clientele.

The shortage of brewers will attract more young men—and women—to the craft, and to formal education and training programs, such as those offered by the American Brewers Guild, UC-Davis and various universities and schools in Europe. Teaching other people to brew will become a nice sideline to the craft brewing industry, but there's a risk that the tutors and teachers who set up their own training programs will be exactly the brewmasters who couldn't make it in a brewpub or microbrewery. As craft brewing becomes more profitable and more established in America, brewers will reclaim their place as bastions of respectability and civic duty, as they were in the nineteenth century, particularly in the run-down industrial areas where a microbrewery can trigger a revival of supporting businesses and provide a spark for new street life.

THE SMART DRINKER

Brewers, distributors and retailers are not the only ones who need education. Consumers do, too, if they want to know what they are drinking and why they are drinking it. Does the word ''microbrewed'' on a beer necessarily mean a beer is craft-brewed? Can a beer really be a ''lambic'' if it wasn't brewed in the traditional style in the Belgian region that gave its name to the beer in the same way that a region of France gave its name to champagne? Is it possible to have ''draft'' beer out of a bottle or can? Does a dark, strong-tasting beer mean it must have a high alcohol content? The answer to all those questions, of course, is no. To be good beer drinkers, we're all going to need to know something about good beer.

We cannot and should not depend on what's on labels—or what's not on labels. We think alcohol content should be on beer labels, the way it is in most European countries, so that you know how strong a beer is before you drink it. Historically, the U.S. government banned American brewers from disclosing the alcohol content of their beers on labels, ostensibly because it would encourage drunkenness among people who would seek out the brands that would give them the biggest buzz. At the same time, many mass-market brewers were tacitly against alcohol-content labeling, presumably because they wanted their customers to assume the beer was stronger than it really was.

The U.S. Supreme Court recently lifted the ban, however, so that American brewers can put the alcohol content on their labels—if they want to and state law permits it. We think they should, primarily to give the consumer more information. If you go to a beer festival in Europe, where drinkers can choose among dozens of different beers of widely varying potency, there are very few people who dash straight for the strongest and start pounding them down. In general, people who drink good beer, and are willing to pay for it, don't want to ruin the experience by getting sick or silly. In fact, there's a strong argument that putting the alcohol content on labels will help reduce drunkenness; if you know a beer is particularly potent, you might decide to have two instead of three or one instead of two, no matter how smoothly it's going down, because you don't want to be feeling fuzzy or cloudy either later that night or in the morning.

The alcohol content is just one small part of a large debate over labeling within the brewing industry in general and the craft brewing niche in particular. Another issue is freshness dating. Many craft brewers put "Best before" markings on their labels. You can often find them on the side of the label, where a year and a month have been nicked. These markings can and do provide information for the drinker, but the date is solely up to the brewer. Most brewers set a date that is three or four months after bottling, but they can put down any date they want. It's very subjective, depending on how long they think their beer will taste good, and how long they think it will take to sell the beer. How long a beer tastes fresh certainly depends on how it is brewed, but it also depends on how it is handled and stored after it leaves the brewery. Distributors, retailers and consumers can all do things that help a beer survive beyond its "Best before" date, or they can do things that turn it stale considerably earlier.

A few craft brewers refuse to put any date on their labels (see Beer People/Jack Joyce, page 65). They argue that freshness dating is a "commodity tactic" that big brewers will use to drive little brewers out of business. In a freshness competition, they warn, no small brewer can compete with Anheuser-Busch. They'd rather leave it up to customers to decide if the beer is any good or not. Some breweries are doing something else: putting the date of bottling on the label. They argue that it's an objective date, and consumers can use it to decide when and whether to buy a beer. In any event, if you have a beer that was bottled three months earlier and it is stale, you certainly won't buy that beer again unless it's younger. On the other hand, you might try a beer that was bottled six months earlier and find it delicious. You'd make a mental note to buy that beer again even if the accepted wisdom says it might be too old.

Perhaps the biggest labeling issues, however, are reserved for where a beer is brewed, whether it is "microbrewed" and what style it represents. Should a company based in St. Louis or Boston, like Anheuser-Busch and Boston Beer Co., respectively, be allowed to put "St. Louis" on cans of Budweiser that are brewed in Newark or "Boston" on bottles of Samuel Adams that come from a brewery in Pittsburgh? Similarly, should the Oregon Beer and Ale Co., which is part of the Boston Beer empire, be allowed to label its Oregon brand beers "Microbrewed in Oregon" when they are contract-brewed at a large Heileman brewery in Portland? Finally, should brewers be allowed to pass off anything they brew as a certain style, even if there is no such style (a "stout lager" was one recent example) or the beer itself was not brewed in the classic style and doesn't taste anything like the classic style is supposed to taste?

These issues have pitted large brewers against micros, and split the craft brewery industry. The Oregon Brewers Guild, representing forty microbrewers, found itself in an unlikely alliance with Anheuser-Busch in filing a complaint with the Bureau of Alcohol, Tobacco and Firearms (probably the only federal agency with a name that conjures up a redneck frat party). The complaint asked the government to ban breweries from claiming they were microbreweries if they actually brewed their beer in big breweries, and to ban breweries from claiming their beer was from a specific city or state if it was actually brewed somewhere else. The complaint said such labeling is unfair and misleads the public. It is unlikely the government will set a long list of specific do's and don'ts for beer labels, but the dispute points out the need for consumers to educate themselves. Do you want to drink a beer that the labels lead you to believe is from a tiny brewery in California when it's really from a giant brewery in Minnesota? Do you want to buy a beer that claims to be a double bock or a Scotch ale or a Vienna lager if it isn't?

Some beer purists say the lack of any sort of regulation in labeling is leading the new generation of American craft beer drinkers to mis-identify classic styles; they think they're drinking a Belgian lambic, when a Belgian lambic actually tastes much different. Many craft brew-ers, meanwhile, say that the only thing that matters is whether people like their beer, no matter what name it carries. Rather than bastardizing old classics, they see themselves redefining beer styles.

We think beer styles are important. If a beer's label says it is a cer-tain style, the consumer should be able to drink it with assurances that it was made in the style, and tastes like the style should taste. If it doesn't matter to you, fine. If it does, then start gathering information. Talk to people who know beer in stores or bars. Pick up one of the many free brewspapers floating around, or subscribe to have one deliv-ered. Check out some of the online forums or Internet newsgroups. And most of all, if you have a beer you don't like and you think it's because there's something wrong with it—it's skunked, or oxidized, or just plain stale, for example—send it back to the bar or take it back to the store. Ask whoever served you to sample the stuff. If you don't get a response that satisfies you, take your business to a bar or store that knows beer better and can help you learn more about better beer.

Another aspect of beer education is that more people are realizing beer's health benefits. At first scientists believed a glass or two of red wine were beneficial to health, but recent studies show that's also true for white wine and beer. George Sheehan, the running doctor, was ahead of his time on this point; he recommended having a couple of beers after every run, and always tried to follow his own advice. (He was able to run in the evening after work, it should be pointed out; those of us who jog in the morning before work have to wait till later for our beer. Except on weekends, of course.) The U.S. government reports that one or two 12-ounce beers a day provides "significant health benefits" in reducing coronary disease for men over age forty and post-menopausal women. The government says three to four beers a day for men and two to three for women—based on average body weights for men and women—is not harmful for most people. While it will always be an alcoholic beverage and subject to potential abuse (like any food), the moderate enjoyment of beer—particularly beer made with all-natural ingredients, like craft beer—is likely to become more widely acknowledged for its health benefits. Beer is good for you, and good beer is even better for you.

Tyrone Irby

TYRONE IRBY AND his buddies in Raleigh, N.C., used to unwind every Wednesday night by going out and pounding pitchers of Coors Light. One night, on a whim, he tried something different: Sierra Nevada Pale Ale. He loved it, and so did his buddies. They began trying different kinds of beer, and Tyrone began reading everything he could about good beer. At that time in North Carolina, it was often easier to find things to read about good beer than it was to find good beer. He read an article about Carol Stoudt, and in 1993 organized the first of many "beer trips" with his buddies. They drove to Adamstown, Pa., toured the Stoudt brewery, drank the beer, headed over to New York City to hit the then-handful of good beer bars there, and then made their way back down the East Coast with stops at Bardo's in Baltimore and a few other beer landmarks along the way. "The most fun I ever had in my life," Tyrone decided. He also decided to do what he could to promote good beer in the Carolinas.

Tyrone and his buddies, notably Kevin Odell, rented out a restaurant for an evening and staged their own little beer festival in January 1994. About 250 people showed up. They were so encouraged that they formed the Southeastern Microbrewers Association and organized another beer festival three months later, on a larger scale, at a hotel in Raleigh. One thousand people showed up and Tyrone lost $5,000. But he didn't give up. He moved the festival to a bigger hotel, the Omni, in Durham, in the spring of 1995. Thirty breweries and 2,400 people came, and the festival made a profit for charity. By 1996 Irby's festival had added restaurant booths, had restricted its invitations to breweries only—no distributors—and had become a fixture on the festival calendar for many of America's best microbrewers. Brewers regard Irby's festival as one of the best run in the country, and it led to daytime jobs for him first as a sales rep for Stoudt's, and more recently for Rogue. Besides festivals (he was organizing a new one in the autumn, on the Outer Banks), Tyrone and his organization sponsor tastings, lectures and beer dinners, and generally provide any information they can to anyone interested in craft beer. The group also lobbies the North Carolina Legislature to do away with the law that prohibits the sale of any beer stronger than 6 percent. "We do anything and everything to let people know there's something out there other than Budweiser," he says. Or Coors Light, his friends remind him.

NINE

Handling and Tasting:
The Vocabulary of Beer

P ART OF THE joy of learning about good beer is being able to describe it, and evaluate what makes it good. That's one of the big reasons that microbrews are so interesting. You can say an awful lot about them simply because there are so many identifiable natural flavors, as opposed to the mass-market beers that are blended and blanded with adjuncts such as corn and rice and who-knows-what other additives and preservatives. It seems as if the goal of mass-market beers is to keep costs down and extend shelf life, while at the same time killing any real beer taste.

Many people who are just getting interested in good beer—even those who know a fair amount about wine—fret about being able to describe beer. "I don't know what words to use," they say. The most important thing to remember is that it's impossible to be wrong. Use whatever words you think appropriate. Many of the descriptive words for beer are the same for wine. Woody or fruity or dry, for example. (Although beer people tend to snicker at some of the more snobbish, personality-oriented descriptives for wine, such as "a naughty little chardonnay.") If you taste pineapple or banana, or lemon or coriander in lighter beers, say so. If darker beers give you tones of steel, wood, moss, peat, caramel, vanilla, chocolate or smoke, say so. Likely as not, someone will agree with you—and wish they'd said it first.

SERVING AND TASTING BEER

Beer should never be served below 40 degrees Fahrenheit—unless you are the type of evolving beer drinker who still occasionally will settle for a thirst-quenching blast of something bubbly and supercold, like a mass-market low-cal beer after coming off the tennis court or golf course or softball diamond on a hot day. We would discourage even that, however. No matter how hot and thirsty you are, you still want some taste, no? Very cold temperatures take away most of the taste of beer. That's why very few good beer lovers will ever drink from a frosted mug or glass. Even if they didn't mind getting frost mixed in with their beer—which they would, of course—they'd mind having the glass lower the temperature of the beer.

Most golden lagers and other lighter beers should be served around 45 degrees. Many brown ales and bitters are usually fine around 50 degrees, and most stouts around 55 degrees. When the British say good beer should be served at room temperature, they're not talking about centrally heated American rooms; they're talking about drafty, uninsulated English rooms, particularly the English cellars where the temperature historically was 55–60 degrees year-round.

Good beer should always be served in a clean glass, first poured down the side into a tilted glass, and then straight into the center of the upright glass to bring up the head. (Watch out for wheat beers and bottle-conditioned beers, though; you may get a lot more head than you anticipate.)

Experienced beer drinkers tend to like glasses that fit the particular characteristics of a beer. Pilsner glasses are perfect for showing off pilsner's clarity and golden color; somehow, it wouldn't look quite the same in a stolid, straight-sided English pint glass. German wheat beer glasses are at least ten inches tall and flared at the top to hold the two-inch head that is part of the beer's charm. Every Belgian brewery seems to have definite opinions about what sort of glass its beer should be served in, but most of them are shaped either like tulips or bowls, the better to give the nose access to all those spicy aromas. If you haven't got a Belgian beer glass handy, brandy snifters are near-perfect substitutes. (Snifters are generally good for beer tasting because they're designed to concentrate aroma.) Fruit beers are often served in champagne glasses to show off the exotic color the fruit has imparted.

Part of the joy of learning about good beer is being able to describe it and evaluate what makes it special to you. Don't be afraid to use the words that come to mind when you're talking about beer. Be descriptive. Have some fun. Get yourself a very clean, well-rinsed glass (a snifter or a small wineglass will do the job). Fill the glass a little more than halfway, leaving room for aroma to gather, and for you to swirl the beer around the glass a little. (Be careful, dry cleaning can get expensive.) Now, hold it up to the light and have a look. Does it look appealing? You might think a bit about the malts that gave the beer its color. How does the head look? Is it thin and soapy-looking, or is it thick, foamy or rocky? On most beers, at least a bit of the head should last all the way to the bottom of the glass (that's also a good sign of a clean glass). If the glass really is clean, there will be a series of foam rings left as evidence of each sip—"Brussels lace," the English call it.

Next, the most important part, the nose. Surprised? Well, remember that your sense of taste is mostly interpreted through your sense of smell. Your tongue can only actually perceive four limited sensations—sweet, sour, salt and bitter. Those are important, of course, but everything else comes to you through your sense of smell. That's why your food seems to have no flavor when you've got a head cold—you can't smell anything. So swirl the beer around the glass, and get a good whiff. Now, think. Does it remind you of anything? Grain, grass, bread, peat moss, hops, molasses? Fruit, flowers, earth? Most importantly, do you like it? The brewers at Bass once did an aroma profile for Draught Bass Ale, and among the aromas they discerned were "mineral baths, wet wool blanket, grass clippings and saddle leather." Of course, they liked the beer, and so do plenty of other people, but even descriptions of tasty things don't always sound so nice. Try describing the aroma of Parmesan cheese to someone sometime, and you'll see what we mean.

Time, finally, to taste the beer. Everyone has his or her own way of doing it, but you ought to move the beer around your tongue a little before it goes down (none of this wine-world spitting nonsense . . . unless you've got to drive). How does it feel in your mouth—thin, medium-bodied, thick? Then there are the actual flavors, of course. Malt has a sweet, grainy, bready flavor, which becomes deeper as the malts become more roasted. Malt can add caramel, toffee, or nutty flavors, and dark malts may taste of coffee or chocolate. The bitterness of hops should be well balanced against the sweetness of malt. A beer with too much hop and too little malt will seem thin, mouth-puckering and astringent, while an underhopped beer might taste over-sweet, syrupy or cloying. Hops also can add flavors; herbal, grassy, citrus and floral notes are common. Unless there is fruit in the beer, fruity aromas usually come from a warm fermentation with a top-fermenting ale yeast. Lagers tend to be more straightforward—most of the flavors come directly from the ingredients, with the yeast adding little flavor of its own. After the beer goes down, the aftertaste is important. Did it finish clear and clean, and would you like to have some more?

Good beer is like a good story—it should have a beginning, a middle, and an end. All of them should be pleasant, and the whole experience should have some complexity and character. Otherwise, why would you want to waste your time drinking it? And as we said, trust your own palate to guide you to what you like. While it's true that some styles of beer are acquired tastes, most aren't. And it's always legitimate to have your own opinion about them. The more you know about the beer, the more fun you'll have drinking it. And fun is what beer is all about.

EVEN GOOD BEER CAN GO BAD

The general rule is, the fresher the beer, the better it tastes. Occasionally beer that has been badly brewed or poorly bottled or kegged gets out to the public. The most common such brewing mistakes include "infected" beer, the result of a microbiological instability. Another brewing mistake can result in extremely cloudy or hazy beer—a colloidal instability, brewers call it.

Even fresh beer that has been well brewed can be mishandled, especially if it is exposed to light, oxygen, too much heat, too much cold or just plain rough treatment. Many people have learned to avoid beer that is stacked in direct sunlight, or stored under fluorescent lights in stores. Such beer is often "lightstruck," the result of a photochemical reaction of the light on the compounds present in hops. Beer in green bottles is especially susceptible to becoming lightstruck, or "skunked," which is what beer smells and tastes like after too much exposure to light. Beer that has been sitting out in warm temperatures—anything above 75 degrees—even for a few hours, is likely to be stale, especially in green bottles. A bottle of Heineken, Moosehead or Pilsner Urquell will skunk almost immediately upon exposure to direct sunlight, and over time in a lighted cooler in a supermarket. Some people who drink brands in green bottles actually have become used to drinking skunked beer because they so rarely have a fresh one.

Oxidation is another common problem. In a bar or restaurant, draft beer that has become oxidized—exposed to air for too long—will have a stale taste that is variously described as reminiscent of cardboard, metal, rotten vegetables or cheap sherry. Oxidation typically happens because air is being used to pump the beer (you see this at picnics, or in bars with creaky old draft systems), because a keg has been hooked up to the draft line for too long or because the beer is just plain old. When you get a bad beer, send it back. Take it back to the store where you bought it, give it back to the bartender or server, and call or write the brewers and/or local distributors to let them know that they've got stale beer out there. Carol Stoudt urges consumers to send beer directly back to her brewery if they buy any out-of-date Stoudt's. She wants to know if distributors are selling her product past its sell-by date so she can solve the problem, whether it's in shipping, distribution or whatever. (She says it couldn't be a brewing or bottling problem, because she would never let old or bad beer out the door in the first place.) She is one of the rare but brave brewers who will actually refuse to sell her beer to a distributor who is not willing or able to handle it properly. Increasingly, reputable microbreweries and contract brewers will buy back out-of-date beer from distributors, particularly if they feel they made a mistake in convincing the distributor to take more beer than the distributor could sell.

Bottles of beer often don't travel well, particularly from some smaller breweries that don't have the time or money for a fail-safe bottling system with lots of backstopping quality controls. Sadly, a few microbreweries and brewpubs that bottle their own beer are under such financial pressure that they succumb to the temptation to put out bottles of infected, oxidized or otherwise stale beer solely because they need the sales and feel they cannot afford to pour the bad beer down the drains. Even if it was properly brewed and bottled, however, there are opportunities for shippers, wholesalers, retailers and consumers themselves to ruin what started off as a perfectly good beer. Heat is an enemy of beer. The rule of thumb is that for every 20-degree increase in temperature, beer ages twice as fast. A beer that would stay fresh for a month in a 40-degree fridge would go stale after a week on a porch where the temperature sometimes hits 80. A common mistake is serving beer too cold. It numbs the taste buds and doesn't allow appreciation of the full flavor of the beer—in much the same way that chilling ruins the flavor of red wine. For expensive, darker beers, check with your retailer to find the right temperature to store it. If you don't have a place where the temperature is the required constant—usually 50–55 degrees—it's probably better to keep it in the fridge at 40 degrees than down in the basement where the temperature might swing from 40 to 70.

Erik Neiderman

ERIK NEIDERMAN IS the kind of brewer and brewpub owner that some beer snobs might look down on. After all, he wasn't a home-brewer for years before getting into the business. He didn't sub-scribe to all the brewspapers, or sit mesmerized in front of his computer screen waiting for beer sites to download from the In-ternet. He didn't even drink all that much beer. Neiderman got into brewing because he saw it as a good business opportunity. While some purists may sniff at that, the rest of us who benefit from another good new brewpub don't care why it's there. We're just glad it is. And that's certainly the case with the Palm Springs Brewery, which Neiderman and a couple of partners opened in March 1994.

As a community, Palm Springs has a reputation for being old, conservative and wealthy—more white wine, margaritas and mar-tinis than good beer, which was largely limited to washing down a spicy Mexican meal with some Dos Equis. Nonetheless, Nei-derman, who moved to the California desert from New York with his family several years ago, decided a brewpub was worth the risk of giving up the New York–style deli he had been running. With money borrowed from friends and relatives—including his father, novelist Andrew Neiderman—Erik and his partners, Victor Yasjanich and Richard Kasofsky, took over a large space on North Palm Canyon, in Palm Springs' main shopping district.

Neiderman apprenticed himself to Los Angeles brewer Marty Velas, who taught him to brew simple, straightforward, commer-cial batches of amber lager, pale ale, wheat, brown ale, and porter styles. Most beer experts would say the quality is generally good, but not great—certainly a positive first step in bringing fresh craft beer to what had been a desert in an oasis. Neiderman, who added a small bottling line and is now distributing to area bars and res-taurants, admits he made one big mistake: To create more seating, he hid the brewhouse. Now he's planning to move the tanks right up in front, in the middle of the restaurant, so they are visible through the windows from the street and to everyone inside.

BUYING BEER

Do you want freshness dates on your beer? You know, the "Best before" date on the label that tells you when the brewer thinks the beer will start going stale? Sure, why not. But are you willing to pay more for each beer that has a freshness date on the label? Brewers say that is the choice consumers need to make. In fact, most consumers don't notice even when there is a freshness date on the label. Besides, many craft beers, especially if they've been properly handled from brewery to drinking, taste just fine even well past their "Best before" dates, which typically vary from brewery to brewery and style to style from forty-five days to a year after bottling. Check the labels, and if you find beer past its "Best before" date, take it back to the retailer—and let the brewer know. Any retailer who refuses to make a refund or credit your account or give you a replacement doesn't deserve your business.

If a label doesn't carry a "Best before" date but does carry the date of bottling, it will be up to you to decide whether you think a beer is too old before you buy it. Three months? Six months? It varies from beer to beer, brewery to brewery, retailer to retailer. A beer that's only two months old might not be any good if the retailer stored it in a hot back room or displayed it in a sunny window, but the same brand of beer might be good for six months in the hands of a knowledgeable, careful retailer. In any event, even if you get a bad beer without a "Best before" date on the label, you still should be able to take it back or send it back. But the next time, buyer beware.

In both stores and bars or restaurants, feel free to ask the clerks, bartenders or servers questions about the beer. What do they have? What do they recommend? Describe to them the types of beer you like, and ask if there's anything that fits the bill. How fresh is it? If it's draft beer, when was the keg opened? If you're going to be drinking the beer with food, look to them for suggestions on a good match. Increasingly, stores and bars and restaurants are educating their staff about beer. They sometimes have representatives of breweries of distributorships come in for lectures and tastings, to help train the staff to know and appreciate beer enough to be able to answer customers' questions. A few proprietors—Tommy Chow of the Peculier Pub in Greenwich Village is peculiarly famous for this—require their staff to take detailed tests on beer, including brewing processes, that they must pass regularly in order to keep their jobs. If you encounter a server who doesn't know or care about beer, you might want to suggest to the manager that some training is in order. If things don't improve, that's a sign that the restaurant or bar doesn't care about your business.

It's important to find a retailer who appreciates beer, understands how to handle beer and can discuss beer in the same way the managers of good liquor stores discuss fine wine or single-malt Scotch whisky. A retailer needs to keep beer at the right temperature, rotate stock and display it properly. Corked beer, such as some of the expensive French and Belgian beers, should be laid on its side, for the same reason—to prevent oxidation—that wine is stored on its side. If you're worried about whether a retailer is taking care of the beer, make sure you buy closed cases, preferably those that have been stored in a cooler or cold room. If you don't have room for proper storage yourself, make sure you buy in small quantities so the beer doesn't go stale sitting around waiting for you to drink it. And if you do buy in smaller quantities, such as just a few bottles of a label, try to choose the bottles from the interior of a closed case, where they may have been more protected from heat and light.

Don't necessarily assume that the bars with the largest selection of beers are necessarily the best place to drink the stuff. Some of those bars with dozens of tap handles and hundreds of bottles don't turn over the stock frequently enough to keep the beer fresh. What good is it to study a menu of three hundred beers if one hundred of them—or even fifty, or ten—haven't been ordered by anyone else in a year? (That's one of the reasons that some good beer bars have "clubs" that give prizes to members who try ninety-nine different beers, or some other large number, within a year; it keeps the stock moving, even on some of the more obscure labels that otherwise might languish.) By the same token, try to be understanding if a bar with an extensive list doesn't have your first choice of an obscure beer. They may keep supplies of certain labels deliberately small, just to avoid the risk of letting it get stale. And don't necessarily assume that a bar is withdrawing from its commitment to good beer by cutting back on the number of different labels it offers. Some bars have decided it's better to have fewer, fresher beers. In bars with extensive draft lines that seem to be serious about beer, ask the bartender when a keg was tapped before you order the beer. The more recently the beer was tapped, the more likely it is to taste fresh. A barrel of some types of strong, dark beer can easily last weeks on a draft line; other lighter beers can start deteriorating within days. Suggest to bartenders and managers that they put up a blackboard or some other sort of notices with the date that each keg was tapped.

Hubert Plummer

HUBERT PLUMMER DISCOVERED both the online world and the world of good beer in college at Vassar. Now a lawyer, he is a prodigious beer-can collector and competent homebrewer, but his real claim to fame is that he serves as host for CompuServe's highly regarded Beer Forum. As host, Hubey provides information for people making requests, keeps threads of discussion going and, occasionally, soothes hurt feelings before they can burst into flame wars. He also maintains CompuServe's online library of beer resources, including reviews of beer books and tasting notes for more than five hundred different beers. Many professional brewers, homebrewers and beer fans say CompuServe's forum is the best online place to talk beer—and they say Hubey deserves a great deal of the credit.

One of the highlights of the forum is Hubey's quote for the day. His sources can range from a dusty old history book to some friendly stranger on the next barstool. Here's a sample:

Make the male member of your family go to a brewery or beer garden and learn exactly how to tap a keg. Much beer has been wasted and much furniture ruined by the man who says he knows how to do the job.

Virginia Elliot, 1933

"I have an appetite for brewing and beer history," Hubey says. "More than anything, I think it is a history of regular people. Brewing history really traces and often defines the history of mankind. I fully support the theory that agriculture was begun to grow grain for brewing, not baking bread." His online hosting work typically takes several hours a week, and it's purely a voluntary position; all he receives in compensation is free connect time while in the forum. In addition to CompuServe, you can check out Hubey on the Web at *http://www.panix.com/~plummerh/beer.html*.

═ TEN ═
Beer and Food

ONE EVENING WE were out with a dozen of New York's best young chefs on a pub crawl, sampling different types of beer and talking about beer with food. Well into the evening, at one bar/restaurant that had been expecting us, waiters suddenly appeared bearing huge platters laden with sauerkraut and German sausages. How would the chefs react to such pedestrian food, certainly plain and uninspired by the standards of their trendy kitchens? Well, they tucked in like trenchermen. Some food seems as if it was meant to go with beer in general, and with certain types of beer in particular. Pizza and lager. Raw oysters on the half shell with porter. Chocolate with imperial stout. Spicy food with pale ale.

The good beer revolution has influenced many restaurants across the spectrum, from neighborhood pubs to places where you'd better wear a necktie and have a credit card, preferably someone else's. Hot young chefs see craft beer as an ingredient that fits nicely with their emphasis on fresh, natural, local ingredients. They welcome the wide range of taste profiles in good beer as an innovative complement to their creations. Indeed, in some cases the beer has been an inspiration for the food, such as the mousse made with Black Chocolate Stout (recipe on p. 103) or the pumpkin soup served in a small, hollowed-out pumpkin with Pumpkin Ale. Many chefs, as they experiment with beer as an ingredient, have come to realize that it can be more flavorful than wine when used in a reduction sauce. More restaurants are starting to routinely present beer dinners, particularly on traditionally slow nights such as Mondays and Tuesdays. Moreover, people at home are beginning to rely on beer for dinner parties, offering a different beer with various courses. The dishes don't need to be fancy. Here's one of our favorite recipes. When you make this recipe yourself, call it Garrett's Drunken Lamb Chops:

8 inch-thick (or more) loin lamb chops, no bone
24 oz. Bateman's Victory Ale, or any Belgian dobbel or other fruity
   ale
3 cups sliced shallots
1 teaspoon green peppercorns
5 sprigs fresh rosemary
A few sprigs of fresh thyme
8 cloves of garlic
Salt and fresh-ground black pepper
Extra virgin olive oil

In a large Tupperware-style bowl, place chops and shallots and add beer to cover them entirely. Add more beer if necessary to cover the chops. Add rosemary, thyme and peppercorns. Slice garlic and add. Salt and pepper to taste. Cover and refrigerate for 24 hours. Remove lamb chops, coat with olive oil, then salt and pepper liberally. Remove the rosemary and thyme from the marinade, then pour out all the marinade, retaining a half-cup. Sauté the shallots, garlic and peppercorns in butter, adding a dash of marinade. Broil the chops closely on high heat until medium rare. Serve with roast new potatoes and asparagus.

Serves 4 piggy people.

Try experimenting with beer and food at home. Sauté some shrimp with sun-dried tomatoes, roast garlic, hot peppers and a pale ale or amber lager, and then serve with a nice tall glass of the same beer. Turkey chili with Scottish ale makes a nice match. So do barbecued ribs with brown ale or a smoked beer, and corned beef with bock. Here's a recommended recipe for Cajun chicken that goes really well with an amber lager or a brown ale:

2 lbs. skinless, boneless chicken breast
8–10 sliced shallots
½ cup of parsley
6–8 cloves of garlic
1 cup olive oil

Spice mix for coating: 1 tbs. paprika, 2 tsp. salt, 1 tbs. onion powder, 1 tbs. garlic powder, 1 tbs. cayenne pepper, 1 tsp. white pepper, 1 tsp. black pepper, ½ tbs. thyme leaves, ½ tbs. oregano.

Cover the chicken breasts with the spice mix. Mix the remaining ingredients and pour over the chicken. Cover with plastic and refrigerate for 24 hours. Place chicken on baking sheet and roast at 350° F for 20 minutes. Allow to cool to room temperature, slice very thin and serve.

Matching beer and food is not new, of course. It's merely being rediscovered. During World War II, the food author M.F.K. Fisher, in her classic *How to Cook a Wolf,* saw the war as an opportunity for a revival of local craft brewing: "There are a thousand small honest breweries in this country which . . . have been forced to close, or else operate under famous names. Now, with the trains full of soldiers and supplies rather than pale ale, perhaps people far from the great breweries will turn again to their local beer factories and discover, as their fathers did thirty years ago, that a beer carried quietly three miles is better than one shot across three thousand on a fast freight."

That didn't begin happening until three decades after the war ended, but many influential food writers and critics, notably the late James Beard, promoted the use of beer with fine food long before brewpubs began popping up on downtown corners. Beard consulted on the first organized beer dinner in the United States, at the Pierre Hotel in Manhattan on Oct. 24, 1984. The dinner was hosted by Michael Jackson, and the cooking was done by four Belgian chefs boasting six Michelin stars among them. All the beers were Belgian. Here's the menu:

Soup of Belgian endive, served with *Palm Ale*
Ostend sole and shrimp, served with *Duvel*
Chicken with sorrel and asparagus, served with *De Koninck Ale*
Melted cheese and walnut salad, served with *Scaldis Strong Ale*
Kriek sorbet, served with *Mort Subite*
Coffee, served with *Gouden Carolus*

Note that the salad was served after the main course, as it should be. After Beard died and his home in Greenwich Village was turned into an institute for the study of food and drink, beer dinners became a mainstay. Here is the menu for the first beer dinner at James Beard House, also hosted by Michael Jackson, in 1993:

Three appetizers served with Frank Boon's *Gueuze, Sierra Nevada Porter and Celis White*: oysters with a salsa of *Rodenbach*; smoked eel on beer bread; scallions dipped in goat cheese with orange peel and herbs
Sautéed Louisiana shrimp in a sauce of sun-dried tomatoes, roast garlic, hot peppers and *Geary Pale Ale*, served with *Brooklyn Lager*
Smoked sausage with mâche and endive in a gueuze vinaigrette, served with *Traquair House Ale*

Yukon potatoes gratin, Fontina cheese and jalapeños made with *Chimay,* served with *Castelain*

Glazed pork prepared with *Ayinger Celebrator* and mango chutney and black beans, served with *Paulaner Salvator*

Refresher sorbet served with *Liefmans Framboise*

Duck braised with cabbae and chanterelles, prepared with *Brooklyn Brown Ale,* served with *Chimay Grande Reserve*

Death by chocolate dessert made with *Catamount Porter,* served with *Samuel Smith's Oatmeal Stout*

Here's a menu for a beer dinner recommended by Steve Hindy, a co-founder of the Brooklyn Brewery, who has hosted more good beer dinners than should be allowed for any one person:

Olive puffs, corn oysters, spicy calamari, assorted sushi, served with *Warsteiner Pilsner* and *Brooklyn Lager*

Sturgeon in hazelnut crust, red pepper relish and lemon basil sauce, served with *Duvel Ale* and *Paulaner Oktoberfest*

Root vegetable and muzzuna salad, toasted carraway and a potato web, served with *Jenlain Ale* and *Goudenband*

Seared Black Angus sirloin in honey mustard spice oil, served with *Sierra Nevada Pale Ale, Brooklyn Brown Ale* and *Chimay Rouge Trappist Ale*

Pecan tart, *Boniata Nougatine* ice cream, served with *Thomas Hardy's Ale* and *Lindeman's Kriek*

We're pleased that people are beginning to see beer as an alternative to white wine when serving fish. Here's a menu for a beer dinner at London Lennie's, probably the best seafood place in Queens:

Roast Michigan whitefish with dill-cured salmon, served with *Affligem Abbey Triple Ale*

Pan-seared loin of tuna with orzo, shallots and red wine, served with *Saranac Pale Ale*

Veal paillard gremolata with fried leeks and sage, served with *Batemans XXXB Ale*

Walnut-crusted poached pear, served with *Young's Old Nick Ale*

Many people are surprised at beer being used to prepare desserts, or that it can be served with them. These people have never had a fresh fruit pie served with a Lindeman's Framboise or Peche, or a rich pecan pie served with an imperial stout. Here's a recipe for Brooklyn Black Chocolate Stout Mousse from Executive Chef Angelo J. Giordano at the Old Bay Restaurant in New Brunswick, N.J. It has been a big hit among diners at the beer dinners the restaurant throws regularly, and is a spectacular make-it-yourself winter dessert to cap off home dinner parties—though we hear that some of the home cooks are adding more Brooklyn Black Chocolate Stout:

1¼ pounds of fine chocolate, cut into small cubes
1 quart of heavy cream
7 eggs
3½ ounces of cane sugar
3 teaspoons of powdered gelatin
4 ounces of Brooklyn Black Chocolate Stout
2 ounces of hot coffee

Place chocolate in a double boiler and melt, stirring occasionally. Bloom gelatin by stirring into the chilled beer, and reserve. Whip heavy cream until it forms soft peaks, remove from mixer and place in refrigerator. In a mixer, whip eggs until frothy, then add sugar. Dissolve gelatin by adding the hot coffee. Add chocolate and gelatin to eggs, mix until well blended. Fold in whipped cream and let set 2–4 hours in the fridge. Serve topped with chocolate shavings and a glass of Brooklyn Black Chocolate Stout.

12 servings.

One of our favorite food-and-beer columnists is Timothy S. Schafer, a chef and caterer who writes for *Ale Street News.* He loves to grill, and to experiment with whatever food and beer he has on hand. He's provided lots of great ideas for using beer, particularly as a marinade. He suggests marinating a butterflied leg of lamb in garlic, oil and rauchbier (a style of smoked beer) overnight, and then putting it on the grill. Or simmer boneless pork shoulder steaks in garlic, onion, carrot, celery, jalapeño, barbecue sauce and porter for a few hours, until the sauce thickens and the meat pulls apart—and then make pulled pork sandwiches. Try steaming your shellfish in beer, or pouring a bit of stout into your baked beans. Marinate your chicken in brown ale or porter before cooking.

There are a number of collections of beer recipes around, and more coming out in print and on the Internet all the time, but if you're not into cooking with beer, it's still fun—especially for guests—to host a beer dinner that plays around with beer and food matches. You can choose the beers you want to serve and then think about what foods would go well with them, or you can choose the food first, and then decide on what beers would be good matches. Most home chefs seem to do both, choosing one course based first on the beer and the next based on the food. The planning can be fun, especially if you are diligent enough to do some research by tasting beers first.

Here's a menu for a beer dinner from Edelweiss, a popular German brasserie near O'Hare airport in Chicago:

Spicy pan-seared jumbo sea scallops, with grilled leeks in a roasted Holland red pepper balsamic coulis; served with *Samuel Smith's Nut Brown Ale*, a smooth ale with a hint of hazelnuts

Flaky strudel stuffed with smoked German sausages mixed with Vermont goat cheese, wild mushrooms, sun-dried tomatoes and accompanied by a sauce Robert; served with *Kaiserdom Rauchbier*, a smoked beer brewed in Bamberg, Germany, from malt kilned over a fire of moist beech

Baked brie rolled in multicolored cracked peppercorns, with freshly baked Granny Smith apple slices; served with *Orval Trappist Ale*, known as the Chardonnay of ales, a very dry, unfiltered ale with plenty of barley and hop taste

Baby lamb chops with a Dijon mustard herbed crust and a ratatouille with oven-dried cherry tomatoes, accompanied by a doppelbock sauce; served with *Doppelbock Celebrator*, a dark, rich, strong beer with the complexity of roast malt

Raspberry chambord double chocolate cake; served with *Lindeman's Framboise*, a wild yeast wheat beer with raspberries

The golden rule in terms of beer and food is that there are no rules. (The same is true of wine and food, of course, though there are some foods that are difficult to match with any wine, while virtually any food can be successfully matched with some style of beer.) Whatever tastes like a good match is a good match. In matching food or planning menus, there are a few rough guidelines. White or wheat beers, with their light, sometimes citrusy tones, often whet the palate and arouse the appetite as an aperitif. Heartier, darker beers such as brown ales stand up to the strong tastes of meat. Lighter lagers may be better with fish. The darkest beers, such as porters and stout, are often a good way to finish a meal with the cheese, dessert, coffee and cigar courses. We've encountered many, many combinations of beer and food through experimenting in our own kitchens, dining at the tables of other beer fans, attending beer dinners in restaurants and lurking on the online bulletin boards, forums and newsgroups where beer and food are a favored topic. Beef stew with Samuel Smith's Taddy Porter is a great idea. Thai curry and Pilsner Urquell. Russian Imperial Stout with a dollop of coffee ice cream dropped in, or on the side to a rich dark chocolate cake. Guinness Stout with oysters, fried or raw.

Here are some standard matches:

Aperitif	White or wheat beer
Chicken or pork	Pilsner, wheat, amber lager
Roast chicken	Pale ale, brown ale, saison, amber lager
Pork	Wheat, amber lager, pilsner, tripel
Raw shellfish	Porter, stout, American pale ale
Cooked shellfish	Wheat, India pale ale, amber lager
Fish	Wheat, pilsner, amber lager, pale ale
Hamburgers	Amber ale, lager, brown ale, pale ale
Pizza	Amber lager, pilsner
Barbecue	Rauchbier, stout, porter, pale ale, amber lager
Marinated/grilled vegetables	Amber lager, porter, bock, red ale
Game	Brown ale, porter, saison, Trappist, abbey dobbel
Roast beef	Pale ale, porter, brown ale
Lamb	Pale ale, brown ale, fruit lambic
Veal	Porter, brown ale, amber lager
Ham	Pilsner, amber lager, bock, weizenbock
Smoked fish, meat, cheese	Rauchbier, porter
Thai, Indian, spicy food	Pale ale, amber lager, bock
Sushi	Pale ale, wheat, pilsner
Salad	Amber lager, pale ale, wheat
Fruit pie or tart	Belgian fruit ales
Nut pies, cheesecake	Stout, framboise, kriek
Sweet desserts	Stout, porter, Scotch ale, Belgian fruit ales
Semisoft cheese	Trappist ale, porter, abbey tripel, gueuze

Stilton, strong cheese	Stout, porter, Trappist ale, gueuze, barley wine
Caviar	Stout
Cigars	Stout, barley wine, strong ales, saison

Chip Bellamy

FOR NEARLY TWENTY years, Chip Bellamy was a lawyer with a firm in Golden, Colo., that represented the Coors Brewing Co. He did legal work on Coors sales, marketing, distributor relations, purchasing and more, including helping with Coors' national expansion in the 1980s. One of his most interesting and enjoyable projects was doing the legal work to set up the SandLot Brewery, the Coors brewpub at Coors Field, the home ballpark for the Colorado Rockies. The experience of working with a small brewing operation helped reinforce his decision to make a mid-career change. In July 1995, he left the firm and hung out a shingle as a sole practitioner specializing in beer law for microbrewers and brewpub owners.

"Since opening my practice, I've worked with microbrewers in Colorado, Ohio, Florida, Arizona and North Carolina on distribution issues, and I've consulted with several microbrewers on licensing, label and regulatory-compliance issues. I've had the opportunity to do some work on contract-brewing issues, and to work on a couple of strategic alliances among microbrewers involving alternating-premises operations. Coors still uses me on issues arising here in the Rocky Mountain region, and I've also been fortunate to develop a client relationship with a regional brewer and importer, in addition to working for craft brewers. But building essentially a new practice is always a challenge, and developing enough business to keep busy full-time with 'beer law' probably isn't feasible. Thus the other area of emphasis for my practice is general business and commercial law for small and medium-sized businesses. Honestly, it's not as much fun as beer law, so much of my practice development effort has remained focused on the beer industry.

"But the ultimate questions are whether law is fun again, and whether I'm having fun, and the answer to both is a resounding yes. I'd love to be busier, but I feel I'm building a good base. I know that my niche is right. Finding affordable expertise in the legal profession—whether in the area of beer law or general business—is becoming increasingly difficult. Now I just have to make it work."

ELEVEN
American Craft Brewers

THE CRAFT BREWING scene is growing and changing far too rapidly to try to list every microbrewery and contract brewery on these pages. Instead, we've put together this list that includes some of the best craft brewers, recounting some of the reasons they have been important or influential in the industry, and briefly reviewing some of our favorites among the beers they brew. We've toured a fair number of these breweries; we've talked shop and sampled the beers with many of the brewmasters. We've tried to be fair and accurate and unbiased—except in the case of the Brooklyn Brewery, where we admit our bias but also think it is justified. We know there are a lot more breweries that we should have put in this section, but we simply didn't have the space. Our apologies to the many friends and good brewers we had to leave out.

ALASKAN BREWING CO.
5429 Shaune Drive
Juneau AK 99801

Founded by Geoff and Marcy Larson in 1986, Alaskan Brewing pioneered the return of brewing to Alaska. The beers are brewed with glacial runoff, the only fresh water available. While Alaskan's beers are, by and large, still only available in the Northwest, its smoked porter has become famous nationwide. Geoff is as proficient with the smoker as he is with the kettle—his hot-smoked wild Alaskan salmon, the stuff of beer festival legend, is delicious, especially with his pale ale.

ALASKAN AMBER BEER—An alt beer brewed to a turn-of-the-century recipe from the long-gone Douglas City Brewery in Juneau. Alaskan

Amber is brewed from two-row malt and a blend of Cascade and Saaz hops. Crisp and versatile, it has a soft fruitiness on the palate.

ALASKAN PALE ALE—Brewed from two-row malt and Willamette, Chinook and Tettnanger hops, this dry-hopped pale ale is dry and snappy. Dry-hopping produces a floral, citric nose.

ALASKAN SMOKED PORTER—This fine award-winning beer is brewed with roasted malts smoked over an alder fire. The rich, smoky aroma blends beautifully with the coffeeish flavor of the dark malts; the smoke, it turns out, is a team player.

ANCHOR BREWING CO.
1705 Mariposa Street
San Francisco CA 94107

Though the Anchor Brewing Co. has been brewing beer in San Francisco since 1896, it seemed as if it had reached the end of its tether before it was rescued in 1965 by Fritz Maytag (heir to the Maytag washing machine fortune). With a firm and loving hand, Maytag turned the brewery around, and it is now one of the best-known and most respected breweries in the country. In Anchor's beautiful copper brewhouse, Maytag and his brewers strive to do things the old-fashioned way. Anchor made headlines several years ago by producing a beer called Ninkasi, an experimental brew meant to reproduce ancient Sumerian beers. Aside from the occasional experiment, Anchor's stable of beers hasn't changed for years. With such a classic history and line of beers, one supposes that there's been no need.

ANCHOR STEAM BEER—Steam Beer was a common style in California during the Gold Rush era of the 1800s, but by 1965 only Anchor was producing it in the original fashion. Fermented in shallow vats by a lager yeast working at warmer ale-like temperatures, Anchor Steam captures some of the best attributes of both ales and lagers. Its sharp snap of hops is backed up by toasty malt flavors with a lightly fruity character.

ANCHOR LIBERTY ALE—This massively dry-hopped, straw-colored pale ale is the height of the American style of IPA. Brashly bitter but generously backed with toasty malt, Liberty Ale delivers the goods for hopheads with a huge pine-needle and grapefruit aroma. First brewed in 1975(!), Liberty Ale is still at the top of its form.

ANCHOR OUR SPECIAL ALE—More widely known simply as Anchor Christmas, this dark, spiced ale follows old English traditions, and has become the springboard for dozens of spiced beers around the country. The secret spicing changes every year, and aficionadoes await each year's batch, released just after Thanksgiving, with noses at the ready, prepared to play "name that spice."

OLD FOGHORN BARLEYWINE—Brewed from the first runnings of three separate mashes, this beer is brewed in small batches and then conditioned for nearly a year. At about 10 percent ABV, it is well within true barley wine strength, and this shows in a lively, fruity palate of great depth and warmth. Old Foghorn was only available on draft for some years, but limited packaging in 6-ounce "nip" bottles has resumed.

ANDERSON VALLEY BREWING CO.
14081 Highway 128
Boonville CA 95415

The brewers at Anderson Valley claim to be inspired by the beautiful countryside, majestic redwoods and the unusual "Boontling" dialect spoken in the region. Their lingo is difficult to pronounce and more difficult to understand, but they brew some mighty fine beers, and have been at it since 1987. Founder Kenneth Allen was a chiropractor until he moved to Boonville and discovered a much better way of straightening people out.

BOONT AMBER ALE—A sixteen-hour mash leaves this beer with a refreshing background tang. It is a medium-bodied pale ale with a nice copper color, a robust head and a rich caramel malt character. Ken Allen says that Boonville's pristine "rudy nebs" makes Boont Amber extra "bahl" . . . and who could argue with that?

BARNEY FLATS OATMEAL STOUT—Sweetish and smooth, this stout is more in the English style than the Irish classic. Its assertive hopping holds the sweetness in check and lets the chocolate and coffee character come through.

BELK'S EXTRA SPECIAL BITTER ALE—This award-winning pale ale has a sturdy malt base that serves as a base for launching the massive hopping that makes a pleasant attack on the palate. Positively bursting with fruit and hop flavors, it cruises into a snappy, dry finish.

BOSTON BEER CO.
30 Germania Street
Boston MA 02130

Under the Samuel Adams label, Boston Beer Co. spearheaded the concept of contract brewing when it launched Samuel Adams Boston Lager in 1985. Founder Jim Koch, a Harvard-trained MBA and marketing genius, has parlayed the Sam Adams family of beers into a nationwide brewing dynamo with annual production exceeding 1 million barrels. Samuel Adams beers are brewed to a high standard at several large regional breweries around the country. The company also maintains a pilot plant in Boston, which is open for tours. The Samuel Adams brands have done much to put craft-brewed beer on the map and before the public throughout the United States.

SAMUEL ADAMS BOSTON LAGER—A Vienna-style lager with moderate hop bitterness, nice malt development and a fresh German hop bouquet, Boston Lager is the company's flagship brand, accounting for nearly half its total sales. This beer is clean, refreshing and smooth. After more than a decade in the market, it is still one of the better examples of its style.

SAMUEL ADAMS DOUBLE BOCK—While this beer offers the deep toffee flavor of German malts, it still carries a lot of weight, and does it well. More than 150 pounds of malt per barrel leave this beer with 8.5 percent alcohol by volume, putting it within the range of a true doppelbock. Moderate hopping serves to balance a sweetish, smooth palate with a warming finish.

SAMUEL ADAMS TRIPLE BOCK—Housed stylishly in small cobalt-blue bottles with corks and gold-foil lettering, this beer is a style unto itself. Brewed from a high concentration of malt and maple syrup, this beer is aged in oak with a wine yeast and achieves a reported ABV of an unprecedented 17 percent. More like a sherry than a beer on the palate, this powerful beer is a unique taste experience.

THE BROOKLYN BREWERY
118 N. 11th Street
Brooklyn NY 11211

The Brooklyn Brewery, widely regarded as one of the United States' leading contract brewers and microbreweries, was founded in 1987 by Steve Hindy, a former foreign correspondent who got interested in brewing beer while posted in "dry" countries in the Middle East, and Tom Potter, a former banker who has become known as one of the craft brewing industry's foremost experts on financial operations. One of the Brooklyn Brewery's biggest innovations was to form the Craft Brewers Guild, a marketing and distribution division that distributes not only the Brooklyn brands but three hundred other craft beer labels, both American microbrews and gourmet imported beer.

Brooklyn Brewery built a twenty-five-barrel brewhouse, the largest in the New York area, in 1996. The stainless-steel brewhouse and fermentation/aging tanks are set in an 1860s-era former steel foundry in the Williamsburg section of Brooklyn, the neighborhood that was home to dozens of pre-Prohibition breweries, including the famous Brewers' Row. The eighteen-thousand-square-foot brewery complex includes the Tap Room, a three-hundred-person tasting and party room that hosts many community events and serves as a gallery for local art works. There is a shop for purchasing Craft Brewers Guild beer gear, and an exhibition of historical Brooklyn brewphernalia.

BROOKLYN LAGER—Brewed to a pre-Prohibition recipe that dates back to the days when Brooklyn was the brewing capital of the East Coast, Brooklyn Lager has won numerous awards, beginning with the Gold Medal at the Great American Beer Tasting in New York in 1989, during the brewery's second year of operation. Brooklyn Lager was also awarded a Gold Medal in the Amber Lager category at the Great American Beer Festival in 1992, and was named World Champion Amber Lager by the Beverage Testing Institute in Chicago in 1994.

BROOKLYN BROWN ALE—Made exclusively with American ingredients, Brooklyn Brown won Bronze medals at the Great American Beer Festival in 1991 and 1992, and has earned its place among the "best of" American beers in many magazines and books, including the ratings of beer guru Michael Jackson, who calls Brooklyn Brown Ale "a complex brew that is closer to Newcastle than London, but bigger than either."

BROOKLYN BLACK CHOCOLATE STOUT—The winter seasonal beer produced by Brewmaster Garrett Oliver with two and a half mashes, this is a classic imperial stout. It has a rich, creamy texture and tones that allow it to stand on its own or accompany food, particularly chocolate and other winter desserts. First bottled in 1994, it has become a seasonal favorite among New York's best beer bars and finest restaurants, and among beer critics everywhere.

BROOKLYN EAST INDIA PALE ALE—Brooklyn EIPA first appeared as a summer seasonal in 1995. Brewed with English malts and hops, EIPA recreates the classic, heavily hopped style of the nineteenth century beers brewed for British soldiers serving in India.

BROOKLYNER WEISSE—A Bavarian-style wheat beer, unfiltered and chock-full of spicy esters that evoke hints of cloves and some say even bananas, Brooklyner Weisse is made with a traditional weizen yeast strain, along with two-row barley and malted wheat. The hops are Perle, from Germany. Bitterness is low to medium, and alcohol content is a shade below 5 percent ABV.

CATAMOUNT BREWING CO.
58 S. Main Street
White River Junction VT 05001

When founder Steve Mason fired up the kettle at Catamount Brewing Co. in 1985, it was the first brewery to open in Vermont in one hundred years. Since then, Catamount has gained a reputation for high-quality beers with a certain signature "toasty" grain flavor. The brewery, as of this writing, was located in an historic old brick building (originally built as a grainery in 1884) in the railroad village of White River Junction. The company has been experiencing rapid growth, however, and was planning a move to a larger facility nearby. Catamount's beers are widely available in the Northeast, but increased production capacity could soon give them broader distribution.

CATAMOUNT AMBER—A deep copper-colored ale with the rich, full-bodied flavor of caramel malt. A blend of Galena and Willamette hops both balances the malt assertively and lends a soft, pleasant hop aroma.

CATAMOUNT PALE ALE—First brewed in 1995, Catamount Pale Ale owes more to England than to the Pacific Northwest. The beer has a deep amber color and medium malt body accented with the distinctive flavor and aroma of English hops from Kent.

CATAMOUNT PORTER—Introduced as a holiday seasonal, Catamount Porter was so popular that it became a year-round product in 1988. It has an excellent roasted nose and medium-roast palate with nice structure and a dry, flinty edge. Galena and Cascade hops round out the palate and nose. Refined and smooth, this is widely considered one of the better porters made in the United States.

CELIS BREWING CO.
2431 Forbes Drive
Austin TX 78754

In 1966, Pierre Celis, a former milkman, saved the Belgian witbier (white beer) style from virtual extinction when he founded the Hoegaarden Brewery in Belgium. Eventually, Celis sold the brewery, picked up stakes and moved to Texas, where he built a beautiful brewery to produce Belgian-style witbier for the American market. For some time, the brewery has been run by Pierre's daughter and son-in-law, Christine and Peter Camps. They continue to be in charge of day-to-day operations though the company was sold in 1995 to Miller Brewing in one of the first major takeovers of a microbrewery by a mass-market brewing company. Time will tell whether Celis Brewing Co. continues to produce the fine beers that have earned a glowing reputation in the craft brewing industry.

CELIS WHITE—Brewed true to the witbier style resurrected by Pierre Celis, Celis White is produced from 50 percent malt and 50 percent raw Texas winter wheat. The beer, which is very pale yellow with a nice white cap of foam, is hopped with Kent Goldings, Oregon Willamette and Cascade, and classically flavored with coriander and dried curaçao orange peel. It is fermented with an ale yeast, which accentuates its fruitiness and leaves the beer clean and dry.

CELIS GRAND CRU—A strong golden ale brewed from pale lager malts, and hopped with Saaz and Cascade. Though this fine beer is broadly within the Belgian tripel style, the addition of spices and curaçao orange peel gives it some unique dimensions.

CHICAGO BREWING CO.
1830 N. Besly Court
Chicago IL 60622

Stephen Dinehart and his wife Jennifer and brother Craig founded the Chicago Brewing Co. in 1989. Housed in a renovated 1920s pickle factory, the brewery has a capacity to produce thirty thousand barrels a year. Unusual for a fledgling microbrewery, its first beer was a lager, which appeared in the summer of 1990 and remains the flagship brand. All the beers are free of adjuncts, chemicals and preservatives, and the Dineharts are deservedly proud to have helped return the tradition of all-malt brewing to the Midwest.

LEGACY LAGER—This award-winning beer sports a bright amber hue with a dense white head. Clean, fresh, and moderately hoppy, it falls broadly into the Vienna lager style.

BIG SHOULDERS PORTER—Though it could use a bit more heft, this chocolate-brown porter is finely crafted. It carries a full-fledged roast character with enough hops to balance well.

HEARTLAND WEISS—A traditional Bavarian wheat beer, lightened slightly to quench Midwestern summer thirsts. Golden and redolent of cloves and a hint of banana, with a clean snappy finish.

DESCHUTES BREWERY
901 SW Simpson Ave.
Bend OR 97702

Founded in 1988, Deschutes was originally a brewpub. Demand quickly grew to the point where the brewery moved into wholesale distribution. Now ensconced in a twenty-thousand-barrel capacity brewhouse, Deschutes makes dramatic gains every year. Their high-quality flavorful beers are well-respected among choosy Northwestern beer connoisseurs.

MIRROR POND PALE ALE—A classic Northwestern pale ale, this copper-colored beer is full-bodied, caramelish, and unstinting with the hops, which come through clean and sharp. Dry-hopping with Cascade lends it a grapefruity nose and a lingering finish.

BLACK BUTTE PORTER—Nearly black and fairly chewy, this porter has a pleasant espresso-roast character backed with a touch of chocolate. Black Butte Porter is the brewery's flagship beer, which speaks volumes about the beer drinkers of Oregon, where microbreweries have nearly 10 percent of the market.

OBSIDIAN STOUT—A blend of eight malts give this rich, strong stout its complex character. The roast is full but not overpowering, and generous hopping balances out lingering sweetness.

D. L. GEARY BREWING CO.
38 Evergreen Drive
Portland ME 04103

David Geary established his brewery in 1986 and brews English-style beers that he lovingly adapts to the wonderfully fresh seafood available along the Maine coast. His brewhouse was made by Peter Austin, founder of the Ringwood Brewery in Yorkshire, where David trained as a brewer. Geary's employs the unique Ringwood yeast strain to fine effect, coaxing it to release its spicy flavors and aromas.

GEARY'S PALE ALE—Dry, spicy, and aromatic with both fruit character and Golding hops, Geary Pale is indeed a fine accompaniment to lobster. Sharp, clean hopping crackles on the palate and leads to a dry finish with a hint of bread.

GEARY'S LONDON PORTER—A wonderfully rich porter that captures the very essence of the style. Medium-bodied but rather roasty, it has some fruit on the palate, then finishes dry and coffeeish with a flourish of hops.

GEARY'S HAMPSHIRE SPECIAL ALE—Geary's winter seasonal is a classic English strong ale, with strong hopping backed up with a sturdy toffeeish malt base. Goldings hops and spicy fruit round out a splendid nose. David Geary has a wry sense of humor and gets straight to the point in his ad line for this beer: "Available as long as the weather sucks."

FRANKENMUTH BREWERY
425 S. Main Street
Frankenmuth MI 48734

The Frankenmuth Brewery was founded in 1986 and bought by Randy Heine in 1990. Serving an area with strong German roots, Frankenmuth specializes in brewing authentic versions of German styles. Heine and his crew stick to the tenets of the reinheitsgebot and employ traditional decoction mashing techniques. Though the beers are traditional, the brewery is high-tech, and has a capacity of 50,000 barrels. The brewery produces beers under the Frankenmuth and Old Detroit names, but the former are more memorable.

FRANKENMUTH GERMAN STYLE PILSENER—Crisp and full-bodied, this beer points to Frankenmuth's strengths with traditional lager styles. Smooth and golden, it carries a light refreshing hop bouquet.

FRANKENMUTH GERMAN STYLE DARK—The name may be ham-fisted, but the beer is very tasty. This beer manages to squeeze a lot of toffee and roast malt flavor out of a fairly light beer, which is not easy to do. Smooth and subtle.

FRANKENMUTH GERMAN STYLE BOCK—This full-strength bock has some of the rich toffee-ish flavors that one associates with true German bocks. Brewed from six malts and aged for 12 weeks, this is an excellent American example of the style.

FULL SAIL BREWING CO.
506 Columbia
Hood River OR 97031

Full Sail's lineup of hefty beers has been so successful that in 1995 the company opened a 250,000-barrel brewery (complete with a 200-barrel kettle) next to the original brewhouse. These breweries are located on a bluff overlooking the Columbia River; and their tasting room commands a view of the Columbia River Gorge National Scenic Area. In Portland, the company operates the Full Sail Riverplace Brewery, which has an annual capacity of 5,000 barrels and brews seasonal specials. Full Sail is well known for big beers that don't stint on flavor.

FULL SAIL AMBER ALE—Brewed from two-row pale, crystal and chocolate malts, this strongish amber ale has an almost butterscotchy palate. The finish is sharp and floral with Cascade and Mt. Hood hops.

FULL SAIL INDIA PALE ALE—Brewed with Challenger and prized East Kent Golding hops, this is a good old-fashioned India Pale Ale, with its dry, strong, malty palate backed by resiny bitterness.

FULL SAIL NUT BROWN ALE—Sneakily soft and somewhat sweet, this mildly spicy brown ale works nicely with food. English chocolate malts lend extra depth to a smooth palate.

GOLDEN PACIFIC BREWING
5515 Doyle, No. 4
Emeryville CA 94608

In 1989, the Thousand Oaks Brewing Co. merged with Golden Pacific Brewing to form the current company, which is enjoying rapid growth. The 17-barrel brewhouse gave way to a 50-barrel brewhouse in 1996, and the popularity of Golden Pacific's beers is extending well beyond their San Francisco Bay Area home base. The beers are clean, judiciously balanced and brewed from local ingredients.

BLACK BEAR LAGER—A moderately hopped California-style dunkel, this chocolaty lager has a clean drinkability. Malts do most of the work; a hop aroma lingers lightly.

GOLDEN BEAR LAGER—This is what would once have been called "California Common" beer—deep gold, smooth and refreshing, with a healthy snap of Northwestern hops.

GOLDEN GATE ORIGINAL ALE—A blend of five specialty malts and several Yakima and Oregon hop varieties give this copper-colored ale a fine complexity. Full-flavored and clean, with a bit of fruit in the center.

GOOSE ISLAND
1800 Clybourn
Chicago IL 60614

The father and son team of John and Greg Hall opened the Goose Island brewpub in 1988. Through hardships which have included the demolition of the shopping center that originally surrounded the brewpub, father and son have persevered and triumphed, erecting an impressive high-capacity brewhouse nearby in 1995. Their beers are full-flavored and traditional.

HONKERS ALE—The brewery's flagship beer, this pale ale is bracingly hoppy with a rich malt center and a spicy finish of Styrian Golding hops. Refreshing and very drinkable.

KOLSCH—A rare authentically brewed Kolsch style beer. German top-fermenting kolsch yeast gives this golden beer a lightly fruity character, which is offset by a breeze of Saaz and Tettnang hops.

BOURBON COUNTY STOUT—One of the big hits of the 1995 Great American Beer Festival, this beer had brewmasters from around the country lining up for more. A powerful imperial stout aged for months in Jim Beam bourbon barrels, this beer has startling depth and complexity, with bourbon notes interwoven with the espresso-like roast malt character. It's an occasional special worth travelling to try.

GRANT'S YAKIMA BREWING CO.
1803 Presson Place
Yakima WA 98903

Hop expert Bert Grant opened Grant's Pub and Brewery in August 1982, making his brewpub one of the longest-running success stories in American microbrewing. Irrepressible, humorous and blunt, the ubiquitous Grant has always claimed that he's brewing for his own tastes rather than those of the public. Fortunately for him, then, the public has enjoyed his hoppy interpretations of traditional styles. In 1991, he built an additional brewhouse to meet the demand for his beers in markets around the country. In 1995, he sold controlling interest to a large wine firm with considerable cash and apparently expansionist aims. While we cannot begrudge Bert a well-earned retirement, we just pray that his beers retain the character that made them famous.

GRANT'S SCOTTISH ALE—Copper-colored, full-bodied and very hoppy, this is the flagship beer of the brewery. Bert Grant may be Scottish, but his ale is American—hops play a big role here. The malt shows through in the aroma, and the beer finishes clean and dry.

GRANT'S APPLE HONEY ALE—This beer grew out of a skirmish with the Feds over Grant's right to brew hard cider. The brewery skirted the whole mess by brewing an ale made from apple juice, malt and honey. As alarming as this may sound, it's actually rather nice. Light, refreshing and brisk, it's a tasty beer to go with a summer salad.

GRANT'S PERFECT PORTER—Modesty is not one of Bert Grant's stronger points, but his porter is right on the money. Rich, medium-bodied and amazingly chocolaty, the beer is brewed with five malts including a smoked malt that gives the beer a spicy backdrop. For once, Grant gave hops a backseat and let the malts come out to play.

GRANT'S IMPERIAL STOUT—Three malts and a touch of honey interplay wonderfully in this intensely strong stout. The roast is the main thing—sharp and espresso-like, with good hopping to back it up. Excellent instead of coffee with desserts.

GREAT LAKES BREWING CO.
2516 Market Street
Cleveland OH 44113

Patrick and Daniel Conaway founded the Great Lakes Brewing Co. as Ohio's first brewpub in 1988. Since then, it has steadily built a nationwide reputation for a wide range of excellent beers. The brewpub is housed in a century-old building complete with a nice beer garden. The brewing facility has expanded over the years to allow for retail sales throughout the Cleveland area.

BURNING RIVER ALE—The name is a humorous allusion to Cleveland's famous environmental difficulties; the only burning going on here is a very snappy hop bite applied through five additions in the kettle. This beer is copper-colored, medium-bodied and packed full of citric Cascade hop character.

EDMUND FITZGERALD PORTER—This award-winning porter, named in honor of the ill-fated Great Lakes ship memorialized by Gordon Lightfoot, has a fine heft on the palate and a well-tuned balance. Too roasty to be a brown ale and not coffeeish enough to be a stout, this rich beer hits the nail on the head for this style.

HOLY MOSES GRAND CRU—This is a strong Belgian-style ale brewed from pilsner and aromatic malts, European hops, coriander and orange peel, and fermented with a Belgian yeast strain. It's spicy, fruity and heady.

KALAMAZOO BREWING CO.
355 E. Kalamazoo Avenue
Kalamazoo MI 49007

Larry Bell and his crew of brewers claim that their brewery is the oldest microbrewery east of Boulder, Colorado. If so, they've been spending all that time perfecting a lineup of truly audacious beers that are rapidly gaining a devoted following. Issued under the Bell's label, the beers are unfiltered, unpasteurized and bottle-conditioned.

BELL'S TWO-HEARTED ALE—A strong, fruity India pale ale bolstered with a blast of English hops. The brewers claim that it is ''well-suited for Hemingwayesque trips to the Upper Peninsula.''

BELL'S SOLSUN ALE—A summer wheat ale made with domestic malt and Belgian wheat malt, spiced with European hops. It says something of the Bell mind-set that this summer ale contains over 6 percent alcohol by volume.

BELL'S CHERRY STOUT—Traverse City tart cherries provide the fruity backdrop to a strong stout, in a well-structured version of a style that has become popular among homebrewers.

BELL'S EXPEDITION STOUT—Startlingly thick, viscous as motor oil, and black as night, this astounding imperial stout is one to watch for. It starts bittersweet on the palate, then bursts out with flavors of espresso, licorice, chocolate and fruit, cruising in for a lingering warm finish. At 11.5 percent ABV, Bell says it is "a fine selection for Himalayan adventures." Not if you want to come back.

MENDOCINO BREWING CO.
13351 Highway 101 South
Hopland CA 95449

In 1983, some of the founders of the New Albion Brewery (1976–1982), the first modern microbrewery in the United States, gathered to build the Hopland Brewery, California's first brewpub since Prohibition. After several expansions and a name change, the brewery has a capacity of over ten thousand barrels a year and has built a reputation for excellence.

RED TAIL ALE—The flagship brand of the brewery (with a particularly terrific label), this full-bodied English-style pale ale is deservingly popular in the Northwest, and has started to show up on the East Coast as well. Slightly low carbonation lends a creamy texture to the beer, which is crisply seasoned with Yakima Valley whole hops. The nose is hoppy with an almost peachy fruit character.

BLUE HERON PALE ALE—A golden ale loosely based on English bitter, Blue Heron is brewed from 100 percent pale malt and two varieties of Northwestern hops. The result is clean, snappy and refreshing with a citric hop character.

EYE OF THE HAWK—Introduced in 1994, this well-balanced strong amber ale is reminiscent of a concentrated version of Red Tail Ale. Higher gravity (and alcohol content) brings out more fruit in the nose, and the balance is tilted toward the malt, though the hopping is still assertive.

BLACK HAWK STOUT—Fairly light-bodied for an American stout, this beer is nonetheless very flavorful, with coffee, chocolate and caramel combining for a fine roast character. Closer to an Irish stout than an English one, this stout is fruitier than either.

NEW BELGIUM BREWING CO.
350 Linden Street
Fort Collins CO 80524

Located in what is now referred to as the "brewery district" of historic Old Town in Fort Collins, New Belgium Brewing Co. was founded in 1992 by engineer Jeff Lebesch and his wife Kim Jordan. Their brewery came roaring onto the scene with flavorful, interesting beers, and Jeff and Kim have been rewarded with meteoric growth. They are particularly known for their authentic approach to Belgian-style ales.

FAT TIRE AMBER ALE—The brewery's flagship beer is not brewed in the Belgian style—even in Fort Collins, tastes haven't evolved quite that far. Fat Tire is a pleasant amber ale with a nutty, caramel palate balanced with crisp hopping and dry-hopped for aroma.

ABBEY TRAPPIST STYLE ALE—A very good interpretation of the Belgian dubbel style, this russet ale has a spicy, fruity aroma with a backdrop of raisins. The finish is complex and slightly sweet.

TRIPPEL TRAPPIST STYLE ALE—Another fine version of a Belgian style, this golden ale has a spicy pear-like aroma and a somewhat sweet palate balanced by generous quantities of Saaz hops.

OLD CHERRY ALE—Though not based on a lambic beer, this beer is inspired by Belgian krieks. As a result, it lacks some of the complexity of some of the Belgians, but it is well brewed and shows a nice interplay between the sweetness of the malt and the tartness of the cherries. The hops are well in the background, allowing the cherry character to come forward.

NEW ENGLAND BREWING CO.
13 Marshall Street
Norwalk CT 06854

Founded in 1989 by Richard and Marcia King, New England Brewing stepped up to another level in 1995 when the brewery moved into a new facility, complete with a beautiful German-made brewhouse and a 180-seat restaurant. The Kings have begun to augment their mainstay traditional styles with more playful specials.

ATLANTIC AMBER—New England's flagship beer is brewed in the steam style, where a fermentation is conducted with lager yeast at relatively warm temperatures normally reserved for ales. The result is a beer which is very smooth and lightly fruity, with nice caramel character and moderate hopping.

GOLD STOCK ALE—The medium-gold color belies the nature of the beer, a strong ale with a light fruit character, a dry palate and assertive hopping. The finish is clean and long. The stock ale style was originally designed for its ability to age and travel, the strength and hopping preserving it over time.

OATMEAL STOUT—Eight varieties of barley malt and, of course, oatmeal are used to brew this very smooth beer. Soft and round, with a pleasant, almost oily texture up front, the roast shows up clearly, but never bites. Hops balance out a malty palate for a bittersweet finish.

THE PIKE BREWERY
1432 Western Avenue
Seattle WA 98101

The Pike Brewery (formerly the Pike Place Brewery) is located in the center of Seattle's historic Pike Place Market. The tiny brewery is built in a classic pre-industrial "tower" design, with the mash tun on the top floor, and liquid flowing down from vessel to vessel. The brewery is gorgeous and the brewers are innovative. Experimental brews have included ingredients ranging from oregano to oysters. Armed with a kettle that only holds four barrels, Pike has in the past brewed its pale ale beers under contract at regional microbreweries. Expansion is planned to produce more beer and sell it more widely across America, and we welcome it.

PIKE PALE ALE—This classic British-style pale ale has long been regarded as one of the best in the country. Its nutty, biscuity flavor derives from English Marris Otter malt, a prized and flavorful old variety. The hopping is assertive but balanced, allowing the pleasant malt to show through. The finish is smooth and quick. The beer is unfiltered and unpasteurized.

PIKE XXXXX STOUT—At just under 9 percent alcohol by volume, this beer is well within the imperial stout range, and confirmation comes in the form of a massive roasted palate which gives way to a touch of malt sweetness and smack of hops. The plummy, raisiny finish has lingering espresso notes.

OLD BAWDY BARLEY WINE—This full-fledged barley wine carries its 12 percent ABV with grace and style. Old Bawdy is brewed from lightly peated distiller's malt, lending it a slightly smoky character. Assertively hoppy, it is less sweet than many barley wines, and is medium-bodied and fruity on the palate with a long, warming finish.

PORTLAND BREWING CO.
2731 NW 31st Street
Portland OR 97210

Portland Brewing Co. opened as a small brewpub in 1986. In 1993, the company expanded dramatically, setting up a beautiful copper brewhouse acquired from the 447-year old Sixenbrau Brewery of Nordlingen, Germany. Already well regarded for its finely brewed ales, the company has started reaching toward its new capacity of 100,000 barrels. The original brewpub on Flanders Street remains open.

PORTLAND ALE—This light amber ale is brewed from Northwestern two-row malt, and a blend of Galena and Cascade hops for bittering. The bitterness is sharply focused up front on the palate, after which a nice dry malt character emerges. A nice Cascade aroma adds polish.

MACTARNAHAN'S ALE—One might expect a Scottish ale here, but the beer is named after a semi-famous investor in the brewery. Slightly heavier than the Portland Ale, with more caramel presence, this beer is packed full of Cascades for a robust bitterness and a floral, piney aroma.

HAYSTACK BLACK—A medium-bodied porter brewed with dark crystal and black malts, and Northern Brewer and East Kent Golding hops. A dry, roasty palate gives way to a hoppy finish.

OREGON HONEY BEER—A pale gold beer where honey stands in for some of the malt. The result is light-bodied and refreshing, but you'd have to be looking for the honey to find it. Nugget hops are used for bitterness, and the earthy Willamette hop does aromatic duty.

PYRAMID/THOMAS KEMPER—HART BREWING
91 South Royal Brougham
Seattle WA 98134

Pyramid Brewing was founded in 1984 in the Washington city of Kalama, a small logging town on the Columbia River, near the foothills of Mount St. Helens. Thomas Kemper Lagers was founded in 1985 at a site just across the Puget Sound from Seattle. Today, both labels are under the umbrella of Hart Brewing, which maintains three breweries—the original two mentioned above and a larger facility in downtown Seattle. Pyramid and Thomas Kemper retain their own personalities. Pyramid focuses on ales, Thomas Kemper on lagers, and the Seattle Hart Brewery handles both. This versatility and a fine range of beers have brought Hart Brewing vigorous growth and lots of respect.

PYRAMID PALE ALE—Pyramid's original flagship beer is bronze and hoppy, full of citrus fruit flavors and herbal aromas from Northwestern hops. The malt follows through nicely on the palate, and gives the beer a fine complexity.

PYRAMID HEFE-WEIZEN—An unfiltered wheat beer with a refreshing hop bitterness and a wonderfully fresh, bready, fruity palate. Brewed with a standard American ale yeast, this is not a true hefeweizen, but rather an unfiltered American wheat beer. It is very pleasant nonetheless.

PYRAMID BEST BROWN—Brewed more closely to the British brown ale style than the American, this malty beer is deep tan in color, with a sweet, toffeeish palate. Hops are unassertive, just enough to balance. It's smooth and balanced.

HART ESPRESSO STOUT—Fortunately, we are spared genuine coffee beans and left to enjoy the coffeeish, chocolaty flavors of roasted malts. Heavy and full-bodied with a tight tan head and a hoppy finish, this fine stout is a robust beer that's perfect for winter.

THOMAS KEMPER WHITE—An unfiltered Belgian-style witbier, spiced with coriander and dried curaçao orange peel. Not quite as fruity as some, but spritzy and refreshing, it maintains a good spice character.

THOMAS KEMPER AMBER—A Vienna-style amber lager, this beer offers a bready malt base and a sharp, spicy Saaz hop nose. The brewery claims that it was designed to accompany pizza, but it is worthy of drinking on its own as well.

REDHOOK ALE BREWERY
3400 Phinney Avenue North
Seattle WA 98103

Redhook was founded by Gordon Bowker (one of the founders of Starbucks Coffee) and Paul Shipman as the Independent Ale Brewery in 1982, and produced 1,000 barrels its first year—quite a feat back in the bad old days. Today, Redhook produces more than 100,000 barrels annually, and that is going to more than double with the new breweries being built with capital obtained when Anheuser-Busch bought 25 percent of the company. Along the way, Redhook has lost some of the butterscotch and banana character that made their beers very distinctive, but the ''Budhook'' epithet is unfair. This company is still producing flavorful beers. However, industry watchers are keeping a close eye on Redhook to see what the effects are of one of the largest micro/macro brewery mergers to date.

REDHOOK EXTRA SPECIAL BITTER—Originally a seasonal named Winterhook, this has become the brewery's flagship beer. Inspired by Fuller's ESB of London, this amber ale has a rich toasted malt center with a hint of peaches; bitterness is moderate and clean, dropping away for a slightly sweet finish.

BALLARD BITTER—Now restyled an IPA by the brewery, this pale amber beer has an assertive snappy bitterness, with a nutty malt center and a clean, dry finish.

WHEATHOOK—This is a refreshing American wheat beer with mild hopping and a bready malt flavor.

BLACKHOOK—Jet black and espresso-like, this medium-bodied stout delivers a nice roast kick. Hops add to the dry character of the roast.

ROCKIES BREWING CO.
2880 Wilderness Place
Boulder CO 80301

Established at the foot of the Flatirons mountain formation in 1979 as the Boulder Brewing Co., Rockies Brewing is the oldest microbrewery in the United States. In the early 1980s, the then-bottle-conditioned Boulder Pale Ale was a revelation to beer drinkers who sought out its spicy, earthy flavor. The title of "oldest microbrewery" has been hard-won, and the brewery has gone through a few management changes, but has emerged once again as a brewer of top-notch ales.

BOULDER EXTRA PALE ALE—No longer bottle-conditioned, this beer retains some of its spicy character and a nice crisp hop attack. The palate is fruity, dry and refreshing.

BOULDER AMBER ALE—Brewed with plenty of crystal malt for a russet complexion and a nutty caramel flavor, this ale is backed up with Hallertauer hops. Pleasant fruit character in the nose follows through onto the palate.

BOULDER PORTER—A nice example of a true porter, this medium-bodied beer is chocolaty with a coffee backdrop on a nutty malt base. Hops are assertive enough to balance, but let the malts do the work.

ROGUE ALES
2320 O.S.U. Drive
Newport OR 97365

The fellows at Rogue have become virtual poster people for the idiosyncratic brewing spirit prevalent in Oregon today. Though the brewery was established in 1989 by a couple of refugees from the Nike athletic shoe firm, it somehow gives the impression, by sheer force of will, of having been around much longer. Rogue is famous for rich, brazenly ambitious ales, sometimes bottle-conditioned or cask-conditioned, always flavorful and never boring. The use of particularly flavorful grains, a low fermentation temperature, and tons of hops add to the house character of the Rogue line.

ST. ROGUE RED—Brewed from Northwest Harrington and four British malts, this beer features toasty malt flavors, coming through on top of sharp hops with a sprucy Chinook and Centennial hop finish.

MOGUL MADNESS—This strong ale is deep red in color and sports a fruity hop bouquet that leaps right out of the glass. On the palate, the beer is huge, bittersweet and resiny, with a sturdy malt center holding it together. A very fine strong ale, this beer features seven hop varieties.

SHAKESPEARE STOUT—Dark, rich and creamy, this hoppy stout is mellowed by oats, which give it a silky soft character on the palate, with nice chocolaty roast tones and a dry, hoppy finish.

ROGUE SMOKE—A classic rauchbier, Rogue Smoke is brewed with Bamberg beechwood smoked malt as well as some hand-smoked malts. The smoke is up front in the nose and on the palate, but is not totally overwhelming. It finishes dry and hoppy. For those who like smoked beers, this is even better than many of the German ones, and is definitely worth looking for. Great with sausages and barbecue.

OLD CRUSTACEAN—This massive barley wine at first seems like an exercise in hop saturation. At 11.3 percent alcohol by volume, the beer is strong enough to age, which it does very nicely. Though it is eighteen months old when it leaves the brewery, several more months (if not years) mellow the hops, and a magnificent fruity, sherryish quality emerges that is worth waiting for. Bottles are marked with the year for easy cellaring.

SIERRA NEVADA BREWING CO.
1075 E. 20th Street
Chico CA 95928

Homebrewers Ken Grossman and Paul Camusi established their tiny brewery in 1981, and never looked back. Today, it is not an exaggeration to say that Sierra Nevada produces some of the finest beers brewed in the United States, with more than one of its products serving as benchmarks for everyone who followed. Grossman and Camusi have been rewarded with a booming business and numerous awards, and continue to grow rapidly. Open fermentation and bottle-conditioning paired with high-tech equipment and quality control put Sierra Nevada and its way of brewing very much at the heart of the American microbrewing revolution.

SIERRA NEVADA PALE ALE—Frequently called (and voted) the best American-style pale ale around, this classic beer is a brilliant balance between aggressive hops and hearty malt flavor. The grapefruity Cascade hop aroma bursts forth over a full-bodied complex and fruity palate. The finish is dry, clean and hoppy. Bottles are bottle-conditioned, while draft is filtered. A masterpiece.

SIERRA NEVADA CELEBRATION ALE—A deep reddish brew for the holiday season. Dry and nutty on the palate with sharp bitterness, fully developed hop flavor and a sprucy finish. It is much admired and sought after every winter.

SIERRA NEVADA PORTER—A dark, medium-bodied ale, this beer affords an easygoing chocolaty roast character, fruity center and smooth finish. It is moderately hoppy.

SIERRA NEVADA STOUT—Creamy, rich, strong and hoppy, this stout combines notes of espresso, chocolate and licorice for a terrific roast profile. The hops play along, but take a back seat to the roasted barley. Try it with vanilla ice cream. Really.

BIGFOOT BARLEYWINE STYLE ALE—Bigfoot is devastatingly dense, fruity, hoppy and rich—and that's just the nose. This russet beer strikes the palate with a hoppy smack, opening up into a candyish bittersweet, resiny palate bursting with caramel, hop and fruit character. It is stunning, powerful and delicious. Released in late winter, it has recently been scarce on the East Coast, where Bigfoot-starved aficionados hit the Internet to report sightings.

SPRECHER BREWING CO.
701 W. Glendale Avenue
Glendale WI 53209

The microbrewing industry in America has been nothing if not audacious, and few microbrewers have been more audacious than Randy Sprecher, who had the temerity to establish the first microbrewery in Milwaukee, the home of mass-market brands such as Miller, Schlitz and Pabst. In Sprecher's case, the coals he carried to this particular Newcastle in 1985 are still burning brightly, especially now that he's moved out of his original tiny brewery into more spacious digs in the Milwaukee 'burbs. Sprecher, a former Pabst brewmaster, is one of the few successful American microbrewers who still has full 100 percent control of his company and still brews every batch of beer himself.

SPRECHER'S BLACK BAVARIAN—A hearty, robust, Bavarian-style lager with a complex malt taste, creamy head and distinctive aromas of coffee, caramel and chocolate.

SPRECHER'S SPECIAL AMBER—Sprecher's best seller, this is a smooth, mellow, German-style beer with a toasted malt flavor, fresh hoppy bouquet and a slightly bitter finish.

SPRECHER'S HEFEWEISS—Coarsely filtered after fermenting with special ale culture, this is a light, citrusy palate-pleaser.

SPRECHER'S WINTER BREW—A Munich-style seasonal, this dark, hearty beer features caramel and black malts. It has medium body and is a very smooth mouthfeel.

SPRECHER'S MAI BOCK—A winter-spring seasonal, this is a long and potent (6.2 percent ABV) bock, dry-hopped in storage to help produce a pronounced malt and hop aroma.

STOUDT BREWING CO.
Route 272
Adamstown PA 19501

In 1987, former schoolteacher Carol Stoudt set up her lager brewery next to her husband's restaurant in the beautiful rolling countryside of Pennsylvania. A decade later, the brewery is still going strong, and while Carol now leaves the brewing to others, she has become an ambassador for fine beer. Stoudt's takes pride in its commitment to the *reinheitsgebot* for its traditional German-style beers, and judges apparently agree with the results, as Stoudt's beers have won numerous awards. When demand outstripped capacity, they began supplementing their production by contract-brewing 12-ounce bottles through the Lion Brewery in Wilkes-Barre, Pa.

STOUDT'S PILS—Traditionally dry and assertively hopped, this refreshing golden pilsner has a nice bite and a clean, bready finish, with just enough malt in the center for balance.

STOUDT'S EXPORT GOLD—Full-bodied and malty, this Dortmunder-style beer puts less emphasis on hop bitterness and lets the bready flavors of five different malts show through. Hallertauer and Tettnanger hops give balance on the palate and the nose.

STOUDT'S HONEY DOUBLE MAI-BOCK—Deep gold in color, this is a concentrated form of the Export Gold, finished with pure honey to take the edge off the 8 percent alcohol bite. The result is smooth, malty and strong, with enough hopping simply to balance.

TABERNASH BREWING CO.
205 Denargo Market
Denver CO 80216

Champion homebrewer, beer author and Weihenstephan University graduate Eric Warner finally decided to get a new day job in 1993, and teamed up with former Institute for Brewing Studies President Jeff Mendel to form Tabernash Brewing in Denver. In less than a year, they won local accolades and three medals at the Great American Beer Festival. Tabernash is committed to traditional brewing, and has geared its brewing systems for intensive procedures that most brewers take shortcuts around. The result has been beers of great integrity and purity of flavor.

DENARGO LAGER—A German-style dunkel, reddish-brown in color, malty and full-bodied on the palate with toffee flavors and a slight hint of roast. Lightly carbonated and very smooth.

GOLD SPIKE—A traditional pilsner, gold in color with a medium-bodied bready malt palate, snappy bitterness and clean finish with a fresh whiff of sulfur. Excellent head formation gives this beer a particularly nice presentation.

TABERNASH WEISS—Eric Warner wrote a very good book on German wheat beer and then apparently followed his own advice. This is a classic hefeweizen: pale, ruddy orange, opaque and full of clove, bubblegum and banana aroma and flavor. Very lightly hopped to let the flavors from the fermentation come to the fore, this weizen is actually finer than many of the German weizens it emulates.

Ron Carter

RON CARTER AND his brother Don are the hands-on, in-store own-ers of The Wine Seller, a small but tidy liquor store with a well-rounded and thoughtful selection of wine, spirits and beer in Ridgewood, N.J. For years, they were post-production editors for big network commercials and popular music videos in New York—for two different companies—who would get together for family dinners and talk about how much they liked good wine, and how great it would be to run a good wine shop together. "That was usually after the second—no the third—bottle of wine," Ron recalls.

In 1994 they bought their store. Don, forty-three, had been drinking good wine for years. He had built up a nice cellar, had taken courses and had kept kept notes on many, many good vin-tages. Ron, ten years younger, plunged into filling the expertise gaps: cheaper wines and beer. "Besides, I was a lot closer to my college beer-drinking days than Don was," Ron says. The shop had maybe a $200 inventory of beer when they bought it, a few cases of Saranac and Samuel Adams. Now, however, the Wine Seller carries about 150 labels of American microbrews and gour-met imported beer, and is continually expanding the display space for beer. "My fridge at home is always full of microbrews, and I'm always trying new ones, experimenting," Ron says. "The revolution in beer has been good timing for us, really. More and more customers come in and want to talk about beer. They want to match beer with food. They want to talk about styles. The toughest thing is when they ask about Bud, Miller and Coors. What style are they? I tell them I don't know, it's kind of its own style that's developed, sort of a lager, sort of a pilsner, not really any classic style."

He finds himself talking to people about beer in the same terms as people talk about wine. "I try to discourage people from giving up on a style of beer just because of what it says on the label," Ron says. "They say they don't like dark beer, but there are some they might like, if they'd try them. People are experimenting a lot, and it's all ages. Everybody's looking for something better." He describes one friend who complained about too many choices—wheats, stouts, bocks and so on—of good beer. "He said he was going back to Bud—a normal beer," Ron says. "Next time I saw him, though, he admitted he found he couldn't drink it anymore." Now he and his buddy agree: Craft-brewed beer is really "normal" beer.

TWELVE
European Breweries and Beer

WHILE THE AMERICAN craft-brewing scene is more dynamic, Europe remains the center of the traditional brewing world. No matter how adventurous American microbrewers become, most of their innovations are variations on beer styles and specific beers that long have been brewed in Europe. Many beer aficionados believe, for example, that no matter how good American "lambic" styles become, they will never approach the quality of the real thing from Belgium. As with the United States, there are far too many good breweries in Britain, Belgium, Germany, France and elsewhere across Europe for us to try to list all of the very best ones. Instead, what we've done in this limited space is give brief descriptions of just a handful of European breweries that produce the most influential beers or most definitive examples of the style. Again, we apologize to all the friends and acquaintances from Europe who make great beer for not having the space to list them all here.

THE CZECH REPUBLIC

PILSNER URQUELL
Plzensky Prazdroj
30497 Plzen
Czech Republic

The German word *urquell* means original source. Here, indeed, we find the source of the pilsner style of beer. Beer has been brewed on this site in the town of Plzen since the 1200s, and continues today with many of the old traditions intact. More than one thousand open oak fermenters line underground caverns where the beer is fermented and then aged in huge oak casks. Famously soft water for brewing is pulled from underground springs (undoubtedly one of the reasons the site was first chosen). While stainless steel, the modern world and Western-style capitalism are inexorably creeping into the brewery, the fundamental character of the beer remains intact. The original pilsner is still among the finest in the world.

PILSNER URQUELL—This classic Bohemian pilsner has a deeper burnished golden color than its German descendants, due to the use of malt that has been dried at a higher temperature. On top of the beer sits a rocky, brilliantly white head. The spicy floral fragrance of the prized local Saaz hop suffuses the beer, which has a crackling snap of hops up front on the palate, dropping away to reveal a full-bodied, slightly sweet bready malt character. The finish is clean and fresh, with the faintest hint of sulfur. This beer is remarkably refreshing without being thin. Like all true pilsner, this beer is best when fresh, but since it is sold in green bottles it is more susceptible to being lightstruck when not handled properly; if you're not planning a trip to the Czech Republic, you should find a shop that keeps this beer out of the light and sells it at a decent clip.

GERMANY

AYINGER
Brauerei Inselkammer
1 Zornedinger Strasse, 8011 Aying
Germany

Franz Inselkammer and his family brewery are well respected among the beer drinkers of Bavaria. The brewery is located in the pretty country town of Aying on the outskirts of Munich. In Munich itself, Ayinger's beers are served in a cabaret called the Platzl, on the square of the same name opposite the Hofbrauhaus. All of Ayinger's beers have an almost startling depth of malt character, making them distinctive at a time when malt flavor seems to be declining among many other German breweries. The brewery buildings, some of them dating back to the 1500s, include a small hotel—the perfect guesthouse for the visiting beer connoisseur.

JAHRHUNDERT BIER—Originally brewed for Ayinger's centenary in 1978, this Bavarian export beer has a bit more strength and heft than a pilsner. Deep gold in color, it is very malty on the palate and is lightly hopped, finishing quite dry.

OKTOBERFEST—Though it is light in color for an Oktoberfest beer, the malt flavor is one you'd expect of a far darker beer. The aroma is pure toffeeish Munich malt, while on the palate the hops are firm, balancing a somewhat sweet deep malt flavor. The finish retains some sweetness, but is clean nonetheless.

ALTBAIRISCH DUNKEL—Deep ruddy brown in color, with a caramelized toffee nose of terrific depth. The beer is lightly hopped, medium-bodied and richly semi-sweet on the palate with an almost coffeeish finish.

CELEBRATOR—Known in Germany as Fortunator, this excellent doppelbock is so dark it looks rather like a stout. The analogy follows through in the aroma, which is very malty with coffee notes, reminiscent of a baking loaf of black bread. On the palate, Celebrator is wonderfully rich, with bread and toffee flavors on a semi-sweet palate which shows its warming strength.

BRAUEREI HELLER-TRUM
Schlenkerla
6 Dominkaner Strasse
8600 Bamberg
Germany

Bamberg is famous for its rauchbiers (smoked beers), and the Trum family of Bamberg, having brewed here for five generations, produces the best of them. The brewery malts its own barley and then smokes it over a beechwood fire, giving rise to an extraordinary beer suffused with smoke. If you've never had smoked beer but like barbecued or grilled foods, you owe it to yourself to make this match.

AECHT SCHLENKERLA RAUCHBIER MARZEN—With the word *aecht* meaning "genuine," and *marzen* denoting its gravity, the name is quite a mouthful. And so is the beer. The smoke is in the forefront of the nose of this amber beer, which has an aroma rather like smoked ham with a coating of barbecue sauce. The palate also shows some smoke, but normal malt flavors also come through clearly, backed up by a snappy bitterness. In lesser rauchbiers, the smoke is allowed to overpower the beer, but Schlenkerla holds it all together. Smoked beers aren't for everyone, but anyone who has tasted smoked Lapsang Chinese teas should immediately recognize the greatness of this unusual beer.

PAULANER
75 Hoch Strasse, 8000 Munich 95
Germany

Originally brewed by Paulist monks, Paulaner's beers have descended to earth without losing certain heavenly qualities. Internationally, Paulaner is the most prominent of Munich's six major breweries, and brews a fine range of traditional styles. Its maltings, brewhouse and cellars are nestled into a hillside, and it still pulls brewing water from natural springs. Over the centuries, the Paulaner brewery has been an innovator, from the creation of the doppelbock style to early work in refrigeration and steam power. The beers are drier than the Bavarian standard, but retain a fine malt character throughout. Long lagering times of ten to twelve weeks assure a pleasant smoothness.

PREMIUM PILS—An excellent example of the German pilsner style. The aroma is full of fresh hops backed by the promise of bready malt. Hops are snappy on the palate before the malt comes into play, still fairly dry, with a clean, refreshing finish.

OKTOBERFEST—Light amber in color with a fine head, this beer shows some malt in the aroma, but it comes through better on the palate, where it attains a certain candyish caramel quality. Medium hopping balances out malt, and the beer finishes almost dry with a bready flourish.

HEFE-WEIZEN—One of Germany's best-known hefeweizens, this beer has all the qualities that define the style. The beer is hazy gold with red highlights, sitting under a huge cap of white foam. The nose is fresh, yeasty and clovy, with a hint of banana and bubblegum. On the palate, it is light-bodied and fairly hoppy for a weizen, with a nice burst of fruitiness and a lively finish.

SALVATOR—The name seems vaguely blasphemous (it means "savior" in Latin), but perhaps that depends on your circumstances. Salvator is the original doppelbock beer, and it is through imitation that other bock beers came to have names with the suffix "-ator." Deep russet in color, Salvator lives up to its reputation, boasting a rich caramel and toffee nose, with both qualities following through to a malty semi-sweet palate. The beer finishes so smoothly that only a certain warmth gives away its strength.

PRIVATBRAUEREI G. SCHNEIDER & SOHN
1-5 Emil Ott Strasse, 8420 Kelheim
Germany

The sixth generation of George Schneiders runs the brewhouse of what is arguably Germany's finest wheat beer brewery. Wheat beer has been brewed on the premises since 1607, when the brewery was no doubt owned by a local nobleman (as all wheat beer breweries once were). The brewhouse is now strikingly modern, with stainless-steel vessels set into a gleaming marble floor. Fermentation is carried out in traditional open vessels, and the beers are then bottle-conditioned. The Schneiders stuck with traditional Bavarian weizen beers through the days when people regarded them as anachronisms. As wheat beer enjoys a huge resurgence in Germany today, the Schneiders are reaping well-earned success.

SCHNEIDER-WEISSE—Darker than most wheat beers due to the use of Vienna and dark malts, Schneider-Weisse is a hazy amber. The head is white and voluminous, and the beer positively roils with carbonation. The aroma shows all of the classic Bavarian wheat beer elements— cloves, bananas, bubblegum and a touch of smoke. On the palate, the carbonation is aggressive and champagne-like, and the beer is expansive, spicy and snappy, with a tart edge, a firm body and a clean bready finish.

AVENTINUS—The brewery's weizen doppelbock has even deeper pleasures to offer. Tawny brown in color, it has an aroma profile similar to that of Schneider-Weisse, but the balance is tipped toward banana and a hint of chocolate backs it up. Fruity flavors burst onto the medium-bodied strong palate, cruising in smoothly to a warming, spicy finish with a tart edge.

SPATEN
Gabriel Sedlmayr
Spaten-Franziskaner-Brau
46-48 Mars Strasse
80335 Munich
Germany

Spaten's origins date back nearly six hundred years, but the most important phase of its history began when the young brewmaster for the Bavarian Royal Court, Gabriel Sedlmayr, took the reins in 1807. He expanded the brewery, which gained an excellent reputation upon which his son, Gabriel II, expanded considerably. Gabriel II and his brother Josef, who bought the brewery formerly belonging to Munich's Franciscan monastery, played a large role in the development of German brewing during the middle to late nineteenth century. The brothers collaborated with each other and with prominent European brewers, developing the modern Oktoberfest-Marzen style and doing pioneering work in brewing microbiology, brewing techniques, steam power and refrigeration. In 1922, the two brothers' breweries merged into the company that today uses the Spaten trade name. The Sedlmayr family still holds a large stake in the company, which is the top-selling Bavarian beer exporter to the United States.

PREMIUM LAGER—Pale gold with a relatively sturdy white head, this pilsner has a fresh, flowery nose and a full-bodied dry palate featuring solid bready malt flavors and a quenching bitterness. Hoppier throughout and less sweet than some of its Bavarian counterparts, and very good with food.

UR-MARZEN OKTOBERFEST—*Ur* means "original," and Spaten can reasonably make that claim, having introduced the style in the 1870s. The beer is brownish amber, and has a full toffee-malt aroma. On the palate, the malt follows through sweetly with a beguiling spiciness, and there is just enough hops to hold up the malt. The aftertaste is pleasant and bready. Over the past ten years it seems to have become a bit lighter in color and flavor, but retains its essential character.

FRANZISKANER HEFE-WEISSBIER—By the time Gabriel Sedlmayr's brewery combined with that of his brother, Josef's brewery had become dedicated to the production of wheat beer under the name Franziskaner (Franciscan). This hazy gold beer raises the traditionally voluminous weissbier head, and has an aroma of cloves and bananas with a strong note of smoke. Full-bodied and spicy on the palate with minimal hopping, it is not the most characterful of the Bavarian wheat beers, but it has the distinction of being the best-selling.

OPTIMATOR—Deep ruby-brown with an impressively vigorous head, this beer exudes an alluring aroma of malt, with hints of hop and even fruit. Round and sweet on the palate, this is one of the fullest expressions of the spicy toffee flavor of fine German malt. Hops step in at the end to balance, leading to an almost dry finish. A deceptively strong doppelbock that perfectly complements full-flavored wursts.

BELGIUM

BRASSERIE DUPONT
Rue Basse 5
7904 Tourpes-Leuze
Belgium

Producing only about five thousand barrels per year, the tiny Dupont brewery is one of the best traditional breweries in Belgium. The Duponts have been brewing artisanal farmhouse-style beer since 1850, and you can still buy your farm-fresh eggs in the front office. The Dupont family acquired the brewery in 1920, and one of the Dupont grandsons, Marc Rosier, runs the brewery today. Though the brewery produces beers under a number of labels, it is most famous for its Saison, and for the beers under the Moinette label.

SAISON DUPONT—This beer is so full of live yeast that the bottle appears vaguely crusty on the inside. The bottle lets loose its cork with champagne-like vigor, and Saison Dupont flows like a force of nature. Golden, churning, almost chunky and powerfully aromatic, the beer raises a thick, mighty white head. A blast of apples, yeast, Goldings hops, grapefruit and coriander forms an appetizing aroma. The beer is bracingly bitter up front, following through with a dry, bright, spicy palate. The finish is clean, dry and refreshing, with a lingering impression of fresh earth and cut hay.

MOINETTE BLONDE—Deeper in color than the Saison, this full-bodied beer has more of an accent on the malt, though the hopping is still prodigious. Spicy, earthy aromas and flavors predominate, with a touch of anise in the background.

BON VOEUX—At 9.5 percent ABV, this Christmas beer is certain to bring glad tidings. Bright gold in color and just as yeasty and hoppy as the other Dupont beers, Bon Voeux has a round, somewhat sweet palate dominated by sweet spice flavors. A highly complex beer with a long resiny finish.

BROUWERIJ DE SMEDT
Ringlaan 18
1890 Opwijk
Belgium

Founded in 1074 by Benedictine monks, Affligem is the oldest brewery in Flanders. When their brewhouse was destroyed in World War II, the monks turned to the secular family-owned de Smedt brewery to produce their beers. The de Smedt brewery was founded in 1790, and largely produces beers in the abbey style. As the popularity of the beer has increased, annual production has risen to more than forty thousand barrels. While they brew beers under various labels, it is the Affligem beers that have made them popular in the United States. In an interesting turnabout, Pierre Celis, who resurrected the witbier style with Hoegaarden and then moved to Texas to brew Celis White (the brewery is now owned by Miller), is now contracting production of Celis White at de Smedt so that his new American style can be distributed in Belgium.

AFFLIGEM TRIPEL—This deep-golden bottle-conditioned beer has an effusive white head and a perfumey aroma with plenty of pear, a touch of anise and perhaps cantaloupe melon. It is yeasty, hoppy, fresh and spicy on the palate with a touch of sweetness, and the warmth of the alcohol gives the beer an almost spiritous quality. A long, earthy, fruity finish rounds it off.

AFFLIGEM DOBBEL—Deep reddish-brown with a white head, this is a very nice example of the dobbel style. The nose is full of raisins, plums and chocolate, which follow through on a mellow, sweetish, spicy palate with medium hop bitterness. The finish is dry and aromatic.

AFFLIGEM NOEL—This dark brown holiday beer takes the best qualities of the dobbel and then deepens them. A strong, candyish nose leads to a semi-sweet palate with rich caramel and licorice flavors, backed with raisins, nutmeg and chocolate. Bitterness is snappy at the finish to balance it all out.

BROUWERIJ FRANK BOON
Fonteinstraat 65
1520 Lembeek
Belgium

Frank Boon has been spiritually connected to beer since he tended bar as a college student. From there he went on to the beer wholesaling business and the art of blending traditional lambic beers. Finally, in the mid-1970s he started brewing them as well, at a time when many old lambic brewers were going under. People thought him a maverick at best, and insane at worst. Today, he is considered a pioneer traditionalist, brewing and blending some of the finest lambic beers in Belgium. Lambic beers, which are spontaneously fermented by wild yeast and microflora in the air and in wooden cask fermenters, are often shockingly sour, and Boon has largely resisted the public's sweet tooth. The brewery produces a framboise and a kriek, but it is the straight unfruited lambics that they are famous for. Frank Boon has certainly been partly responsible for a renewal of interest in traditional lambic brewing. The lambic family of beers takes its name from the town of Lembeek, where Brouwerij Frank Boon is situated in a building erected in 1810.

BOON GUEUZE—The cork-finished bottle releases a hazy gold beer with a white head and a funky aroma of apple peel, lemons and wet wool. On the palate, the beer is sour and dry with a nice interplay of spicy sherryish flavors. Hops are barely noticeable, as is often the case in traditional lambics.

BOON GUEUZE MARIAGE PARFAIT—The "perfect marriage" referred to here is this particular blend, for which the brewery chooses only its finest lambic batches. Because lambic beers are spontaneously fermented, every batch has variations, and they are blended for consistency. Golden and spritzy, Mariage Parfait has a fresh herbal nose with an earthy background of wet wool and lemon peel. The palate is pleasantly sour with a focused tang, showing a complex interplay of earth and fruit flavors. The finish is very clean and dry. This is the beer equivalent of a great Stilton.

BROUWERIJ LIEFMANS
200 Aalst Straat
9700 Oudenaarde
Belgium

Founded in 1679 in the East Flanders town of Oudenaarde, the Liefmans brewery has long been the standard-bearer for the tart local style of brown ale. The Liefmans versions are still considered classics, and follow lengthy brewing regimens the reasons for which are lost to time. They are open fermented in copper vessels and then aged for many months, some of them being blended or having fruit added along the way. The results speak for themselves, as Liefmans beers are still superior to those of their counterparts and imitators. In 1990, the Riva group of Dentergem, West Flanders, took over the brewery and currently produces its wort, sending it by tanker to the Oudenaarde brewery for fermentation, conditioning and packaging. As awful as this may sound, the beers have retained their character, and Riva claims that all production will return to the Oudenaarde brewery once renovations are completed. The beers all cellar excellently, particularly Goudenband.

GOUDENBAND—A deep reddish-brown beer which shows the deeply aromatic nose of a fine dry sherry, with cherry and damson notes. On the palate the beer is full-bodied but spritzy, with a wonderful balance of sweet and sour flavors dominated by a raisiny character and backed by earthy malt. It finishes dry and snappy, with some hop aroma showing through. Excellent as an aperitif or as a base for the famous Belgian beer and beef stew *carbonnade flamande*.

FRAMBOZENBIER—Fruit beers needn't be based on lambics, and this is a good example of a non-lambic raspberry beer. Based on the brown ale, the beer only picks up a little bit of raspberry color, but the nose is huge and complex. It is fruity, tart and brisk on the palate, with the underlying brown ale showing through the raspberry nicely. Finishes clean and dry.

KRIEK—Cherries are added to six-month-old strong brown ale, where they ferment for an additional two months. The resulting beer is ruddy brown, with a cherry and raisin aroma. It is sweet and then sour on the palate, smooth, but perhaps slightly lacking in malt. Cellaring for up to a year will dry the beer out and produce greater complexity. Pairs nicely with roasted duck.

BROUWERIJ LINDEMANS
257 Lenniksebaan
1712 Vlezenbeek
Belgium

The Lindemans family farmers went into the brewing business fulltime in the 1860s, but the brewery, housed in an old barn, belies the farming roots. The Lindemans brewers today are lambic brewers, selling much of their production to blenders of gueuze. Their house specialty is fruit lambics, which they have had a large hand in popularizing in Belgium and foreign markets. Along the way, they have largely given in to the public demand for sweeter beers, but at least one of these is a classic unto itself, much to the annoyance of staunch traditionalists. In a nod to those wishing more traditional lambic beers, they have recently begun releasing the excellent Cuvee Rene.

FRAMBOISE—When poorly made, a sweetened fruit lambic can be a mere cartoon of a beer, but in the right hands it can be a work of art. Lindemans Framboise belongs in that latter category, not least for its appealing pinkish-red hue and light pink head. When the beer is poured, the aroma of fresh raspberries—stems, stalks, leaves and all—wafts over the table. The palate follows through, delivering in full on its promise—sweet with a balancing sour edge and a complex earthy backdrop. It is ludicrously decadent with a slice of good cheesecake.

KRIEK—The beer pours blush gold with a massive aroma of sour cherries. It is sweet and then sour on the palate with a fine carbonation and a touch of malt flavor, finishing sharp and dry with hints of earth. Not quite as elemental as the framboise, but still very pleasant.

CUVEE RENE—Lindemans' traditional gueuze pours hazy gold with a rolling effervescence and a magnificently earthy champagne-like aroma full of spice, wet blankets, apple peels and fruit. Sharp and spritzy on the palate, it is quite full bodied, and shows an impressively complex interplay of flavors reminiscent of the finest champagnes. It finishes with its sourness intact, showing a flash of malt and leaving a lingering, dry tang. A truly magnificent beer which the brewery and the public will hopefully back strongly in the future.

BROUWERIJ MOORTGAT
Breendonk Dorp 58
2870 Breendonk-Puurs
Belgium

The Moortgat brewery produces Belgium's best-selling specialty beer, Duvel (pronounced DOO-vl). The brewery is family-owned and -run, and was founded in 1871. The years have been kind to the Moortgats, and their brewery now produces more than 200,000 barrels annually. It retained its own maltings until recently, in order to prepare the special malts that allow Duvel to achieve its light golden color. This is now handled to the brewery's specifications by an outside malting house, and fans are hoping the quality will not be adversely affected. Originally, the brewery only produced dark ales, of which Duvel was one, until it was reformulated in the late sixties.

DUVEL—Some Belgian beers defy categorization and become icons unto themselves. Duvel is much imitated, but never equaled. Taking the opposite tack of the abbey breweries, the Moortgats appealed to a lower authority and named this beer after the Flemish word for the devil. Certainly the beer is seductive and deceptive enough. The very pale yellow color masks a beer that contains more than 8 percent ABV. The beer is bottle-conditioned and virtually erupts into the glass, raising a massive, stark, white head. The nose is perfumey, full of hops, pear brandy and citrus. Light-bodied but flashy on the palate, the beer is full of spicy flavors backed by hay and a hint of tobacco. The palate signs off with a snap of hops and a spicy aftertaste warmed by alcohol. Great with a wide variety of foods, Duvel is often referred to as the ''champagne of Belgium.''

BEL PILS—A terrific version of the pilsner style, Bel Pils pours with a medium-gold color and thick white head. The nose is full of hops, hay and a fresh touch of sulfur. On the palate, the beer is quite dry and hoppy, with a sizzling pinpoint carbonation that is remarkably refreshing. It finishes cleanly, with a hoppy snap.

BROUWERIJ RODENBACH
Spanje Straat 133-141
8800 Roeselare
Belgium

The most famous and accomplished brewer of the old Flemish red ale style, Rodenbach's production is up to nearly 200,000 barrels annually. The current brewery was founded in 1836, and includes some of the most extraordinary brewing apparatus still in use anywhere in the world. Fermentation of the beers takes place in stainless-steel fermenters, but conditioning takes place in huge (up to 500-barrel) unlined Polish oak vats, where microorganisms in the wood invade the beer and imbue it with its characteristic sourness. The maturation in wood takes up to two years. The vats, more than one hundred of them, are arranged in awe-inspiring rows, and many of them date back to the early 1900s. Springs which feed a local lake also provide water for brewing.

RODENBACH—Oak and acidity with only a backdrop of malt comprise the aroma of this beer, which pours a mahogany red derived from specialty malts and wood maturation. On the palate, the beer is light-bodied and sharply acidic, with fruit, wood and wool flavors showing through. The beer finishes with a quick tartness. This beer is a blend of the two-year-old beer (which goes on to become the Grand Cru) and younger brews. A terrific beer with salads.

RODENBACH GRAND CRU—Reddish-brown in color, this beer expresses the full character of the Flemish red ale style. Rodenbach Grand Cru spends two years maturing in the oak vats, and apparently uses that time well. It shows a bit of its sourness even in the nose, but raisins, caramel and Madeira are also prevalent. The sourness hits the palate with a tart smack, but quickly reveals a complex interplay of oak tannins, bright fruit and rock candy, rolling through to leave a somewhat tannic oakiness in its wake.

CHIMAY
Abbaye de Notre Dame de Scourmont
6483 Forges
Belgium

The largest and best known of the Trappist breweries, Chimay forges ahead behind its monastery walls, brewing fantastic beer for a grateful world. Located near the French border about six miles south of the town of Chimay, the abbey was founded in 1850 and commenced commercial brewing in 1862. The brewery has a production capacity of more than 100,000 barrels annually, allowing it to keep up with ever-increasing demand. Chimay draws water from its own wells for brewing, and uses a multi-strain yeast that ferments at unusually high temperatures (77 degrees Fahrenheit). These yeast strains are largely responsible for the spicy ''house character'' of the beers, along with the use of some distinctive American hop varieties. All of the Chimay beers are bottle-conditioned and come in 33-centiliter and 75-centiliter bottles (the latter corked). The names of the beers (Rouge, Blanche and Bleu) refer simply to the color of the label and bottle cap. As the craft brewing revolution surges into the next century, Chimay's beers are popular enough to be found in the most serious restaurants and the humblest delis in major U.S. cities and some smaller towns where there is a market for world-class beers. While the abbey is more famous for its beers, it also produces some nice cheeses, broadly in the Camembert style.

CHIMAY ROUGE—The original Chimay beer, brewed in the dubbel style, it is russet brown in color and crowned with a rather brief tan head. The nose has notes of caramel, nutmeg and muted hops. On the palate, the beer is soft and spicy, with a sweet malt center and a hint of sourness in the background. Best served at about 60° F, this is a terrific beer to pair with red meats. In the 75-centiliter corked bottle, it is known as Chimay Premiere.

CHIMAY BLANCHE—Brewed broadly in the tripel style, this beer takes a step away from the typical Trappist character. The amber beer pours with a larger, firmer head than the other Chimay beers, and the nose has a spicy, almost citric hop quality. On the palate, it is firm and bracingly hoppy, with a peachy malt center, drying out to a snappy finish. Can be slightly chilled, and will age nicely at cellar temperatures for a year or so. In the 75-centiliter bottle, it is known as Chimay Cinq Cents (commemorating the five hundredth anniversary of the town of Chimay).

CHIMAY BLEU—Of the three Chimay beers, this is the richest and most prized. Chimay Bleu carries its 9 percent ABV with grace, showing dark fruit, nutmeg and black pepper in the nose, with a hint of apple peel. The flavors follow through on a full-bodied, slightly sweet palate with an earthy, yeast backdrop of raisins and chocolate. The hops take a back seat here, serving only to provide a bracing balance for the sweetness of the malt. This beer improves with cellaring, and some connoisseurs will not drink it until it is at least three years old; the rest of us rarely manage to wait that long. In the 75-centiliter bottle, it is known as Chimay Grande Reserve.

ORVAL
Abbaye de Notre Dame d'Orval
6823 Villers-devant-Orval
Belgium

Established in 1132, Orval Abbey survived a great many insults at the hands of invading armies over the centuries, but finally was sacked and destroyed in 1793 after the French Revolution. The present abbey was rebuilt in 1926 to blend in with the ruins of the old, and the brewery was established shortly thereafter. The name "Orval" comes from the French, meaning "golden valley." The brewery only produces one beer, which is as distinctive as its bowling-pin-shaped bottle and striking label. Aside from the beer, the monks also produce bread and cheeses, which are available at the brewery.

ORVAL—Three special malts and Belgian candy sugar lend this beer a startling orangy color capped by a rocky tight-knit white head. There is a spicy hop and bright fruit aroma. English Goldings hops leap to the fore on the palate, giving a sharp, focused bitterness, which gives way to a dry, spicy palate with candyish notes and a citrusy fruit finish. Hop bitterness and bready malt linger refreshingly on the palate.

ROCHEFORT
L'Abbaye de Notre-Dame de Saint-Remy
5430 Rochefort
Belgium

The quietest and least well-known of the Trappist breweries, the abbey at Rochefort sits hidden away in the unhurried Ardennes countryside, producing any number of good works, which include some of the world's finest beer. The abbey dates back to the 1200s, and was a convent until the 1400s, when it became a monastery. Brewing commenced in the next century, ceased in 1794, and began anew in 1899. Rochefort produces three beers under the name Trappistes Rochefort and identified as 6, 8, and 10 respectively, referring to their gravities in the outdated Belgian brewing degree system. Each beer has its own cap rather than a different label.

ROCHEFORT 6 (RED CAP)—A tawny brown beer with almost pinkish highlights, this beer has a fine fruity nose that promises a bit more than is delivered on the palate, where it is smooth but light-bodied, with a mild spiciness and a dry finish.

ROCHEFORT 8 (GREEN CAP)—The beer is medium brown and heads impressively, giving an aroma of sweet spice and dates. On the palate, it is relatively dry but has a rich maltiness, the fruit following through to a long, dry finish.

ROCHEFORT 10 (BLACK CAP)—Deep mahogany in color, the beer is capped with a stiff head and bursts with an aroma of raisins, dates, sherry and dark chocolate. On the palate it delivers in full—silky smooth, earthy, fruity and spicy, with a deeply warming spiritous quality that is nearly overwhelming. Resiny hop notes wend through the thicket of flavors and emerge in the finish, bringing it in cleanly. Chocolate, musty malt and dark fruit linger in the aftertaste. An astonishing beer of infinite complexity and grace.

WESTMALLE
Abdij der Trappisten
Antwerpsesteenweg 496
2390 Malle
Belgium

The Abbey of Our Lady of the Sacred Heart, known as Westmalle, was founded in 1794 and started brewing about 40 years later. The progenitors of the dubbel and tripel styles of ale, the monks at the Trappist abbey of Westmalle have been selling beer to the public for over 130 years, though the brewing operation only became truly commercial in 1920. That said, they do not market their beers as aggressively as Chimay or Orval, and consequently the beers can be more difficult to find. They are, however, worth searching out. The beers are brewed from summer barley and spiced with Hallertauer, Saaz, Fuggles and other traditional hop varieties. The fermentations are convoluted and complex, often involving repeated additions of yeast and sugars. The current brewery was built in 1934, and has been overhauled a few times since so that the monks could increase production. The beers are bottle-conditioned and suitable for laying down for a year or two.

WESTMALLE DUBBEL—This dark brown beer raises an impressively rocky head and is redolent of chocolate, hops and prunes. On the palate it is deeply malty and slightly sweet, with a touch of spicy roast in the background, and the fruit following through to a drying hoppy finish.

WESTMALLE TRIPEL—Bright burnished gold and capped with an expansive head, the original tripel is still the king of its style, richly aromatic with hop and fruit aroma and a faint touch of anise. On the palate it is round but boldly hoppy and strong, with fine malt and fruit flavors gently overlapping and gliding in for a dry, spicy finish. The aftertaste is a warm glow of bread and fruit.

FRANCE

BRASSERIE CASTELAIN
13 Rue Pasteur
62410 Benifontaine
France

In 1966, Roland Castelain and family bought this brewery, which dated back to 1926. Today, the brewery is run by Roland's grandson Yves, who has become one of the major voices and talents on the French artisanal brewing scene. His beers appear in France under the name Ch'ti, a slang term referring proudly to someone from northern France. Castelain's *bieres de garde* are smoother and less spicy in character than many others, and are packaged in cork-finished bottles. The beers are brewed from local barleys and a blend of European hop varieties. Today, what started as a very small operation is producing upward of twenty thousand barrels a year for a growing number of international markets.

CASTELAIN BLONDE—Deep brilliant gold color, with a nose of malt, toffee and hay. Somewhat sweet on the palate, with well-defined malt flavor and a fruity backdrop balanced by effective but unassertive hopping. Round and mellow at the finish, with a fresh touch of sulfur.

CASTELAIN AMBREE—Light amber in color with a well-formed head and a nose of caramel and slightly spicy malt. Full-bodied and semi-sweet on the palate, with a deep malt flavor and restrained fruitiness. Look for just a hint of licorice in the background. Hops bring up the rear for a clean finish.

JADE—The only beer brewed in France that is certified organic, Jade is brewed from artesian well water and organically raised malts and hops. The color is pale yellow, and the aroma is light, with notes of hay and fruit. The palate is light-to-medium-bodied, with a quick malt center and a touch of grassiness, buoyed by firm hopping for a refreshing finish.

BRASSERIE ST. SYLVESTRE
St. Sylvestre-Cappel
59114 Steenvoorde
France

French Flanders is hop country, and there could be no finer setting for one of France's finest artisanal breweries. The Ricour family acquired the brewery in 1918, and is still in charge of its day-to-day operation. The beers are broadly in the *biere de garde* farmhouse style, but have more individuality than most, owing perhaps as much to Belgium as to France. The beers are brewed from English and French malts, and hopped with Brewers Gold from the local area and Tettnanger from Germany. Like other *bieres de garde,* those of St. Sylvestre are top-fermented and then lagered cold for varying periods. Their beers are all rather strong at about 8.5 percent alcohol by volume, and rely on differences in hops, malt and yeast strains to provide their individual characters.

3 MONTS—The brewery's flagship beer is named after the three hills that surround the village and provide the only point of variety in the rather flat landscape of Flanders. Labeled with the subtitle "Flanders Golden Ale," this beer is suitably golden in color, having been brewed from pilsner malt with a dash of sugar in the kettle. It has a nicely formed white head and a spicy, earthy aroma with a pleasant overlay of hay-like hops. On the palate it is dry and moderately hopped, with earthiness following through along with a touch of fruit and a vinous edge to the finish. The beer is filtered, though not aggressively, and retains a vaguely yeasty character.

3 MONTS GRAND RESERVE—Light amber in color and bottle-conditioned, this beer is full of character from the start, showing apple peel, cloves and a touch of smokiness in the nose. The palate is round and fat, with a malty center surrounded by complex fruit and spice flavors and assertive, resiny hops. Finishes moderately dry and spicy. One of France's finest beers.

FLANDERS WINTER ALE—Known in France as Biere de Noel, this copper-colored beer is brewed for the Christmas season. A fruity, musty aroma leads to a very full-bodied, rounded palate with a silky malt sweetness gently balanced by hops and accentuated by fruit flavor. The finish is malty with a vinous edge and a warming glow. More than a month of lagering leaves this beer with an alluring smoothness not often seen in French beers.

SCOTLAND

CALEDONIAN BREWING COMPANY
42 Slateford Road
Edinburgh EH11 1PH
Scotland

The last surviving brewery of Edinburgh's great Victorian brewing era, Caledonian marches into the future under the firm hand of Managing Director Russell Sharp. Sharp worked at the brewery in his youth, and later advanced through the whisky industry to become head chemist for Chivas Regal. When the brewery was threatened with closure in 1987, Sharp led a management buyout, saving one of Scotland's finest breweries and setting it on a steady course.

The red-brick brewery buildings at Caledonian date from the 1860s and are part of one of Britain's most picturesque breweries. Inside is a blend of brewing museum and modern production facility. The hammered copper kettles are open, sitting in the brewhouse like giant bowls embedded into the floor (because that's precisely what they are) with hoods several feet above. Beneath the floor the kettles are direct-fired by gas flame, but the coal still sits in the scuttles; gas was only introduced to the brewhouse in the 1980s. The barleys used in Caledonian's all-malt ales include the Scottish Golden Promise and English Pipkin varieties. Golden Promise, in particular, seems to impart an almost vanilla character reminiscent of certain fine single-malt Scotch whiskies. On a visit some years ago, Russell Sharp fixed a bushy brow and opined that American microbrews were all over-hopped and lacked subtlety. Caledonian's beers are classically smooth and, yes, subtle. Mr. Sharp can be forgiven his hubris.

80/- EXPORT ALE—The name of this beer is to be read "80-shilling" and denotes the price that a beer of this price would once have fetched at market. A light amber ale of about 4 percent alcohol by volume, it carries a toffeeish malt aroma and is medium-bodied and sweetish on the palate, with a bit of hop and fruit flavor showing through. The bitterness is restrained and allows the malt to shine.

DEUCHAR'S EXPORT STRENGTH IPA—Despite the name, this fine pale ale does not carry the traditional strength of an IPA, clocking in at a modest 4.5 percent. Nonetheless, it carries a nice hop nose and bright gold color, a snappy bitterness and hop flavor, which is followed by a fresh, bready hop finish.

MERMAN—A russet-brown ale with a beautiful buttery caramel aroma that carries through to a softly sweet, malty palate bursting with malt and fruit flavor. Hops are a bit player here, serving only as a balance. A classic Scottish ale.

MACANDREW'S SCOTCH ALE—An export version of the brewery's Edinburgh Strong Ale, MacAndrew's is a honey-colored ale with a deep butterscotch and earthy hop aroma. The bitterness is surprisingly assertive up front, but quickly drops back to reveal toffeeish malt and fruit flavors, moving into a dry, bready finish.

ENGLAND

ELDRIDGE, POPE & COMPANY
Weymouth Avenue, Dorchester
Dorset DT1 1QT
England

Old brewing texts give elaborate recipes for producing ''the celebrated Dorchester beer,'' and Dorchester retains a fine brewing reputation to this day, due not least to the efforts of Eldridge Pope. The brewery was founded in 1837, but the present buildings date from the 1920s. While the brewery produces a number of beers, it is best known outside of Dorset for its famous Thomas Hardy's Ale, a classic barley wine named after the author, who was not only from Dorchester but wrote fondly of its beer. Today, one imagines that Thomas Hardy's name is spoken as often in reference to this beer as to his novels, and it is difficult to say where lies the greater honor.

ROYAL OAK PALE ALE—This deep amber ale skirts the color line for pale ales, and is no doubt a true throwback to the days when ''pale'' meant ''paler than porter.'' In any event, the color is beautiful, as is the deeply toffeeish, earthy aroma. It is soft and fruity up front on the palate, round and medium-bodied, with plums, caramel, toffee and hops in soft interplay. Hops bring the beer in for a clean, dryish finish. Great with roast beef, this beer is particularly subtle, and overchilling should definitely be avoided if you want to capture its full flavor.

THOMAS HARDY'S ALE—Aged for nearly a year before being lovingly bottled on its yeast in dated, numbered bottles, Thomas Hardy's Ale is always a work in progress. By the time it leaves the brewery, it has reached an alcoholic strength of 12.5 percent by volume, fortitude enough to protect it on a journey that can last for decades. When young, the beer exudes a powerful aroma of deep, musty malt, molasses, maple syrup and dark fruit. The palate is quite sweet and full-bodied, full of plums and raisins, with sharp bitterness yanking it into some sort of balance. It is fascinating but disjointed. Some years of aging make a world of difference. A bottle of 1986 Thomas Hardy's poured recently with a very light, creamy effervescence. A strong aroma of baking dark bread blended with rich sherry and Madeira notes. On the palate, the beer bursts with flavor, full rather than truly sweet at the center, a well-tuned interplay of malt, honey, chocolate, vanilla, plums and raisins, with brighter, more citric fruit emerging in the long, smooth finish. The brewery claims that Thomas Hardy's Ale will age well for at least twenty-five years, and it is certainly off to a very good start.

FULLER, SMITH & TURNER
Griffin Brewery
Chiswick Lane South
London W4 2QB
England

In London, devotees of traditional cask-conditioned ale tend to be "Fuller's people" or "Young's people," and Fuller's beers are distinctly different from those of its London colleague. Fuller's has been brewing in the West London suburb of Chiswick since the 1820s, and in the last twenty years has gained an international reputation for its full-flavored range of ales. In particular, Fuller's ESB (extra special bitter) has carried the standard for the brewery, consistently winning awards and virtually developing ESB into a style of its own. The brewery itself is quite handsome and worth a look if a tour is available. Fuller's takes good care of its beers in its London pubs, some of which serve unusually good food—a brilliant match for their fine beers.

CHISWICK BITTER—Named after the local area, Chiswick Bitter is a traditional cask-conditioned "ordinary" bitter, a session beer of light gravity and strength. That said, it has a nice snappy aroma, a crisp bitterness and a splendid hay-like quality on the palate. It finishes clean and dry, with a touch of bready malt in the aftertaste. A great beer for the start of your evening in the pub.

LONDON PRIDE—The true Fuller's house character becomes apparent in this medium-bodied bitter, which carries an enticingly deep malt aroma with resiny hop notes. On the palate, the beer is soft and smooth, with the fruity slightly flowery sweet malt taking the front seat as the broad hop bitterness balances things out.

ESB—Flowery hops, malt and freshly turned earth mingle in the aroma of Fuller's famous strong bitter, which carries its 5.5 percent alcohol with elan. On the palate, the beer is soft, smooth and balanced, with caramel, fruit and wildflower honey flavors playing in unison against a background of moderate bitterness. The finish is long and beckoning. In top condition, this is one of England's finest bitters, well deserving of its numerous awards.

GEORGE BATEMAN & SON
Salem Bridge Brewery
Wainfleet, Skegness, Lincolnshire PE24 4JF
England

When George Bateman bought this brewery in 1874, his highest ambition was to provide "good, honest ales" to his fellow farmers in the surrounding countryside. Today, the brewery is capable of producing more than 35,000 barrels a year, but Bateman's success has been hardwon. Bateman's nearly went under in the 1970s before being buoyed by the rebound of interest in traditional brewing led by the Campaign for Real Ale. The enterprising Jackie Bateman has seen that Bateman's beers are available to connoisseurs from the United States to Japan. According to head brewer Martin Cullimore, Bateman's distinctive house yeast character led some people to deride Bateman's beers as "those banana beers" during the dark days of the early 1970s. Apparently, the Bateman family is having the last laugh.

XXXB—The beer pours with a beautiful burnished gold color and impressive white head. A huge aroma of earthy hops and fruit foreshadows a soft, round palate full of banana and green apples over a caramel backdrop. Hops bring it in to a clean finish. Complex throughout and excellent with food.

VICTORY ALE—Named after the brewery's salvation from family members who wanted to sell it off, this very deep amber ale has a nose which is so luscious as to promise a barley wine. At 6 percent ABV, it is not quite that strong, but the palate is wonderfully soft and round with a malty bubblegum-like fruitiness balancing with spicy Golding hops, drying out for a clean finish.

GEORGE GALE & COMPANY
Horndean, Portsmouth
Hampshire PO8 0DA
England

Near the naval city of Portsmouth, Gale's flies its flag in the village of Horndean, where Richard Gale first purchased the Ship and Bell Hotel (and brewery) in 1849. When fire brought down the inn in 1869, the present brick building was built with a classic tower design. Inside, a maze of staircases and platforms keeps the brewers in good shape as they go about brewing for the company's more than 130 pubs. The brewery vessels are a blend of old, new and used, including some uncoated-pine open fermenters. Up in the tower, a cast-iron mash tun built in the 1920s sends wort down to a cast-iron kettle of the same period for production of the famous Prize Old Ale. Flavorful old varieties of hops and malt are favored here; Marris Otter malts are spiced with Fuggle, Golding and Challenger hops. The house yeast produces a very fruity, vinous character which is evident in all of the beers. Now capable of producing more than ninety thousand barrels per year, Gale's is the largest family-owned brewery in Hampshire.

HSB—The name stands for "Horndean Special Bitter," even if no one spells it out anymore. One of the best-loved pints in southern England, HSB is a premium-strength bitter with a deep, ruddy, tawny port complexion and fine, fruity aroma. The beer is soft and sweetish on the palate, with nutty caramel and marmalade notes. The hops bring up the rear for a clean finish. Flavorful, complex and consistently interesting to drink.

PRIZE OLD ALE—First brewed around the turn of the century, Gale's Prize Old Ale looks eminently worthy of its name, hand-bottled and corked in a distinctive low-shouldered bottle with a stylish label. Fortunately, the beer has the substance to back up the promise, and Prize Old Ale pours deep russet brown with a stiff rocky head. A heady aroma of peaches, plums, marmalade and hops leads to a powerful vinous palate which makes no attempt to disguise its heft of 9 percent alcohol by volume. Oaky, fruity, musty, sherryish and expansive, the beer rolls into the finish with an acidic twang. Oak and hops linger. Aged in tanks for up to a year and then bottle-conditioned, this is one of England's very finest strong ales and quite suitable for aging.

SAMUEL SMITH
The Old Brewery, Tadcaster
Yorkshire LS24 9SB
England

Despite being dwarfed by brewing giants such as Bass, Samuel Smith's of Yorkshire is one of England's best-known breweries internationally. The distinctive labels and clear bottles don't hurt, but it is the subtle beauty of the beers that have made Smith's famous. The brewery was founded in 1758 and bought by the Smith family in 1847, and they are still the owners today. The brewery is one of the few left to employ a method of fermentation called the Yorkshire Square system, which circulates the fermenting worts through a split-level open fermentation vat. The fermenters, or squares, are fashioned of slabs of Welsh slate. Between the fermentation system, the slate, and the local yeast strains, a certain magic emerges, and the beers emerge soft, full-bodied and subtle. Hard water drawn from an underground aquifer is particularly suited to brewing the pale ale for which the brewery is famous. None of the beers from Samuel Smith's should be served colder than 50° F, lest the chill numb the taste buds to the subtleties that this beer has to offer.

SAMUEL SMITH'S OLD BREWERY PALE ALE—Known in its cask-conditioned draft form as Museum Ale in English pubs, this pale ale is Smith's best-known beer. A beautiful honey color, the beer raises a sturdy head and has a soft, earthy aroma of caramel, fruit, butterscotch and hops. On the palate, the hopping is restrained but firm, and the buttery malt flavor suffuses a soft, slightly sweet round palate with an earthy background of hop flavor.

SAMUEL SMITH'S NUT BROWN ALE—Light brown in color, this beer has a sweet aroma full of caramel, butter, vanilla and hazelnuts. On the palate it is semi-sweet with more caramel than roast character, full-bodied and nutty. There is enough bitterness to provide a nice balance to the malt and a clean finish.

SAMUEL SMITH'S OATMEAL STOUT—This deep brown ale pours with a nice rocky tan head, and a wonderful aroma of chocolate and vanilla and a whiff of coffee. On the palate it is somewhat sweet and round and has an almost oily, silky smoothness. There is not much oatmeal in this beer, a few percent at best, but that smoothness seems to be oatmeal's contribution to the equation. Hops play a strictly supporting role, holding the gentle sweetness in check.

SAMUEL SMITH'S IMPERIAL STOUT—Catherine the Great of Russia had a penchant for English stouts, but in her day the trip from London to the Baltic ports was a very long one, and the stout rarely survived the voyage. Imperial Stout was conceived as a strong beer meant to travel, but in the early 1980s Samuel Smith's started brewing this one to travel to the United States. It is nearly black with a deep tan head, and the thickness of this stout is evident even in the pouring. A rich aroma of coffee, chocolate and raisins announces a deep, smooth, malty, full-bodied palate full of roasted malt flavors, reminiscent of semi-sweet chocolate. The beer is sturdily hopped, but only enough to keep the malt from becoming cloying. The beer finishes long and finally disappears, leaving a warming afterglow of butterscotch, chocolate and vanilla.

YOUNG & CO.
The Ram Brewery
Wandsworth, London SW18 4JD
England

When gales of change blew through the British brewing industry during the 1970s, bringing cheaper, more mass-market beers, Young's stood firm in its commitment to traditional brewing, alone among the London brewers. Founded in 1831, Young's went public at the turn of the century, but the reins still lie in the hands of John Young and his family. Behind the high brick walls of the brewery, a menagerie makes its home, from the free-running geese to the sturdy mascot ram and one of England's finest stables of dray horses, which are still hitched up to wagons to make deliveries to the local pubs.

Inside the brewery, modernity blends with the Industrial Revolution, though the latter retains a comforting edge. Museum-quality steam engines and kettles are now largely silent but buffed up, operational and ready for duty should it call. The open fermentation vessels are a mix of stainless-steel and copper-lined wooden vessels, and the computer age is nowhere to be seen. A robust yeast strain gives Young's beers their characteristic dryness, while the classic Marris Otter malt contributes wonderfully bready flavors that have propelled the beers to many awards. Young's is one of England's best-loved and most respected independent breweries. In its fine pubs in England, Young's is known for its traditional bitters, simply called Young's Bitter and Young's Special.

RAM ROD—An excellent golden-amber pale ale with an earthy hop aroma and tangy bitterness, perfectly balanced by a sturdy malt center full of bread and peaches, finishing dry and clean.

SPECIAL LONDON ALE—In the U.K., this beer is known as Strong Export Ale, pointing to its roots in the original India pale ale style, of which it is one of the best British examples. The beer pours a light honey color, and is packed with toasty malt and the spicy aroma of Golding hops. On the palate the hops deliver a clean bite, giving way to a full-bodied, dry, fruity malt center, which finishes clean and dry with lingering hops. An excellent beer deserving of a wider audience.

OATMEAL STOUT—A deep red-black beer that raises a thick tan head and a coffeeish aroma with just a touch of licorice. On the palate, the beer starts off in an almost sweet direction, but then dries out as the roasted malts insert coffee and chocolate flavors and the 7 percent oatmeal in the mash lends an incredible silky smoothness. Finishes dry with a touch of molasses lingering.

OLD NICK—The bottle says "barley wine style," but the beer says "old ale." Never mind. This deep russet-brown beer is full of flavor and aroma, with intense fruit in the nose, backed up by a fruity malt palate of fine depth. The assertive, resiny hopping rounds out the picture. A very fine beer for a winter's evening.

IRELAND

ARTHUR GUINNESS & SON
St. James's Gate
Dublin 8
Republic of Ireland

Perhaps no other country in the world is as inextricably linked, heart and soul, to a single beer as Ireland is to Guinness. Arthur Guinness purchased the abandoned brewery at St. James's Gate in 1759 and started brewing ales, but quickly moved on to brew the porter that had become popular in England. Word of the quality of his beer spread throughout Ireland and into England, and when the Industrial Revolution came to breweries, Guinness was prepared to make full use of technological innovations and the spread of the British Empire to become for a time the world's largest brewer. Along the way, the porter style gave way to Extra Stout Porter, and finally to the Draught Guinness Stout and bottled Extra Stout that we are familiar with today.

Time has not erased the many different stouts that Guinness has produced over the years, and they live on today in as many as twenty different varieties, from the soft, creamy draft found in Ireland to the strong, acidic versions favored in countries from Malaysia to the Carribean and Africa. Those who may think that stout is in any way obscure might be surprised to note that Guinness, which commands a worldwide brewing empire, produces upward of 20 million barrels a year, most of it stout, sold in 150 countries. In the Caribbean and Africa, Guinness Foreign Extra Stout is considered an aphrodisiac, while in Ireland it is regarded as a close second to mother's milk in its wholesomeness. While many countries no longer allow Guinness to use its old advertising slogans "Guinness Gives Strength" and "Guinness Is Good for You," they are clearly still widely believed and the beer even more widely enjoyed.

DRAUGHT GUINNESS—While a pint of Guinness appears black and imposing with a regal cap of creamy white foam (formed by a special dispenser), it is actually a fairly light beer designed for drinking in reasonably large volumes. The aroma is full of chocolate and espresso, with an overlay of fruit and spicy hops. The beer delivers a sharp smack of hops up front, and the crisply dry palate is softly roasty and chocolaty with a touch of fruit and hop, deriving a certain creaminess from the head. The beer finishes dry with a slight acidic tang. No doubt the Guinness products were always designed to travel, and have retained a splendid hoppiness that is apparent in the finish and aftertaste of the draft beer. Draught Guinness for the United States is brewed in Ireland. At about 4.2 percent alcohol by volume, it is as light in alcohol as mass-market American beers that have far less to offer in terms of flavor. A canned version is now available, complete with a plastic widget in the can that disperses nitrogen into the liquid to form a creamy head. While it is one-dimensional compared to the true Draught product, it is not to be despised in a pinch.

EXTRA STOUT—At about 6 percent ABV, this beer more closely resembles the nineteenth-century versions of Guinness than does the Draught. Ruby-black with a thick tan cap of foam, the beer exudes a strong nose of fruit, espresso, chocolate and hops. On the palate it is assertive throughout, with hops leading the charge, then giving way to a fruity roasted malt center with a slight sourish edge. The beer finishes flintily dry, hoppy and clean. It is a much bigger and entirely different beer than Draught Guinness.

Pat Babcock

PAT BABCOCK IS, by day, an engineer at a Ford truck plant in Canton, Mich. By night (and by weekend) he is a homebrewer who offers advice on America Online and elsewhere online. His motto: "Beer is my obsession, and I'm late for therapy!"

Here's what else he says about himself:

"I started brewing/vintning at the ripe old age of twelve through a grade school science fair project on fermentation. My very understanding parents encouraged my curiosity and helped me locate equipment and supplies to continue 'playing' with fermentation. I very rarely got a taste of what I produced back then, but my parents and their friends seemed to enjoy the fruits of my work.

continued . . .

The products back then were kind of standard. A lambrusco-like purple wine, and a Prohibition-style ale made from whatever malt product I could get my hands on, usually our ol' friend Blue Ribbon.

"Vintning fizzled out for me about two years later upon the production of a very effective batch of anti-freeze. Totally unpalatable. Brewing became the sole focus of my experiments in fermentation. I brewed my first batch from 'self-cultured' yeast at fifteen. My father brought home a bottle of beer having sediment on the bottom (the brand has long since slipped my memory). I had heard that you could use the dregs of some bottles instead of yeast in beer. This seemed a likely candidate. I made a three-gallon batch of my finest (they were all my finest back then) and poured in the sediment. In spite of my methods, the experiment was successful. The beer fermented rather slowly, but the final product brought raves from those that sampled it. Bread yeast never again found its way into my beer."

A driver's license, college and a career as an engineer got in the way for a few years, but Pat picked up brewing again in 1993. He began inventing equipment, bought his own three-barrel system, joined a homebrew club and started posting tips on brewing and kegging on his Internet home page, *http://oeonline.com/~pbabcock/brew.html*. Now he also is a homebrew guru for America Online beer forumites.

"Currently, I culture my own yeasts, to the extent of reviewing the cultures through a 1500x microscope in search of contaminants, and in sheer admiration! I have been called upon by fellow homebrewers to analyze beer samples for defects, and I have consulted in the opening/remodeling of brewpubs and homebrew supply shops. I perform demonstrations for whatever group wishes to have one, usually outside local homebrew shops to celebrate National Homebrew Day and Oktoberfest. I grow hops in my yard. From what I had learned from reading on hop cultivation, I was able to harvest a useable crop of hops that first year—something the experts say cannot be done."

Pat says there are many different types of homebrewers. Some brew to save money. Some stick with simple kits and a couple of standard recipes. Some are competitive perfectionists. Most approach brewing as an art or a science, or a combination of the two.

"Most brewers I've encountered are at least college graduates," Pat concludes. "Many hold advanced degrees. And most are no less than fascinated by the brewing process—the chemistry, biology, history, or the act of brewing itself."

THIRTEEN
Beer Bars and Brewpubs

WHAT MAKES A good bar? To us, the first of many criteria is that it has good beer. There are many other factors, of course—location, atmosphere, staff, service, prices, music, food and so on. It would be impossible to list all the good joints in America—especially since so many brewpubs are sprouting up across the country, typically a dozen or more each month. In addition, many longtime bars are becoming good beer bars, putting in new draft lines and adding new craft beers to their menus.

Sadly, we haven't been in all these bars and brewpubs, but we have been in many of them. For every establishment listed, we do know at least one person who has been there—in some cases a lot of different people. Many of these people are Internet correspondents who so graciously share their knowledge and astute observations in online forums. Many are also personal acquaintances and friends, notably Stan Hieronymus and Daria Labinsky, the Beer Travelers (see page 30). Check their publications, on and off line, for the latest and more extensive information on good beer in any particular area.

As usual, we're sorry for the many good places we've left out. In towns like Seattle, Denver or Portland (both Oregon and Maine), we couldn't list every good place simply because there are so many good places. Just because we've overlooked a bar or brewpub doesn't mean that it won't serve good beer or food or both. We've included the phone numbers for each establishment, in the hopes that you'll call a place before going very far out of your way looking for good beer, just to make sure they're still there and still serving good beer. Hey, stuff happens, even to good beer places.

ALABAMA

Magic City Brewery
420 21st Street South
Birmingham AL
205-328-2739
In a registered historic landmark building.

Port City Brewery
225 Dauphin
Mobile AL
334-438-2739
Pretty brick and wood pub, with brewhouse in the middle.

ALASKA

Gold Rush Saloon
3399 Peger Road
Fairbanks AK
907-586-1000
Two dozen micros on tap, almost as many dart boards.

Humpy's Great Alaskan Ale House
610 West Sixth Avenue
Anchorage AK
907-276-2337
More than forty taps, across from the performing arts center.

ARIZONA

Bandersnatch
125 East Fifth Street
Tempe AZ
602-966-4438
Reportedly the U2 road crew's favorite brewpub in America, and Arizona's first modern-era brewpub, est. 1988.

Beaver Street Brewery & Whistle Stop Cafe
11 S. Beaver Street
Flagstaff AZ
520-779-0079
Beer garden has good views of the mountains.

Coyote Springs Brewing
4883 North 20th Street
Phoenix AZ
602-468-0403
Good beer, good staff. This brewpub has been making beer in a glass-enclosed brewhouse right behind the century-old bar since 1992. Stout cheesecake is a recommended dessert. Also a branch downtown.

Hops! Bistro & Brewery
Fashion Square Mall
7000 East Camelback Road
Scottsdale AZ
602-423-5557
Brewpub that does sixteen mostly lighter styles, usually has five on line, and recommends various trendy pasta dishes with specific beers.

Hops! Bistro & Brewery
Biltmore Fashion Park
2584 East Camelback Road
Phoenix AZ
602-468-0500
Slightly hoppier brews than its sister brewpub (see page 162).

Prescott Brewing Co.
130 W. Gurley Street
Prescott AZ
520-771-2795
Famous for its beer float—porter and vanilla ice cream.

ARKANSAS

Ozark Brewing Co.
430 W. Dickson Street
Fayetteville AR
501-521-2739
Upscale brewpub.

Vino's
923 W. 7th Street
Little Rock AR
501-375-8468
A brewpub with pizza, calzones, nightly entertainment.

CALIFORNIA

Barclay's
5940 College Avenue
Oakland CA
510-654-1650
Specializes in craft brews.

Barney's Beanery
8847 Santa Monica Blvd.
Hollywood CA
213-654-2287
Good for draft micros, celebrity-spotting.

Brewery at Lake Tahoe
3542 S. Lake Tahoe Blvd.
South Lake Tahoe CA
916-544-2739
Small brewpub in an old mission.

Buckhorn Saloon
14081 Highway 128
Boonville CA
707-895-2337
Stylish brewpub serving beer from Anderson Valley Brewing.

Buffalo Bill's
1082 B Street
Hayward CA
510-886-9823
The brewpub founded by Bill Owens, maker of famous Pumpkin Ale and Alimony Ale, the bitterest beer in America.

Burlingame Station
333 California
Burlingame CA
415-344-6050
A good brewpub just north of Palo Alto.

Calistoga Inn
1250 Lincoln Avenue
Calistoga CA
707-942-4101
British-style brewpub with rooms for the night.

Cantina del Cabo
139 G Street
Davis CA
916-756-2226
American Brewer reports sixty-nine beers on tap.

Crown City Brewery
300 S. Raymond
Pasadena CA
818-449-0052
Besides its own beer, several guest beers and lots of bottled micros.

Dempsey's Ale House
50 E. Washington Street
Petaluma CA
707-765-9694
Brewpub known for good beer and spicy Thai and Indian food.

D.P.'s Pub & Grill
3110 Newport Boulevard
Newport Beach CA
714-723-0293
More than one hundred draft beers.

Father's Office
1018 Montana Avenue
Santa Monica CA
310-393-3227
All draft, all craft.

Goat Hill Tavern
1380 Newport Boulevard
Costa Mesa CA
714-548-8428
More than 140 draft lines serving more than 120 different beers.

Gordon Biersch
640 Emerson Street
Palo Alto CA
415-323-7723
The prototype for the growing brewpub chain.

Hogshead Brewing Co.
114 J Street
Sacramento CA
916-443-2739
Lager brewpub.

Jacks at the Cannery
2801 Leavenworth
San Francisco CA
415-931-6400
Biggest jewel in the Jacks chain, with 110 beers on draft.

Jupiter
2181 Shattuck Avenue
Berkeley CA
510-843-8277
The gothic-styled church of beer.

Karl Strauss' Old Columbia Brewery and Grill
1157 Columbia Street
San Diego CA
619-234-2739
Good food, nice old brick building, beer by one of the godfathers of the U.S. good beer revolution.

Lyon's Brewery
7294 San Ramon Road
Dublin CA
510-829-9071
Not a brewpub, but specializes in fresh California microbrews.

Manhattan Beach Brewing Co.
124 Manhattan Beach Blvd.
Manhattan Beach CA
310-798-2744
Brewpub with views of the ocean.

Naja's Place
154 International Boardwalk
Redondo Beach CA
310-376-9951
About eighty tap beers, hundreds of bottles, overlooking the marina.

North Coast Brewing
444 N. Main Street
Fort Bragg CA
707-964-2739
People argue over whether the beer or food is better.

Pig & Whistle
2801 Geary Blvd.
San Francisco CA
415-885-4779
Where the English drink in The City.

Riptide's
310 Fifth Avenue
San Diego CA
619-231-7700
Big, busy ale brewpub in the heart of the Gaslamp District, among the artists' lofts and studios and galleries.

San Andreas Brewing
737 San Benito Street
Hollister CA
408-637-7074
Brewpub in an old creamery, on the fault line, with six to seven of its own beers on tap and a decent, inexpensive restaurant.

St. Stan's Brewery & Restaurant
821 L Street
Modesto CA
209-524-4782
Large brewpub with six different beers on tap at all times.

Sudwerk Privatbrauerei Hubsch
2001 Second Street
Davis CA
916-756-2739
Big German-style brewpub, both beer and food.

Terrific Pacific
721 Grand Avenue
Pacific Beach CA
619-270-3596
Suburban San Diego brewpub known for a powerful Doppel Hefeweizen, and for $1 beers every time a fire truck from the station across the street goes out with sirens blaring.

Toronado
547 Haight Street
San Francisco CA
415-863-2276
More than forty taps in the heart of Haight-Ashbury.

Twenty Tank Brewing
316 11th Street
San Francisco CA
415-255-9455
*Look for the big neon mug
outside.*

**The White Cockade Public
House**
18025 State Highway 9
Boulder Creek CA
408-338-7882
*Cozy Scottish pub in a log cabin
in the middle of a redwood
forest.*

COLORADO

Breckenridge Brewery & Pub
600 South Main Street
Breckenridge CO
303-453-1550
*Good brewpub at the bottom of
the ski resort. Also a branch in
Denver.*

Carvers Bakery Cafe Brewery
1022 Main Avenue
Durango CO
970-259-2545
*A combination brewpub and
bakery.*

Champion Brewing
1442 Larimer Street
Denver CO
303-534-5444
*A big ale brewpub in busy
Larimer Square, specializing in
Colorado micros.*

Columbine Mill Brewery
5798 S. Rapp Street
Littleton CO
303-347-1488
*Brewpub in an old grain
elevator, highly praised for ales
and seasonals.*

**CooperSmith's Pub and
Brewing**
5 Old Town Square
Fort Collins CO
970-498-0483
*Great for people-watching on the
square. Excellent beer, food.*

**Denver Chop House &
Brewery**
1735 19th Street
Denver CO
303-296-0800
*Upscale ornament of the Rock
Bottom brewpub chain.*

Mountain Sun Pub & Brewery
1535 Pearl Street
Boulder CO
303-546-0866
*A nice mix of its own beers and
other people's.*

Mountain Valley Tap Tavern
167 N. College Avenue
Fort Collins CO
970-484-4974
*More than two dozen taps, many
more micros in bottles.*

Oasis Brewery & Restaurant
1095 Canyon Boulevard
Boulder CO
303-449-0363
A brewpub with nice vistas of the mountains.

Old Chicago Bar & Restaurant
1102 Pearl Street
Boulder CO
303-443-5031
This is the first of the fine chain with good draft and bottle selections in two dozen locations.

Phantom Canyon Brewpub
2 East Pikes Peak Avenue
Colorado Springs CO
719-635-2800
Upscale brewpub in an historic building.

Rock Bottom Brewery
1001 16th Street
Denver CO
303-534-7616
Flagship of the fast-growing brewpub chain, on the 16th Street pedestrian mall.

Walnut Brewery
1123 Walnut
Boulder CO
303-447-1345
Large brewpub in an old warehouse.

Wynkoop Brewing Co.
1634 18th Street
Denver CO
303-297-2700
The first brewpub, and widely regarded as one of the best, in Colorado. Near Coors Field in northwest downtown ("LoDo" for lower downtown) Denver. Many pro brewers really admire this place.

CONNECTICUT

The Brewhouse
13 Marshall Street
Norwalk CT
203-853-9110
Reasonably priced but classy brewpub attached to New England Brewing Co.

Eli Cannon's Tap Room
695 Main Street
Middletown CT
203-347-3547
Eighteen drafts, spicy food.

Griswold Inn
36 Main Street
Essex CT
203-767-1776
An historic former stagecoach stop and steamboat mooring.

Sam Adams Pub
105 Greenmanville Avenue
Mystic CT
203-536-9649
Upscale restaurant at the seaport.

DELAWARE

Brandywine Restaurant & Brewpub
3801 Kennett Pike
Wilmington DE
302-655-8000
Brewpub in an upscale shopping area, specializing in English-style ales.

Dogfish Head Brewings & Eats
320 Rehoboth Avenue
Rehoboth Beach DE
302-226-2739
Delaware's first brewpub.

Stewart's
219 Governor's Square
Bear DE
302-836-2739
Brewpub in a shopping area twenty minutes south of Wilmington. Golden, pale, amber ales, and a stout, plus specials and seasonals.

DISTRICT OF COLUMBIA

Brickskeller
1523 22nd Street N.W.
Washington DC
202-293-1885
About 650 bottled beers, from under $3 to more than $60 a bottle, on the eight-page beer menu. On the edge of Georgetown, a block from Embassy Row. Beer tastings.

Capitol City Brewing
1100 New York Avenue
Washington DC
202-628-2222
Popular upscale brewpub in an old bus station, for Democrats and Republicans alike. Try an Irish Red here to see what it should really taste like.

My Brother's Place
237 Second Street N.W.
Washington DC
202-347-1350
A restaurant with a good lineup of American microbrews and gourmet imported beer.

FLORIDA

Four Green Fields
205 W. Platt Street
Tampa FL
813-254-4444
Thatched-roof Irish pub.

Hops Grill & Bar
4502 14th Street West
Bradenton FL
813-756-1069
Part of the brewpub chain.

Hubbs
7557 US Hwy 17-92
Fern Park FL
407-834-2337
*Part of the brewpub chain
known for its giant sandwiches.*

**McGuire's Irish Pub &
Brewery**
600 E. Gregory Street
Pensacola FL
904-823-9787
*Brewpub with great beer and
good value in its rabbit warren
of "theme" rooms.*

**The Mill Bakery, Eatery &
Brewery**
330 West Fairbanks Avenue
Winter Park FL
407-644-1544
*Part of the Mill chain in the
Orlando suburbs. There's also a
branch right across from
Universal Studios.*

Sarasota Brewing Co.
6607 Gateway Avenue
Sarasota FL
813-925-2337
*Sports brewpub, great place to
refuel for spring training.*

Shakespeare's Pub & Grill
1015 N.E. 26th Street
Fort Lauderdale FL
305-563-7833
*One of the best of the British
pubs in and around Fort
Lauderdale.*

**South Pointe Seafood House &
Brewing Co.**
One Washington Avenue
Miami Beach FL
305-673-1708
*Pricey but good food, with rustic
decor, water views and good
beer.*

GEORGIA

County Cork Pub
5600 Rosewell Road
Atlanta GA
404-303-1976
*Irish pub with good beer,
burgers and Irish stew.
Specializes in black-and-tans.*

John Harvard's Brew House
3041 Peachtree Road
Atlanta GA
404-816-2739
*Busy brewpub, part of the chain,
in trendy Buckhead.*

Rose & Crown
288 E. Paces Ferry Road
Atlanta GA
404-233-8168
An authentic English pub.

Taco Mac
5830 Roswell Road
Sandy Springs GA
404-257-0735
*On the edge of Atlanta, this is
the crown jewel of a regional
chain of good beer bars, serving
102 different draft beers—not as
many as in the Taco Mac in
Snellville.*

Three Dollar Cafe
I-75, West on Windy Hill Road
Smyrna GA
770-850-0868
*A good range of bottled micros
from across America in the
Atlanta suburbs.*

U.S. Border Brewery Cantina
12460 Crabapple Road
Alpharetta GA
770-772-4400
*Busy brewpub in the Hotlanta
'burbs.*

HAWAII

Ryan's Parkplace Bar & Grill
1200 Ala Moana Boulevard
Honolulu HI
808-523-9132
*Featuring mostly Northwestern
micros.*

IDAHO

Bugatti's Pub
105 S. First Avenue
Sandpoint ID
208-263-4796
Overlooking Lake Pend Oreille.

Capone's
751 N. Fourth Street
Cour D'Alene ID
208-667-4843
Pizza and Northwest craft beers.

Sun Valley Brewing
202 N. Main Street
Hailey ID
208-788-6319
Brewpub specializing in ales.

ILLINOIS

Blind Pig
6 Taylor Street
Champaign IL
217-351-7444
*Popular for music and beer with
University of Illinois crowd.*

Blue Cat Brewpub
113 18th Street
Rock Island IL
309-788-8247
*Brewpub near the Mississippi
River gambling boat.*

Clark Street Ale House
742 N. Clark
Chicago IL
312-642-9253
*Upscale watering spot on the
edge of downtown.*

Edelweiss
7650 W. Irving Park Road
Chicago IL
708-452-6040
*Popular German restaurant that
does beer dinners.*

The Ginger Man
3740 N. Clark
Chicago IL
312-549-2050
*The place to go after (or before)
games at Wrigley.*

Goose Island Brewing Co.
1800 N. Clybourn
Chicago IL
312-915-0071
*Chicago's first modern-era
brewpub, and still one of
America's best. Try something
cask-conditioned, from the
handpumps.*

House of Beer
16 West Division Street
Chicago IL
312-646-2345
*A beer destination in the Rush
Street entertainment district.*

John Barleycorn
658 W. Belden
Chicago IL
312-348-8899
*Artsy pub-restaurant with more
than thirty draft beers.*

The Map Room
1949 N. Hoyne
Chicago IL
312-252-7636
*Antique maps and fresh craft
beer taps, more than twenty of
each.*

Mickey Finn's Brewery
412 N. Milwaukee
Libertyville IL
847-362-2739
*A good brewpub in the Chicago
exurbs.*

Quenchers
2401 N. Western Avenue
Chicago IL
312-276-9730
*Classic neighborhood tavern
with mostly Midwestern micros.*

Sheffield's
3258 N. Sheffield
Chicago IL
312-281-4989
A regular stop for Cubs fans.

Taylor Brewing Co.
200 E. Fifth Avenue
Naperville IL
708-717-8000
*Brewpub in a onetime furniture
factory.*

Indiana

The Ale Emporium
86th & Townline Road
Indianapolis IN
317-879-1212
*Good selection of draft and
bottled micros and imports.*

Bloomington Brewing Co.
1795 E. Tenth Street
Bloomington IN
812-339-2256
Brewpub near the IU campus.

Broad Ripple Brewpub
840 East 85th Street
Indianapolis IN
317-253-2739
*Brewpub with English-style ales
and decor.*

Oaken Barrel
50 N. Airport Parkway
Greenwood IN
317-887-2287
*Large restaurant on the road to
the airport.*

IOWA

Front Street Brewery
208 E. River Drive
Davenport IA
319-332-1569
*Brewpub along the Mississippi
River.*

Old Depot Restaurant
301 S. Tenth Street
Adel IA
515-993-5064
*Brewpub in an old railroad
depot.*

Millstream Brewing
Lower Brewery Road
Amana IA
319-622-3672
*Brewpub amidst the Amish
settlement of the Amana
Colonies.*

The Sanctuary
405 S. Gilbert Street
Iowa City IA
319-351-5692
*Church music, stained glass and
righteous beer.*

KANSAS

Free State Brewing
636 Massachusetts
Lawrence KS
913-843-4555
*Brewpub with a nice beer
garden.*

River City Brewing Co.
150 N. Mosley
Wichita KS
316-263-2739
*Comfortable old setting for a
brewpub.*

KENTUCKY

Bluegrass Brewing Co.
3929 Shelbyville Road
Louisville KY
502-899-7070
Adventurous ale brewpub.

Marikkas German Restaurant
411 Southland Drive
Lexington KY
606-275-1925
*German food, good German beer
to match.*

LOUISIANA

Abita Brewing Co.
72011 Holly Street
Abita Springs LA
504-893-3143
Uses Abita beer in many dishes, such as TurboDog (a dark, malty ale) biscuits. Also Golden, Amber and Purple Haze, a raspberry wheat.

The Bulldog
3236 Magazine Street
New Orleans LA
504-891-1516
One of the best neighborhood bars in a city famous for them, with 50 draft beers, though some locals grumble about suburbanites coming in to drink Lite.

Carrollton Station
8140 Willow Street
New Orleans LA
504-865-9190
Famous live music spot with good beer, right across from the streetcar barn.

Chimes Restaurant and Oyster House
3357 Highland Road
Baton Rouge LA
504-383-1754
Try the oysters with one of the porters, on tap or bottled.

Cooter Brown's
509 S. Carrollton
New Orleans LA
504-866-9104
Great neighborhood tavern with wide beer selection, uptown on the riverbend at the corner of St. Charles, near the levee.

Crescent City Brewhouse
527 Decatur Street
New Orleans LA
504-522-0571
A lager brewpub in Jackson Square, across from the old Jax Brewery (now an upscale shopping mall), that takes advantage of the unrestricted bar opening hours.

Rivershack Tavern
3449 River Road
Jefferson LA
504-835-6933
Overlooking a levee, with a Deep South feel and fine beer and food.

MAINE

Federal Jack's Brew Pub
8 Western Avenue
Kennebunk ME
207-967-4311
Overlooking Kennebunkport Harbor, this is Shipyard's brewpub.

The Great Lost Bear
540 Forest Avenue
Portland ME
207-772-0300
*A welcoming neighborhood
tavern with dozens of New
England microbrews, mostly
from Maine and New Hampshire,
among the fifty-plus beers on
tap.*

Gritty McDuff's
396 Fore Street
Portland ME
207-772-2739
*One of the chain's best and
busiest brewpubs, on the main
street in Portland's historic
district.*

The Moose's Tale
1 Sunday River Road
Bethel ME
207-824-3541
*Sunday River's Golden, IPA, Alt,
Red Ale, Porter, seasonals.*

Morganfield's
121 Centre Street
Portland ME
207-774-5853
*An eclectic music venue,
specializing in draft beer from
Maine micros.*

Sea Dog Brewing Co.
26 Front Street
Bangor ME
207-947-8004
*Part of the brewpub chain,
usually offering eight or more of
its ales.*

Taps
446 Fore Street
Portland ME
207-774-7777
*One of the best beer bars in a
town full of them.*

Theo's Pub
Sugarloaf Mountain ME
207-237-2211
Brewpub convenient for skiers.

MARYLAND

Baltimore Brewing Co.
104 Albermarle Street
Baltimore MD
410-837-5000
*A German restaurant and beer
hall. GABF-winning dunkel and
weizen.*

Cat's Eye Pub
1730 Thames Street
Baltimore MD
410-276-9085
*A music venue in Fells Point,
with a long beer menu.*

Hard Times Cafe
1117 Nelson Street
Rockville MD
301-294-9720
*Part of the chain specializing in
chili and beer.*

Last Chance Saloon
5888-A Robert Oliver Place
Columbia MD
410-730-5656
*More than fifty beers on tap at
this family restaurant in a
shopping center.*

Max's on Broadway
737 S. Broadway
Baltimore MD
410-675-6297
More than sixty beers on tap in Fells Point.

Mt. Airy Brewing Co.
233 S. Main Street
Mt. Airy MD
410-795-5557
Brewpub in the old firehouse in Mt. Airy's historic district.

Olde Towne Tavern
227 East Diamond Avenue
Gaithersburg MD
301-948-4200
Montgomery County's first brewpub, with rooftop terrace dining.

Ollie's Pub
106 21st Street
Ocean City MD
410-289-6317
A combination bar and package store, with more than seven hundred beers.

Racer's
7732 Harford Road
Parkville MD
410-882-5212
Good selection of micros amid auto-racing decorations in the northeast Baltimore suburbs, with a blackboard bearing info about each draft beer and free pretzels and peanuts. One of Sebbie Buhler's favorites.

Ram's Head Tavern
33 West Street
Annapolis MD
410-268-4545
A nice tavern serving beers from the Fordham Brewing Co., a contract brewer, and a bevy of other beers, too.

Sisson's
36 East Cross Street
Baltimore MD
410-539-2093
Baltimore's first brewpub, and still one of the best. Occasional beer dinners.

The Wharf Rat
204 West Pratt
Baltimore MD
410-244-8900
Popular brewpub in an iron-front building near Camden Yards. Northern Bitter is a classic ESB.

The Wharf Rat
801 S. Ann
Baltimore MD
410-276-9034
With thirty-plus drafts, maybe the best bar in Fells Point, a neighborhood full of good bars.

MASSACHUSETTS

Boston Beer Works
61 Brookline Avenue
Boston MA
617-536-2337
Huge brewpub next to Fenway Park.

Brewhouse Cafe & Grill
199 Cabot Street
Lowell MA
508-937-2690
Brewpub on three floors of an old textile mill.

Cambridge Brewing Co.
1 Kendall Square
Cambridge MA
617-494-1994
Ale brewpub in a shopping area.

Commonwealth Brewing
138 Portland Street
Boston MA
617-523-8383
Famous for its porter, this English-style brewpub is one of the best in a town now known for beer as much as beans.

Coolidge Corner Clubhouse
307 Harvard Avenue
Brookline MA
617-566-4948
Sports bar with lots of TV sets, even more good beers.

F.J. Doyle & Co.
3438 Washington Avenue
Jamaica Plain MA
617-524-2345
Perenially Boston's favorite neighborhood bar. Irish, of course, with plenty of character and characters.

John Harvard's Brew House
33 Dunster Street
Boston MA
617-868-3585
First location for this brewpub chain that does both ale and lager.

Redbones
55 Chester Street
Somerville MA
617-628-2200
Two dozen regional craft brews on draft, barbecue and Southern food in the Somerville section of town, with high-class beer tastings and dinners, many featuring hard-to-find Northwest micros.

Sam Adams Brewhouse
710 Boylston Street
Boston MA
617-421-4961
Not a brewpub, serving only Samuel Adams labels.

Sunset Grill and Tap
130 Brighton Avenue
Boston MA
617-254-1331
More than one hundred draft beers, more than four hundred bottles. At Christmas, a tremendous selection of microbrewed seasonals on tap.

MICHIGAN

Ashley's
338 S. State Street
Ann Arbor MI
313-996-9191
A University of Michigan favorite.

Berkley Front
3087 W. 12-Mile Road
Berkley MI
810-547-3331
Fifty draft lines, mostly given over to American micros, in the northern Detroit suburbs. No smoking, no grilled or fried foods, for fear of hurting the beer.

Butch's Dry Dock
44 E. Eighth Street
Holland MI
616-396-8227
Dozens of beers, even more sandwiches on the menu.

Cadieux Cafe
4300 Cadieux
Detroit MI
313-882-8560
Good Belgian food (mussels, of course, and blackened tuna) and Belgian beer, in a decent neighborhood. Includes a "feather" bowling alley with dirt lanes.

The Corner Bar
1030 E. Vine Street
Kalamazoo MI
616-385-2028
Great beer, and a great collection of brewphernalia.

Eccentric Cafe
315 E. Kalamazoo
Kalamazoo MI
616-382-2338
The house bar for the Kalamazoo Brewing Co. A good place to talk, with a fish tank instead of a TV.

Tom's Oyster Bar
15016 Mack Avenue
Grosse Pointe Park MI
313-822-8664
A raw bar with a nice selection of American micros and imports.

Traffic Jam and Snug
511 W. Canfield
Detroit MI
313-831-9470
Near Wayne State, a popular brewpub with students and faculty.

Ye Olde Tap Room
14915 Charlevoix
Detroit MI
313-331-9154
A nice mix of craft brews on draft, plus more than two hundred bottles.

MINNESOTA

The Black Forest Inn
1 E. 26th Street
Minneapolis MN
612-872-0812
German restaurant with a nice beer garden.

Brit's Pub and Eating Establishment
1110 Nicollet Mall
Minneapolis MN
612-332-3908
Good British pub with grub.

MacKenzie Scotch Pub
918 Hennepin Avenue
Minneapolis MN
612-333-7268
Next door to the Orpheum Theater.

Shannon Kelly's
795 Wabash Street North
St. Paul MN
612-292-0905
Brewpub specializing in ales.

Sherlock's Home Brewery
11000 Red Circle Drive
Minnetonka MN
612-931-0203
Authentic English pub, down to the handpumps, southwest of Minneapolis.

Sweany's Saloon
96 N. Dale Street
St. Paul MN
612-221-9157
Repeat winner in voting for the city's best neighborhood tavern.

MISSOURI

Blueberry Hill
6504 Delmar Avenue
St. Louis MO
314-727-0880
Good beer amid old rock memorabilia and music.

Dressel's
419 N. Euclid Avenue
St. Louis MO
314-361-1060
Refined Welsh pub with classical music on the sound system.

Flat Branch Brewing Co.
115 S. Fifth Street
Columbia MO
314-449-0400
A brewpub that does a wide range of its own beers.

75th Street Brewery
520 75th Street
Kansas City MO
816-523-4677
An ale brewpub.

St. Louis Brewery Tap Room
2100 Locust Street
St. Louis MO
314-241-2337
Right in the brewery, you can watch them make the beer you're drinking.

MONTANA

Golden Spur
1014 S. Hanes Avenue
Miles City MT
406-232-3544
*Pub connected to the Milestown
Brewing Co.*

Iron Horse Brewpub
100 Railroad Street
Missoula MT
406-721-8705
*In an old train station, this
brewpub specializes in German
styles.*

The Rhinoceros
158 Ryman Street
Missoula MT
406-721-6061
*Probably the best bar in the
state, with fifty taps.*

Spanish Peaks Brewing Co.
120 N. 19th Avenue
Bozeman MT
406-585-2296
Italian food and a range of ales.

NEBRASKA

**Crane River Brewpub and
Cafe**
200 N. 11th Street
Lincoln NE
402-476-7477
*Downtown brewpub that does
both ales and lagers.*

Dubliner Pub
1205 Harney
Omaha NE
402-342-5887
*Good Irish pub, with a variety of
imported beers on two dozen
taps.*

Jones Street Brewing Co.
1316 Jones Street
Omaha NE
402-344-3858
*Busy ale brewpub with a
hickory-fired grill in an old
factory. Takeout available in
gallons or half-gallons.*

Lazlo's Brewery and Grill
710 P Street
Lincoln NE
402-474-2337
*Ale brewpub in the old
warehouse district.*

NEVADA

Great Basin Brewing Co.
846 Victorian Avenue
Sparks NV
702-355-7711
*Brewpub that concentrates on
ales.*

**Holy Cow! Casino Cafe and
Brewpub**
2423 Las Vegas Boulevard
Las Vegas NV
702-732-2697
*Decent brewpub with slot
machines galore.*

Mad Dogs & Englishmen
515 S. Las Vegas Boulevard
Las Vegas NV
702-382-2528

*Pub with a range of imports,
open twenty-four hours.*

NEW HAMPSHIRE

Italian Oasis & Brewery
127 Main Street
Littleton NH
603-444-6995
*Skiers' hangout with an Italian
menu and unfiltered ales.*

Martha's Exchange
185 Main Street
Nashua NH
603-883-8781
*Brewpub with a speakeasy feel
and motif, down to the Al
Capone IPA.*

Seven Barrel Brewery
Plainfield Road
West Lebanon NH
603-298-5566
*On the Vermont border, an
impressively designed brewpub.*

Stark Mill Brewery
500 Commercial Street
Manchester NH
603-622-0000
Big busy brewpub.

Winnipesaukee Pub & Brewery
546 Main Street
Laconia NH
603-527-1300
*Brewpub offering its own beer
and a range of guest beers.*

NEW JERSEY

Andy's Corner
265 Queen Anne Road
Bogota NJ
201-342-9887
*George Gray's good
neighborhood local, favored by
the* Ale Street News *folks.*

Antone's Grill and Pub
112 South Avenue
East Cranford NJ
908-276-3414
*More than thirty draft beers.
Exits 136-137 off the Garden
State Parkway.*

Front Porch
217 Wagaraw Road
Hawthorne NJ
201-427-4331
*In an old house in a middle-
class North Jersey suburb of
New York.*

Long Valley Pub and Brewery
1 Fairmount Road
Long Valley NJ
908-876-1122
*Good multi-level brewpub in an
old barn. Porter is the specialty.*

Old Bay Restaurant
61-63 Church Street
New Brunswick NJ
908-246-3111
*Cajun cookin' and lots of good
beer. Highly recommended.*

Ship Inn
61 Bridge Street
Milford NJ
201-995-7007
*New Jersey's first brewpub, an
English-style brewpub that makes
its own English-style ales.
English-style food, and a
Ringwood brewing system.*

Triumph Brewing Co.
138 Nassau Street
Princeton NJ
609-924-7855
*Good upscale brewpub, steps
from Princeton, that's popular
with Ivy Leaguers.*

NEW MEXICO

Billy's Long Bar
4800 San Mateo N.E.
Albuquerque NM
505-889-6400
*Pizza place with half a dozen of
its own beers on tap, plus forty-
some guest beers.*

Brewster's Pub
312 Central Avenue S.W.
Albuquerque NM
505-247-2533
*Live music and more than two
dozen taps at this downtown
nightspot.*

Embudo Station
US Hwy 68
Embudo NM
505-852-4707
*Brewpub in a former rail depot
overlooking the Rio Grande.*

Evangelo's
200 W. San Francisco Street
Santa Fe NM
505-982-9014
*Known for its wide selection of
bottled beer.*

O'Ryan's Tavern & Brewery
700 S. Telshor Boulevard
Las Cruces NM
505-522-8191
*Large ale brewpub fitted out like
the Old West.*

Rio Bravo Brewing Co.
515 Central Avenue N.W.
Albuquerque NM
505-242-6800
*An upscale brewpub on old
Route 66.*

Adobe Blues
63 Lafayette Avenue
Staten Island NY
718-720-BLUE
*A huge selection of bottled beer,
and very good Mexican food.*

Brewsky's
43 East 7th Street
New York NY
212-420-0671
*Small space, but many micros.
Check out Burp Castle next door
(below).*

Burp Castle
41 East 7th Street
New York NY
212-982-4576.
*An upscale temple of beer, where
monks serve quality European
brews. Next door to Brewsky's
(above).*

Cafe Centro Beer Bar
MetLife Building, 200 Park
Avenue
New York NY
212-818-1333
*Yupscale, suit-and-tie lunch and
after-work destination for food,
beer and meeting people.*

Cafe de Bruxelles
118 Greenwich Avenue
New York NY
212-206-1830
*Maybe the best Belgian
restaurant in America, with beer
to match.*

Clark's Ale House
122 West Jefferson Street
Syracuse NY
315-479-9859
*Ray Clark serves his own beer,
among other micros, on twenty-
six taps. Aiming to be a "beer
drinkers' paradise," the place
has no mixed drinks and does
not allow tipping.*

Chumley's
86 Bedford Street
New York NY
212-675-4449
*A former speakeasy that retains
the feel, but with lobster specials
and lots of micros on draft.*

Company B's
206 Route 303
Orangeburg NY
914-365-6060
*A sprawling suburban restaurant
with more than fifty draft lines,
almost all micros.*

d.b.a. 41 first avenue
41 First Avenue
New York NY
212-475-5097
*An East Village landmark for
good beer, including cask-
conditioned on handpumps.*

Dr. Finley's Publick House
43 Green Street
Huntington Village NY
516-351-3440
*A large modern restaurant with
lots of English beer and
American micros.*

East Side Ale House
961 Second Avenue
New York NY
212-752-3615
*No-nonsense Midtown bar
specializing in American micros.*

Ginger Man
11 East 36th Street
New York NY
212-532-3740
*Classy, expensive, sixty-six draft
beers, ninety bottles, raw oysters,
good cigars.*

Heartland Brewpub
35 Union Square West
New York NY
212-645-3400
*Good American food with a nice
range of well-brewed beer.*

Highlander Brewery
Third Avenue at 17th Street
New York, NY
212-979-7268
*A brewpub doing authentic
English cask-conditioned ales on
the site of an old German beer
hall and the late, lamented Fat
Tuesday's. Say hey to Nick and
Stuart, the young English
brothers who run the joint.*

Holmes & Watson
450 Broadway
Troy NY
518-273-8526
*More than three hundred bottles,
plus a nice range of drafts.*

James Bay Brewing Co.
154 West Broadway
Port Jefferson NY
516-928-2525
*A good brewpub on Long Island,
overlooking the harbor.*

Kinsale Tavern
1672 Third Avenue
New York NY
212-348-4370
*Part Irish pub, part
neighborhood tavern, a big
selection of micros and imports
on the Upper East Side.*

MacGregor's Grill & Tap
7408 Pittsford-Palmyra Road
Perinton NY
716-425-7260
*Three dozen taps in the first bar
in this mini-chain.*

Mahar's Public Bar
1110 Madison Avenue
Albany NY
518-459-7868
*A small bar with fifty draft beers,
micros and imports most of the
year, but it cuts back to twenty-
five during the summer.*

Mountain Valley Brewpub
US Hwy 202
Suffern NY
914-357-0101
*Near the Jersey border, with a
good separate dining room and
great Ruffian Porter. Say hey to
Lon Lauterio, proprietor and
director of sales/distribution.*

Mugs Alehouse
125 Bedford Avenue
Brooklyn NY
718-384-8494
*A friendly Williamsburg bar near
the Brooklyn Brewery.*

North Star Pub
93 South Street
New York NY
212-509-6757
*The best English pub in
Manhattan.*

Park Slope Brewery
356 6th Avenue
Brooklyn NY
718-788-1756
*Ask owner-brewer Steve Deptula
to show you the brewhouse he
welded together.*

Peculier Pub
145 Bleecker Street
New York NY
212-353-1327
*Big wooden booths, more than
three hundred beers, tips are
included in the price of beer.*

Pugsley's Pub
Washington & Albany Streets
New York NY
212-385-4900
*This tiny "micro pub" near the
World Trade Center has a great
draft lineup, but is not open on
weekends.*

**Original Saratoga Springs
Brewpub**
14 Philadelphia Street
Saratoga NY
518-583-3209
*Reliable reports from hopheads
give it a thumbs-up.*

Silver Swan
41 East 20th Street
New York NY
212-254-3611
*A Manhattan secret: terrific
German food, and a fine
international beer menu.*

Southampton Publick House
40 Bowden Square
Southampton NY
516-283-2800
*Jim and Maureen Sullivan
opened the East End's first
brewpub in the summer of 1996
in an historic old inn and former
speakeasy. The emphasis is on
classic beers brewed "true to
style."*

Waterfront Ale House
136 Atlantic Avenue
Brooklyn NY
718-522-3794
*Also called Pete's Waterfront,
with good grilled food and a
great beer lineup.*

Zip City
3 West 18th Street
New York NY
212-366-6333
*A big, good-looking brewpub
with inspired food menus and a
beer menu specializing in
German styles.*

NORTH CAROLINA

Carolina Brewery
460 W. Franklin St.
Chapel Hill NC
919-942-1800
*Good food, like sausage po boys
and artichoke beer cheese
rarebit. Even better beer. Great
beer dinners.*

Cottonwood Grille and Brewery
122 Blowing Rock Road
Boone NC
704-264-7111
*Possibly the smallest commercial
brewhouse in America, but great
beer from Kinney Baughman,
who brought home a lot of good
beer knowledge from his days as
a pro basketball player in
Belgium. Try the Framboise.*

42nd Street Oyster Bar and Seafood Grill
Jones & West Streets
Raleigh NC
910-831-2811
*Rambling dark-wood seafood
joint with long tables, tall stools
and lots of good beer.*

Front Street Brewpub
9 Front Street
Wilmington NC
910-251-1935
Popular night (and day) spot.

Greenshields Pub and Brewery
214 East Martin Street
Raleigh NC
919-829-0214
*Open since 1989, recently
expanded.*

Groundhog Tavern
149 East Franklin St.
Chapel Hill NC
919-929-4963
*Eight drafts and more than fifty
beers overall.*

Olde Hickory Brewpub
2828 Highway 79 West
Hickory NC
704-327-2743
*Beers made with nearby
mountain spring water.*

Ricci's
Lakewood Shopping Center
Durham NC
919-493-0910
*Chicago-style pizza, many
micros, cigar friendly.*

Satisfactions
Brightleaf Square
Durham NC
919-682-7397
*A Duke sports bar with big
screens and lots of draft micros.*

Smoky Mountain Brewery
91 Stamey Cove Road
Waynesville NC
704-648-4755
Brewpub off to a promising start.

Southend Brewery and Smokehouse
2100 South Blvd.
Charlotte NC
704-358-4677
*Regional cuisine, with 350 seats
inside and more on the patio.*

Spring Garden Brewing Co.
5804 Hunt Club Road
Greensboro NC
910-547-8277

A popular restaurant that added a brewery in 1991.

NORTH DAKOTA

Downtowner's Pub & Grill
301 Third Avenue North
Fargo ND
701-232-8851
A dozen micros and gourmet imported beers.

Old Broadway Restaurant & Pub
22 Broadway
Fargo ND
701-237-6161
Brewpub in the middle of town.

OHIO

Barrelhouse Brewing Co.
22 E. 12th Street
Cincinnati OH
513-421-2337
Brewpub offering both ales and lagers, near Main Street Brewing Co.

Great Lakes Brewing Co.
2516 Market Street
Cleveland OH
216-771-4466
The brewpub connected to this brewery that distributes fine beers regionally.

Hoster Brewing Co.
550 S. High Street
Columbus OH
614-228-6066
Big brewpub in a former repair shop for streetcars. Ales and lagers.

Hubb's
3101 LaGrange Street
Toledo OH
419-243-7238
More than three dozen draft lines in this link in the Florida-based chain.

Liberty Brewing Co.
1238 Weathervane Lane
Akron OH
216-869-2337
Cajun cookin' and award-winning beers at this brewpub.

Main Street Brewing
1203 Main Street
Cincinnati OH
513-665-4677
Big and busy upscale ale brewpub, just north of 12th Street, near Barrelhouse. Excellent, award-winning stout.

McGuffy's House of Draft
5418 Burkhardt Road
Dayton OH
513-254-0173

More than forty beers on draft.

OKLAHOMA

Bricktown Brewery
1 N. Oklahoma Avenue
Oklahoma City OK
405-232-2739
Ale brewpub in a brick building in Bricktown.

Interurban Brewing
105 W. Main Street
Norman OK
405-364-7942
Brew in the old downtown train depot.

Norman Brewing Co.
102 W. Main Street
Norman OK
405-360-5726
Big ale brewpub with good food.

Tulsa Brewing Co.
7227 S. Memorial Drive
Tulsa OK
918-459-2739
Impressive space for this ale brewpub.

OREGON

Bend Brewing Co.
1061 N.W. Brooks Street
Bend OR
503-383-1599
Nice brewpub in a pretty, pleasant riverside setting.

Bogart's Northwest
406 N. 14th Street
Portland OR
503-222-4986
Two dozen regional micros on draft, plus a small raft of bottles.

Bombs Away Cafe
2527 Monroe
Corvallis OR
503-757-7221
Mexican food and a good lineup of regional craft brews.

Bridgeport Brewery
1313 W. Marshall
Portland OR
503-241-7179
Great pizza, great beer in an old warehouse. Maybe Portland's best brewpub. Try the Pintail ESB, Blue Heron Pale Ale, XXX Stout. Try everything.

Cascade Microbrewery & Firehouse Pub
3529 Fairview Industrial Way S.E.
Salem OR
503-378-0737
A brewpub that offers its own beer, and thirty-plus regional guest micros.

Coyote's Cafe
2809 N.E. Sandy Boulevard
Portland OR
503-234-8573
*Comfortable place with more
than two dozen Northwest craft
beers on draft.*

**Deschutes Brewery and Public
House**
1044 N.W. Bond Street
Bend OR
503-382-9242
*The brewpub corner of one of
America's best microbreweries.*

Dublin Pub
6821 N.W. Beaverton-Hillside
Portland OR
503-297-2889
*Irish pub known for folk music
and 104 beers on tap.*

Eugene City Brewery
844 Olive Street
Eugene OR
503-345-8489
*A good brewpub in a great beer
town.*

**Full Sail Tasting Room and
Pub**
506 Columbia Street
Hood River OR
503-386-2281
*Overlooking the Columbia River,
with fresh beer from one of the
top U.S. microbreweries.*

Gemini Pub
456 N. State Street
Lake Oswego OR
503-994-7238
Two dozen regional draft beers.

Grub Street Grill
35 N. Central Avenue
Medford City OR
503-779-2635
*Kid-friendly bar with a nice
selection of regional micros.*

Horse Brass Pub
4534 SE Belmont
Portland OR
503-232-2202
Traditional English pub.

Laurelthirst
2958 N.E. Glisan Street
Portland OR
503-232-1504
*Local tavern in a pretty
neighborhood, with live music.
Good for breakfast, too.*

McMenamins
6179 S.W. Murray Road
Beaverton OR
503-644-4562
*One of the best in the chain of
dozens of good bars and
brewpubs, many of them in
Portland.*

Mount Hood Brewpub
87304 Government Camp Loop
Government Camp OR
503-272-3724
*Popular among skiers looking
for good fresh ale.*

The Pilsner Room
0309 S.W. Montgomery
Portland OR
503-220-1865
*Upscale restaurant with beer
from Full Sail, next door.*

Portland Brewing Brewpub
1339 N.W. Flanders
Portland OR
503-222-7150
Nice-looking brewpub with half a dozen ales or more.

Produce Row Cafe
204 S.W. Oak
Portland OR
503-232-8355
One of the best beer bars in maybe the best good beer town in America, on the southeast Portland waterfront, with a fabulous steak sandwich, according to Kevin Odell.

Rogue Brewery & Public House
31-B Water Street
Ashland OR
503-488-5061
A pizza place that is also the brewpub for the prestigious Rogue beers.

PENNSYLVANIA

Brigid's
726 N. 24th Street
Philadelphia PA
215-232-3232
Belgian farmhouse food and beer.

Chiodo's Tavern
107 W. Eighth Avenue
Homestead PA
412-461-3113
In the suburbs, next to the Homestead High-Level Bridge, with a large selection of beer. Still a shot-and-beer place, but with good beer now.

City Tavern
132 S. Second Street
Philadelphia PA
215-413-1443
Re-creation of a colonial-era dining room, with a small but impressive selection of beer.

Copa, Too!
263 S. 15th Street
Philadelphia PA
215-735-0848
Perennial winner of award for Philly's best sports pub.

Dawson Street Pub
100 Dawson Street
Manayunk PA
215-482-5677
Good selection of draft and bottled micros and imports.

Dickens Inn
421 S. Second Street
Philadelphia PA
215-928-9307
Historic tavern with a pleasing choice of imported beer on draft.

Dock Street Brewery and Restaurant
2 Logan Square
Philadelphia PA
215-496-0413
Upscale brewpub connected to a fine Eastern microbrewery. Drink a bit of history with Thomas Jefferson Ale, made to the great man's recipe.

Elmer's Suds
475 E. Northhampton
Wilkes-Barre PA
717-825-5286
Unpretentious eatery with a decent selection of micros and imports.

Farmhouse Restaurant
1449 Chestnut Street
Emmaus PA
610-967-6225
Known for elegant beer dinners hosted by John "The Malt Advocate" Hansell.

Fat Head's South Shore Saloon
1805 E. Carson
Pittsburgh PA
412-431-7433
An extensive selection of craft beer, on draft and in bottles.

Flanigan's Boathouse
113 Fayette Street
Conshohocken PA
610-828-BOAT
Twenty-six drafts in the Philadelphia suburbs.

Hoppers Brewpub
123 West 14th Street
Erie PA
814-452-2787
Classy restaurant in an old train station, connected to a craft brewery.

Jack's Firehouse
2130 Fairmount Avenue
Philadelphia PA
215-232-9000
Neighborhood restaurant in an old firehouse, with beer from Stoudt's.

Khyber Pass
54 S. Second Street
Philadelphia PA
215-440-9683
Nice beer menu, including some labels you don't see everywhere in the East.

Lancaster Malt Brewing Co.
Plum & Walnut Streets
Lancaster PA
717-391-MALT
Munich on the Conestoga, and several Heart Institute-approved items on the food menu.

Mad Mex
370 Atwood Street
Pittsburgh PA
412-681-5656
Near Pitt, with probably the broadest selection of micros in town. There's an upscale version in suburban North Hills. Cal-Mex food.

McGillin's Old Ale House
1310 Drury Lane
Philadelphia PA
215-735-5562
Revolutionary-era downtown tavern with good beer.

Northeast Taproom
1101 N. 12th Street
Reading PA
610-372-5248
*Full of weird and eclectic junk—
and good beer.*

Penn Brewery
800 Vinial Street
Pittsburgh PA
412-237-9400
*Modern-era, pretty revival of a
brewpub in a pre-Prohibition
brewery, specializing in German-
style lagers.*

Samuel Adams Brew House
1516 Sansom Street
Philadelphia PA
215-563-2326
*The first modern-era brewpub in
Philly. If you like hops, try the
IPA—Infamous Pale Ale. Also
gold and amber.*

Sharp Edge Bar
302 S. Saint Clair Street
Pittsburgh PA
412-661-3537
*Small bar with a big beer list,
including some impressive
Belgians.*

Stoudt's Black Angus
Route 272, P.O. Box 880
Adamstown PA
717-484-4387
*Terrific beef, even better beer.
Carol Stoudt has won lots of
medals at the Great American
Beer Festival. Try the Fest,
Helles, Honey Double Mai-Bock.
Try them all.*

Valley Forge Brewing Co.
267 East Swedesford Road
Wayne PA
610-687-8700
*Nice-sized restaurant in an old
theater in a shopping mall.*

Zeno's Pub
100 West College Avenue
State College PA
814-237-4350
*Serves craft beer to the Penn
State crowd, and beyond.*

RHODE ISLAND

Mews Tavern
279 Main Street
Wakefield RI
401-783-9370
*More than forty tap beers are
offered in what was once a
stable.*

Union Station Brewing
36 Exchange Terrace
Providence RI
401-274-2739
*Brewpub in the former railroad
depot.*

Yesterday's
28 Washington Street
Newport RI
401-847-0125
*Upscale restaurant with more
than thirty draft lines.*

SOUTH CAROLINA

Blue Ridge Brewing
217 N. Main Street
Greenville SC
803-232-4677
Some people think its beers are the best done by any SC brewpub.

Downtown Brewing Co.
18 East North Street
Greenville SC
803-232-4677
A brewpub specializing in German styles.

Hilton Head Brewing Co.
7-C Greenwood Drive
Hilton Head SC
803-785-2739
Pretty resort setting for pretty good local beer and guest micros.

Mike Calder's Pub
288 King Street
Charleston SC
803-577-3818
Irish pub with a broad range of British beers on tap.

SOUTH DAKOTA

Firehouse Brewing Co.
5610 Main Street
Rapid City SD
605-348-1915
Brewpub in, you guessed it, an old fire station.

Sioux Falls Brewing Co.
431 N. Phillips Avenue
Sioux Falls SD
605-332-4847
Upscale brewpub that concentrates on ales.

TENNESSEE

Big River Grille & Brewing Works
222 Broad Street
Chattanooga TN
615-267-2739
Home of the rapidly expanding brewpub chain. The branch in Nashville is famous for its classy billiards room.

Bohannon Brewing Co.
134 Second Street
Nashville TN
615-259-9611
Downtown brewpub in part of a onetime distillery.

Bosco's Pizza Kitchen & Brewery
7615 W. Farmington Road
Germantown TN
901-756-7310
Upscale pizza brewpub in a shopping area.

Smoky Mountain Brewing Co.
474 S. Gay Street
Knoxville TN
615-673-8400
Homey, comfortably cluttered ale brewpub.

Stone Lion Tavern
418 High Street
Chattanooga TN
615-266-5466
Boasts the biggest beer selection in Tennessee.

TEXAS

The Big Easy
5731 Kirby
Houston TX
713-523-9999
Good beer and plenty of Cajun and blues, live or on the system.

Boardwalk Bistro
4011 Broadway
San Antonio TX
210-824-0100
Brewpub that does both ales and lagers and is known for its food.

Copper Tank Brewery
504 Trinity Street
Austin TX
512-478-8444
Brewpub with a beautiful long bar, half a dozen ales on tap.

The Draught Horse
4112 Medical Parkway
Austin TX
512-452-6258
Brewpub that serves literally dozens of other brewers' draft beers, too.

Flying Saucer
111 E. Fourth Street
Fort Worth TX
817-336-7468
Devoted to collections of old plates and new beer, with sixty-five beers on draft.

Fredericksburg Brewing Co.
245 E. Main Street
Fredericksburg TX
210-997-1646
Brew-n-Breakfast? Bed-n-Brew? A good Hill Country brewpub, with twelve quaint rooms to rent.

Ginger Man
304 W. Fourth Street
Austin TX
512-473-8801
Part of the fine upscale chain of beer bars, with eighty good beers on draft.

Hills & Dales Ice House
15403 White Fawn Drive
San Antonio TX
210-695-8309
More than fifty draft beers, more than three hundred bottles.

Houston Brewery
6224 Richmond Avenue
Houston TX
713-953-0101
*Upscale restaurant. Ask
brewmaster Tim Case for a tour.*

Hubcap Brewing Co.
1701 N. Market
Dallas TX
214-651-0808
*Sports bar, maybe the best
brewpub in Dallas. At Christmas,
try their spicy seasonal Rudolph
the Rheinbeer.*

Joey's
2417 N. St. Mary's Street
San Antonio TX
210-733-9573
*Good neighborhood brewpub
with a range of guest micros.*

McGonigal's Mucky Duck
2425 Norfolk Street
Houston TX
713-528-5999
*Probably Houston's best music
spot, and maybe its best beer
bar, too.*

Medieval Inn
7102 Greenville Avenue
Dallas TX
214-363-1114
*More than three dozen taps,
specializing in Texas micros,
with a good happy hour.*

Richmond Arms
5920 Richmond Avenue
Houston TX
713-784-7722
*More than sixty different beers
on tap, sometimes seventy.*

Stan's Blue Note
2908 Greenville
Dallas TX
214-824-9653
*Fifty draft beers, three times as
many in bottles.*

The Strand Brewery
101 23rd Street
Galveston TX
409-763-4500
*Brewpub that concentrates on
German-style lagers.*

Timberwolf Pub
2511 Bissonet
Houston TX
713-526-1705
*Ninety beers on tap in rustic
setting.*

Waterloo Brewing Co.
401 Guadalupe Street
Austin TX
*The first modern-era brewpub in
a town that now has several
good ones.*

UTAH

Desert Edge Brewery
273 Trolley
Salt Lake City UT
801-521-8917
*Brewpub in a former trolley
station, does what it can under
Utah's law limiting beer to 4
percent alcohol by volume.*

Ebenezer's Restaurant
4286 Riverside Road
Ogden UT
801-394-0302
Log cabin brewpub.

Eddie McStiff's
57 S. Main
Moab UT
801-259-2337
Brewpub on the way to or from Arches National Park.

Squatter's Pub Brewery
147 W. Broadway
Salt Lake City UT
801-363-2739
Ale-only brewpub in an old hotel.

Wasatch Brew Pub
250 Main Street
Park City UT
801-645-9500
Utah's first modern-era brewpub.

VERMONT

McNeill's Brewery
90 Elliot Street
Brattleboro VT
802-254-2553
Good little brewpub in an old firehouse. Motto: ''No ferns, food if you need it, incredible beer.''

The Shed
1859 Mountain Road
Stowe VT
802-253-4364
Ale brewpub popular with skiers and locals alike.

Vermont Pub & Brewery
144 College Street
Burlington VT
802-865-0050
Large and busy downtown brewpub.

Ye Olde English Inne
Route 2
Stowe VT
802-253-7558
Goode jointe withe regionale crafte beere.

VIRGINIA

Bardo Rodeo
2000 Wilson Boulevard
Arlington VA
703-527-9399
One of the biggest (seating eight hundred plus), most playful, hoppiest-beer, most adventurous and all-round best brewpubs on the East Coast, with remnants of the former tenant, an Oldsmobile dealership.

Bistro Belgique Gourmande
302 Poplar Alley
Occoquan VA
703-494-1180
*Well-reviewed Belgian restaurant
with many Belgian beers to
match.*

Blue-n-Gold Brewing Co.
3100 Clarendon Blvd.
Arlington VA
703-908-4995
*Creole cuisine, six of their own
beers, ten other local microbrews
on tap. Named after the owner's
pet macaw.*

Blue Ridge Brewing
709 W. Main Street
Charlottesville VA
804-977-0017
*Sports bar/brewpub that does
both ales and lagers. Golden,
Amber, Brown and Stout are
regulars.*

Cobblestone Pub and Brewery
110 N. 18th Street
Richmond VA
804-644-2739
*More than fifty taps, including
Old Dominion's micros. Live
music, Cajun and Jamaican
food, just east of downtown
Richmond.*

Commercial Taphouse & Grill
111 N. Robinson
Richmond VA
804-359-6544
*Classic neighborhood tavern that
has moved to good beer. Also a
Norfolk location. Beer dinners.*

Court Square Tavern
East Jefferson and Fifth
Charlottesville VA
804-296-6111
*Pleasant tavern with a good
local clientele and a decent beer
lineup.*

Galaxy Hut
2711 Wilson Boulevard
Arlington VA
703-276-3099
*A good local bar with fifteen
micros and imports on draft.*

Green Leafe Cafe
765 Scotland Street
Williamsburg VA
804-220-3405
*Unpretentious bar/restaurant
with more than a dozen regional
micros on draft.*

Hard Times Cafe
1404 King Street
Alexandria VA
703-836-5340
*First outpost in this chain of
good-beer restaurants.*

Hero's American Restaurant
9412 Main Street
Manassas VA
703-330-1534
*Good micro menu, including
several regionals, that does beer
tastings.*

The Jewish Mother
3108 Pacific Avenue
Virginia Beach VA
757-422-5430
Deli food and a broad selection of craft beers.

Legend Brewing Co.
321 West 7th Street
Richmond VA
804-232-8871
A brewpub with a nice outdoor patio, serving Legend ales and lagers. Chocolate Porter is a wintertime treat.

Richbrau Brewpub
1214 E. Carey Street
Richmond VA
804-644-3018
Seasonals such as smoked porter and raspberry wheat are served at Richmond's first brewpub, in conjunction with the next-door Queen's Arm Pub.

Ton 80
215 N. Main Street
Blacksburg VA
703-552-3068
Several hundred beers from across America and around the world.

Tuscarora Mill
203 Harrison Street
Leesburg VA
703-771-9300
Good restaurant with several micros on draft in an old grain mill.

Virginia Beverage Co.
607 King Street
Alexandria VA
703-684-5397
A fifteen-minute walk from the Old Town stop on the Metro, this brewpub does some big beers (try the Belgian Brown) to stand up to a menu described as "Tidewater with a Cajun accent."

WASHINGTON

Ale House Pub & Eatery
2122 Mildred Street West
Tacoma WA
206-565-9367
A sports bar with sixty-three beers on draft, according to one count.

Archer Ale House
1212 Tenth Street
Bellingham WA
360-647-7002
Two stars from the Beer Travelers, high praise indeed.

Birkebeiner Brewing
35 W. Main Street
Spokane WA
509-484-0854
Fifteen or more beers on tap, its own and others.

Blue Moon Tavern
712 N.E. 45th Street
Seattle WA
206-545-9775
A comfortable, quirky local legend of a bar, partly because of the good beer.

The Brick
1 Pennsylvania Street
Roslyn WA
509-649-2643
*The bar from the TV series
"Northern Exposure."*

College Inn Pub
4006 University Way N.E.
Seattle WA
206-434-2307
*University of Washington
institution, in a basement with
fifteen draft lines.*

Cooper's Northwest Alehouse
8065 Lake City Way N.E.
Seattle WA
206-789-9691
*Neighborhood tavern with more
than two dozen Northwest
regional micros on tap.*

Elysian Brewing Co.
1221 E. Pike Street
Seattle WA
206-860-1920
*Sebbie Buhler recommends this
place: eight of its own beers,
eight guest beers, and a very
reasonably priced menu matched
to the beers.*

Engine House 9
611 N. Pine Street
Tacoma WA
206-272-3435
*Brewpub, complete with stalls, in
a firehouse dating from the days
when horses pulled engines.*

Fred's Rivertown Ale House
1114 First Street
Snohomish WA 98290
360-568-5820
*An hour northeast of Seattle, and
worth the trip with more than
two dozen taps.*

Front Street Ale House
1 Front Street
Friday Harbor WA
206-378-2337
*Brewpub that requires a ferry
ride to get to it.*

F.X. McCrory
419 Occidental Avenue South
Seattle WA
206-623-4800
*The place for beer and oysters
near the Kingdome.*

Goochi's
104 East Woodin Avenue
Chelan WA 98816
509-682-2436
*Thirty micros on tap in eastern
Washington.*

Grant's Brewery Pub
32 N. Front Street
Yakima WA
509-575-2922
*Started by master brewer Bert
Grant, and serving his masterly
hopped beers.*

Hart Brewery & Pub
91 S. Royal Brougham
Seattle WA
206-682-3377
*One of the best brewpubs
initiated by a regional brewery
anywhere. Stylish.*

Latona Pub
6423 Latona Avenue N.E.
Seattle WA
206-525-2238
*One of the best neighborhood
beer bars in a town that
probably leads the universe in
the category.*

Leavenworth Brewing
636 Front Street
Leavenworth WA
509-548-4545
*Brewpub that does both ales and
lagers under the town's tallest
steeple.*

Milton Tavern
7320 Pacific Hwy. East
Milton WA
206-922-3340
*Nonsmoking bar with more than
thirty micros on tap.*

The Swiss
1904 Jefferson
Tacoma WA
206-572-2821
*Good food, more than thirty taps
for Northwest micros.*

Trolleyman Pub
3400 Phinney Avenue North
Seattle WA
206-548-8000
*The brewpub connected to the
Redhook brewery.*

Virginia Inn
1937 First Avenue
Seattle WA
206-728-1937
*One of the oldest, best-known
and best-loved bars in Seattle.*

WEST VIRGINIA

West Virginia Brewing Co.
1291 University Avenue
Morgantown WV
304-296-2739
An ale-and-lager brewpub, the
*first in the state, with a food
menu featuring fresh pasta.
Closed Mondays.*

WISCONSIN

Angelic Brewing Co.
322 W. Johnson Street
Madison WI 53703
608-257-2707
Tuna steak sandwiches, thick-cut
*fries, beer styles from Bacchanal
Blonde to Shakedown Nut Brown
to Skinner's Stout.*

Brewmasters Pub
4017 80th Street
Kenosha WI
414-694-9050
Brewpub that makes lagers in a
former stable. Shawn Quigley,
the head brewer, is into beer
dinners.

Capital Brewery Beer Garden
7734 Terrace Avenue
Middleton WI
608-836-7100
Next to brewery in Madison
suburbs, open only on summer
weekends.

Dos Bandidos Restaurant
1004 S. Old Oneida Street
Appleton WI
414-731-3322
Brewpub with a Mexican menu.

Dotty Dumpling's Dowry
116 N. Fairchild
Madison WI
608-255-3175
Mad City hamburger mecca near
the University of Wisconsin.

Gasthaus zur Krone
839 S. Second Street
Milwaukee WI
414-647-1910
German restaurant with big beer
selection (five hundred labels),
including drafts from two good
local microbreweries, Lakefront
and Sprecher's.

Great Dane Pub & Brewing
123 Doty Street
Madison WI
608-284-0000
Busy downtown brewpub,
popular with state workers and
politicians.

Karl Ratzch's
320 E. Mason Street
Milwaukee WI
414-276-2720
Our favorite German place in a
town that's famous for them.

Porta Bella
425 N. Frances
Madison WI
608-256-3186
Landmark town/gown Italian
place, which has added lots of
draft micros.

Port of Hamburg
5937 S. Howell Avenue
Milwaukee WI
414-747-9151
German food, twenty German
beers on draft.

Puempel's Tavern
18 Sixth Avenue
New Glarus WI
608-527-2045
The unofficial brewpub for New
Glarus Brewing in Wisconsin's
Swiss country.

Quivey's Grove
6261 Nesbitt Road
Fitchburg WI
608-273-4900
*Nice suburban Madison
restaurant with a number of
Wisconsin micros on tap.*

Saz's on State Street
5539 W. State Street
Milwaukee WI
414-453-2410
*Neighborhood tavern with great
barbecued ribs, several
Wisconsin micros on tap.*

Water Street Brewery
1101 N. Water Street
Milwaukee WI
414-271-9560
*Milwaukee's first modern-era
brewpub. Terrific wait staff and
bartenders.*

Homebrew Recipes

Most people who homebrew start off with kits. Those that stick with it often move on to experiment by adding ingredients to kits, and then gathering all their own ingredients and working without a kit. In this section we're aiming to provide the intermediate-level homebrewer (with several batches under his/her belt) with some helpful hints and good recipes for a few classic beer styles. For in-depth coverage of homebrewing, we can heartily recommend Charlie Papazian's New Complete Joy of Homebrewing, *among other excellent books.*

GENERAL PRINCIPLES AND PROCEDURES

If your yeast isn't ready to pitch, you're not ready to brew. Your yeast is one of the most important determinants of how your beer will finally turn out, and you need to pitch a sufficient amount of healthy yeast to get a vigorous fermentation and avoid difficulties. Unfortunately, the average package of yeast, whether liquid or dry, usually doesn't provide enough yeast to do the job properly. Yeast requires a little preparation, but it's worth it, and will make a big difference in the quality of your beer.

If you're using dried yeast, you should use two packets rather than one. If you're using a kit that comes with its own yeast, then you should either get another packet of the same yeast from your homebrew shop, or switch yeasts altogether and use the proper amount. Before dried yeast is used, it should be re-hydrated so it can get to work on the wort as soon as you pitch it. This prevents any present bacteria from getting a toehold in your wort while your yeast is busy re-hydrating.

Sterilize a one-quart mason jar, then fill it with hot tap water. Meanwhile, bring a pint of water to a boil in a pot or kettle for five minutes. Dump the hot water out of the mason jar and replace it with about eight ounces of boiled water. Close the lid of the jar, and wait for the liquid inside to return to just above room temperature (75–85 degrees

Fahrenheit). Then open the jar and add two packets of yeast, close the jar and give it a good shake. Let it sit at room temperature for two to three hours before pitching.

If you are using liquid yeast, you should either add two expanded packets of yeast, or better, prepare a yeast starter. To prepare the starter, burst the pack one or two days in advance, so that the pack is already inflated. Prepare a sterile one-quart mason jar, and add three table-spoons of pale dried malt extract. Boil one and a half pints of water for ten minutes, then add a bit more than a pint of it to the jar. Close the jar and, wearing oven mitts (the jar is now very hot, so be careful), give it a good swirl until all the extract dissolves. When the jar returns to room temperature (75 degrees Fahrenheit), open it and add the liquid yeast (the pack should be inflated), directly into the center of the jar. Close the jar and shake it for thirty seconds to aerate the wort. Take a six-inch-square piece of tinfoil, run it briefly through a flame over your stove to sterilize it, open the jar and fit the tinfoil tightly over the mouth of the jar. Do not re-close the jar. Let it sit at room temperature. The next morning (or sooner), you should see clear evidence of fermenta-tion, and the starter is ready to pitch. You now have two or three times as much yeast to work with, which will result in a quicker, cleaner fermentation and better flavor in your beer.

Make sure that all of your equipment is very clean and sterilized shortly before use. Equipment that isn't clean cannot be sterilized, and sterilized equipment will not remain so for more than a few hours.

All of these recipes yield five U.S. gallons. Malt extract references are for the unhopped syrup form. If you wish to use powdered extract, reduce the amount by 20 percent. To use these recipes, you will be steeping crushed (not powdered) grains in your brewing water before adding malt extract. Place the crushed grains in a nylon mesh sack. Heat your brewing water to one hundred and fifty degrees Fahrenheit, then add your grains, turn the heat off and allow the grains to steep for a half hour. (While your grains are steeping, put your cans of liquid extract in a pot or bucket of hot water. This will make the extract much easier to pour later.) Remove the sack of grains, leaving as much of the liquid as possible behind in your pot. If more than a few bits of grain husk have made it into your brewing water, you may want to strain them out; otherwise you may get astringent flavors from the husks when you boil your wort.

Replace any water which was retained by the grains, and then bring your infused brewing water to a boil. Add any gypsum or other brewing salts. Now turn the heat off, and add your extract, stirring well and rinsing all extract from the cans. When you're confident that the extract is entirely dissolved, turn the burner back on, and carefully bring the wort to a strong boil. Do not cover the pot or leave it unattended— boil-overs are very unpleasant, not to mention dangerous. If you cannot achieve a vigorous boil in your pot, you need a bigger one. A simmer will not produce the best results.

Add your first hops as the boil starts. Hop pellets can either be added loose or in a fine nylon mesh bag. (Whole hops or half-ounce hop plugs should be placed in a coarse nylon bag.) If you are using a hop bag, make sure that the hops are submerged in the wort during the boil, and that the wort flows through the bag. Boil for sixty to ninety minutes.

Finishing hops should be added one minute before the end of the boil. Remove any hop bags, recovering as much wort as practicable. If you are using a wort chiller, run the wort off into your sterile fermenter. If you have boiled a concentrated wort, this must be added to cold water that must already be in your fermenter. We recommend closed fermentation in glass carboys. You must be extremely careful with hot wort, and never add it to a glass carboy that is not partially full of cold water; thermal shock can shatter the glass, causing more problems than you want to think about.

If your wort is still too warm (over 80 degrees Fahrenheit) to pitch your yeast, cover the mouth of the carboy with a piece of sterile tinfoil, then either immerse the fermenter in a bath of cold water to cool it, or put it in a running cold shower until the wort temperature falls below 80 degrees Fahrenheit. (Do not place an unsterilized thermometer into your wort when checking temperatures.) Then pitch your yeast through a sterilized funnel. Aerate your wort thoroughly, either by stirring (reversing direction frequently) with a sterile instrument or, if you're up to it, by shaking the fermenter. Fit your airlock, filled with an inch of water or vodka, and move it to a dark area where the temperature is reasonably steady and similar to your fermentation temperature.

Here are some recipes for classic beer styles, all but the last one selected by Garrett. The EIPA and Brown Ale recipes are closely based on his renditions of those classic styles for Brooklyn Brewery, so feel free to sample yours side by side with his. Happy Brewing!

East India Pale Ale (1840s Style)

8 lbs. Munton's Pale Malt Extract
1 lb. Munton, Crisp, or Baird Pale Malt (grain)
6 oz. 90 L (medium) Crystal Malt
3 oz. East Kent Golding or Willamette Hops (at 5 percent alpha for bittering)
1.5 oz. East Kent Golding Hops (finishing)
1.5 oz. East Kent Golding Hops (dry-hopping)
2 tsp. Gypsum (if your water source is very hard, reduce to 1 tsp.)
½ tsp. non-iodized table salt
½ to ¾ cup corn sugar for bottling
An aggressive British Ale yeast, such as Wyeast #1028

Primary fermentation should take a week or less at 66–68°F. Add dry hops when main fermentation is finished, and allow to stand on hops for at least one week. Rack to secondary fermenter if you wish to condition further. Otherwise, bottle and allow to bottle-condition for not less than three weeks.

Original Gravity: 1068 (16.7 Plato)
Finishing Gravity: 1010–1012 (2.5–3 Plato)
ABV: 7.25 percent
Color: Straw
Bitterness: 45 IBU at bottling.

Nut Brown Ale

7 lbs. Munton's (or other British) Pale Malt Extract
¾ lb. 60 L Crystal Malt
½ lb. Chocolate Malt
¼ lb. Roasted Barley
1 level tsp. non-iodized table salt
2 oz. Fuggle or Willamette Hops (at 4.5 percent alpha, for bittering)
1 oz. Fuggle Hops (to finish)
½ cup corn sugar for bottling
British Ale Yeast

Primary fermentation should take a week or less at 65–68°F. Bottle approximately one week after terminal gravity is reached. Racking to secondary is not necessary.

Original Gravity: 1056 (14 Plato)
Finishing Gravity: 1016 (4 Plato)
ABV: 5.3 percent
Color: Deep russet brown
Bitterness: 28 IBU at bottling.

English Best Bitter

6 lbs. Munton's (or other British) Pale Malt Extract
1 lb. Munton's, Crisp, or Baird Pale Malt (grain)
¾ lb. 40 L Crystal Malt
2 oz. Fuggle Hops (at 4.5 percent alpha, for bittering)
1 oz. Fuggle or East Kent Golding Hops (to finish)
½ cup corn sugar for bottling
British Ale Yeast with fruity character, such as Wyeast #1968

Primary fermentation should take six days or less at 64–66°F. Bottle approximately one week after terminal gravity is reached. Racking to secondary is not necessary.

Original Gravity: 1048 (12 Plato)
Finishing Gravity: 1014 (3.5 Plato)
ABV: 4.5 percent
Color: Honey amber
Bitterness: 28 IBU at bottling.

Oktoberfest-Marzen

7 lbs. German Pale Malt Extract
1 lb. German Munich Malt (grain)
½ lb. 90 L Crystal Malt
1 lb. German Carapils Malt (grain)
1.75 oz. Perle Hops (at 5.5 percent alpha, for bitterness)
¾-1 cup Pale Dry Malt Extract for bottling
Bavarian Lager Yeast, such as Wyeast #2206 or #2308

Pitch yeast at 60°F, then gently bring temperature down to fermentation temperature of 52°F. Try your best to maintain temperature between 48° and 54°F. Primary fermentation should take a week to ten days. Ideally, you should then rack to a secondary fermenter and lager for at least three weeks at 34–36°F. If this isn't possible, then condition in secondary at the lowest temperature you can maintain for two to three weeks, during which sulfur characteristics should dissipate.

Original Gravity: 1052-1054 (13.5 Plato)
Finishing Gravity: 1014 (3.5 Plato)
ABV: 5.3 percent
Color: Deep amber
Bitterness: 28 IBU at bottling.

Bavarian Hefeweizen (German Wheat Beer)

6 lbs. German Wheat/Barley Malt Extract
2 lbs. Malted Wheat
½ lb. German Munich Malt
1 oz. Hallertauer Hops (at 4.5 percent alpha, for bittering)
½ tsp. Irish Moss (15 minutes before end of boil)
1 cup corn sugar for bottling
Bavarian Weizen yeast, such as Wyeast #3056

Be careful as you add Irish Moss—it can cause boil-overs. (Reduce heat, add Irish Moss, then re-establish boil slowly.) Pitch yeast at 64°F and allow to rise to 68°F.

Fermentation can be rapid—as little as three or four days. Condition in primary at ambient temperature for one week after end of primary fermentation, then bottle. Bottle-condition for at least two weeks.

Original Gravity: 1052 (13 Plato)
Finishing Gravity: 1012 (3 Plato)
ABV: 5.0 percent
Color: Orange-gold
Bitterness: 18 IBU at bottling.

Classic Strong Stout

8 lbs. Munton's (or other British) Pale Malt Extract
½ lb. Black Malt
½ lb. Black Barley
½ lb. Roasted Barley
½ lb. 90 L Crystal Malt
1 tsp. Calcium Carbonate (optional)
2½ oz. Willamette Hops (at 4.5 percent alpha, for bittering)
1 oz. Cascade Hops (to finish)
½ cup of corn sugar to bottle
A strong, but neutral Ale Yeast such as "Chico," Wyeast #1056

Primary fermentation at 66–68°F should take a week or less. Bottle ten days after fermentation has finished, and bottle-condition for at least two weeks.

Original Gravity: 1060 (15 Plato)
Finishing Gravity: 1016 (4 Plato)
ABV: 5.8 percent
Color: Red-black
Bitterness: 34 IBU at bottling.

Celebration Ale

Finally, here's a recipe, posted on the CompuServe beer forum by Bill Schaefer, that aims to emulate Sierra Nevada Celebration Ale, a winter seasonal favorite:

7 lbs. pale malt extract
1 lb. 30 L crystal malt steeped
1 lb. 50 L crystal malt steeped
1 tsp. Irish Moss @ 60 min.
1 oz. Northern Brewer hop pellets @ 60 min.
1 oz. fresh Centennial hops @ 30 min.
1 oz. fresh Centennial hops @ 10 min.
1 oz. fresh Centennial hops @ the end of the boil

Dry-hop with half-ounce fresh Centennial hops for two weeks in the secondary fermenter.
Wyeast American Ale #1056.
One and one-third cup of light dry malt extract for priming.

Online Resources

WANT TO KNOW where to get a beer in Phoenix? Having a beer dinner and need suggestions on what to serve with the framboise beer for dessert? Want to know when Milwaukee's Lakefront Brewery will roll out its next batch of pumpkin ale? Writing a school report on the brewing industry? Want to start a brewpub yourself? Looking for the perfect recipe for imperial stout? Just want to get in touch with other homebrewers, or people who love to talk beer?

The Internet and various online services have become a tremendous resource for professional brewers, homebrewers and good beer drinkers all over the world. Besides the beer and brewing forums on CompuServe and America Online, Internet providers and Webzines such as Total New York are putting together searchable databases of places to drink good beer. And, of course, there are the Internet newsgroups devoted to beer, particularly *alt.beer,* along with *rec.food.drink.beer* and *rec.crafts.brewing.* The demographics for good beer and online users are almost a direct overlay—well-educated, quality-conscious, etc.—so a high percentage of craft beer fans are Internet users, and vice versa.

There are far too many good beer sites on the World Wide Web to list on these pages, but here is a short list of good all-round references with *clickable links* to hundreds of other sites put up by commercial breweries, brewpubs, homebrew clubs, beer-of-the-month clubs, brewphernalia sellers, beer groups or associations and individual beer drinkers.

Ale Street News On-Line, http://www.alestreetnews.com
    News, features, reviews, resources and other beer links from one of the craft brewing industry's best-known publications.
Alt.Beer FAQ, http://eff.org/~brown/alt.beer.faq
    The Internet newsgroup's archive of frequently asked questions.

Association of Brewers, http://www.aob.org/aob.html
Great research resource for professional or would-be professional brewers. Also the site for Institute for Brewing Studies, American Homebrewers Association, Great American Beer Festival.

The Beer Info Source, http://www.beerinfo.com/~jlock/
One of the best of the many personal beer sites put up by individuals; John Lock has assembled many useful beer resources, references and links.

Beer Travelers, http://www.allaboutbeer.com/beertravelers
Hundreds of listings and brief reviews of North American bars and restaurants that serve good beer.

The Brewery, http://www.alpha.rollanet.org/
Aimed primarily at home brewers.

BreWorld, http:www.breworld.com/
Large professionally oriented British-based site, including job listings.

Campaign for Real Ale, http://www.camra.org.uk
The British-based CAMRA is the world's foremost public-interest group promoting craft brewing.

The LibBEERy, http://www.iii.net/users/rich/libeery/libeery.html
Beer references.

New York City Beer Guide, http://www.nycbeer.org/
News, reviews, events, places to drink in NYC, with good links to other beer sites.

Oktoberfest, http://www.munich.com/oktoberfest
Official site for Munich's annual sixteen-day beer bash.

The Real Beer Page, http://realbeer.com/
One of the largest beer sites on the Internet.

The Virtual Library—Beer, http://www.mindspring.com/~jlock/www-beer.html
Beer references from John Lock.

World Wide Web of Beer, http://www.nycbeer.org/links/reference.html
Great beer references from The New York City Beer Guide.

Beeriodicals

I N SOME FIELDS, those who can't do teach instead. In some fields, those who can't do or teach instead write about it. In the beer world, thankfully, many of those who can do also teach, write, edit and publish. There has been a mini-boom in the world of beer publishing in recent years, with a range of beer magazines, brewspapers and brewsletters in print, from large slick glossies to little sheets that somebody runs off a home computer. Like the microbreweries they cover, many beeriodicals have a local slant. Whatever they cover and however they cover it, the beer press has become a vibrant offshoot of the craft-beer phenomenon, and has become a primary forum—along with online services and the Internet—for learning about good beer and debating the important issues for good beer drinkers. Here are some of the best-known periodicals covering craft beer:

The Advocate, P.O. Box 375, Hayward CA 94543. Phone 813-685-4261. Quarterly published by the Home Wine and Beer Trade Association for retailers.

Ale & Lager Examiner, P.O. Box 275, White Plains NY 10602. Bimonthly brewsletter.

Ale Street News, P.O. Box 1125, Maywood NJ 07607. Phone 201-368-9100. Website: *http://www.alestreetnews.com.* Bimonthly brewspaper covering national/international issues with a focus on New York, New Jersey, Connecticut, Pennsylvania and other Eastern states.

All About Beer, 1627 Marion Avenue, Durham NC 27705. Phone 919-490-0589. E-mail: *73121.1032@compuserve.com, AllAbtBeer-@aol.com.* Website: *http://www.allaboutbeer.com.* Bimonthly, oldest consumer beer magazine in America.

American Brewer, P.O. Box 510, Hayward CA 94543-0510. Phone 800-646-2701. E-mail: *AmBrew@aol.com.* Slick magazine devoted to the business of beer, published five times a year.

American Breweriana Journal, P.O. Box 11157, Pueblo CO 81001. The bimonthly journal of the American Breweriana Association, covering beer-related collectibles.

BarleyCorn, P.O. Box 549, Frederick MD 21705. Phone 301-831-3759. Eight-times-a-year national brewspaper.

Bay Schooner, PO Box 549, Frederick MD 21705. Phone 301-831-3759. Eight-times-a-year paper, regional sister to the above BarleyCorn, covering Mid-Atlantic brew news.

Beer the Magazine, P.O. Box 717, Hayward CA 94543-0717. Phone 800-646-2701. E-mail: *Beermag@aol.com*. Website: *http:// www.ambrew.com/*. Five-times-a-year slick magazine aimed at beer drinkers.

Beer & Tavern Chronicle, 244 Madison Avenue, Suite 164, New York NY 10016. Phone 212-685-8334. National monthly brewspaper.

Beer Travelers, P.O. Box 187, Washington IL 61571. E-mail: *Beer-Trav@aol.com*. Monthly newsletter listing and reviewing good bars and brewpubs across America.

Brewers Digest, 4049 W. Peterson Avenue, Chicago IL 60646. Phone 312-463-7848. Monthly for professional brewers.

Brewing Techniques, P.O. Box 3222, Eugene OR 97403. Phone 800-427-2993. E-mail: *btcirc@aol.com*. Website: *http://www.realbeer.com/ brewing techniques/*. Bimonthly magazine for brewers, both home and commercial.

Brew Magazine, 1120 Mulberry Street, Des Moines IA 50309. Phone 800-340-4929. E-mail: *brewmag@netins.net*. Slick bimonthly covering beer and brewing.

Celebrator Beer News, P.O. Box 375, Hayward CA 94543. Phone 800-430-BEER. E-mail: *70540.1747@compuserve.com, tdalldorf-@celebrator.com*. Website: *http://realbeer.com/celebrator/*. Bimonthly brewspaper with national/international coverage that focuses on the West.

Great Lakes Brewing, 214 Muegel Road, East Amherst NY 14051. E-mail: *glbrewing@aol.com*. Brewspaper covering North Central and Northeastern states.

Juice, P.O. Box 9068, Berkeley CA 94709. Phone 800-604-JUICE. E-mail: *GetJuice@aol.com*. Bimonthly covering good beer, wine, liquor, tea, coffee.

Malt Advocate, 3416 Oak Hill Road, Emmaus PA 18049. Phone 800-610-MALT. E-mail: *maltman999@aol.com, 75022.2401@-compuserve.com*. Website: *http://www.realbeer.com/maltadvocate/*. Quarterly magazine of the Malt Society, covering beer and malt whisky.

Microbrewery Times, P.O. Box 22341, Eugene OR 97402. Phone 503-686-2108. E-mail: *micbrew@teleport.com*. Bimonthly covering West Coast microbreweries.

Midwest Beer Notes, 339 Sixth Avenue, Clayton WI 54004. Phone 715-948-2990. E-mail: *70413.3453@compuserve.com*. Eight issues a year covering the Midwest beer scene.

Modern Brewery Age, 50 Day Street, Norwalk CT 06854. Phone 203-853-6015. Weekly newspaper, bimonthly magazine for professional brewers.

The New Brewer, P.O. Box 1679, Boulder CO 80306-1679. Phone 303-447-0816. E-mail: *orders@aob.org*. Website: *http://www.aob.org/aob/*. A bimonthly published by the Institute for Brewing Studies.

Northwest Beer Journal, 2626 Lodgepole Drive SE, Port Orchard WA 98366.

Northwest Brew News, 22833 Bothell-Everett Highway, Suite 1139, Bothell WA 98021-9365. Phone 206-742-5327. E-mail: *Beernews@aol.com*. Bimonthly brewsletter covering beer and brewing in the Northwestern states.

On Tap, P.O. Box 71, Clemson SC 29633. Phone 803-654-3360. Bimonthly covering national and international beer scene.

Rocky Mountain Brews, P.O. Box 2171 Fort Collins CO 80522. Monthly covering mountain states.

Southern Draft Brew News, 702 Sailfish Road, Winter Springs FL 32708. Phone 800-206-7179. E-mail: *BrewNews@aol.com, brewnews@southerndraft.com*. Website: *realbeer.com/sodraft*. Bimonthly brewspaper focusing on beer news in ten Southeastern states.

Southwest Brewing News, 1505 Lupine Lane, Austin TX 78741. Phone 512-443-3607. E-mail: *swbrewing@aol.com*. Bimonthly brewspaper with a regional focus.

Suds 'n Stuff, 4764 Galicia Way, Oceanside CA 92056. Phone 800-457-6543. Bimonthly covering beer on the West Coast.

What's On Tap, P.O. Box 7779, Berkeley CA 94707-7779. Phone 800-434-7779. E-mail: *71151.3321@compuserve.com*. Ten issues a year, covering beer on the West Coast.

Yankee Brew News, P.O. Box 520250, Winthrop MA 02152, Phone 800-4BEER12. E-mail: *70571.3252@compuserve.com*. Bimonthly brewspaper covering beer and brewing in New England and eastern Canada.

Zymurgy, P.O. Box 1679, Boulder CO 80306-1679. Phone 303-447-0816. E-mail: *orders@aob.org*. Website: *http://www.aob.org/aob/*. Five-times-a-year journal of the American Homebrewers Association.

A Beer Glossary

Adjunct—Anything introduced during the brewing process, aside from barley malt, to provide sugars for fermentation, including rice, corn, corn sugar and other unmalted grains.

Alcohol—Intoxicating liquid (ethyl alcohol, actually) produced by fermentation of malt sugars by yeast. Measured by volume internationally or, in America, by weight.

Alcohol by Volume (ABV)—Percentage of alcohol content in a beverage, by volume. The common measure for European beers. *See* Original Gravity.

Alcohol by Weight—Percentage of alcohol content in a beverage, by weight. Five grams of alcohol in 100 centiliters of beer equal 5 percent alcohol by weight. The common American measure, it is usually about 20 percent lower than the ABV. Five percent ABV would equal about 4 percent alcohol by weight.

Ale—Beer fermented more quickly at warmer temperatures than lager, with top-fermenting yeast.

Barley—The cereal grain, a member of the grass family, used in brewing. Two-rowed and six-rowed barley, referring to the rows of grain, are the two main families of barley used in brewing.

Barrel—About 31 gallons in the United States, 36 imperial gallons (a barrel roughly one-third larger) in Britain.

Beer—1. Any alcoholic beverage created from fermenting malt barley and/or other cereals. 2. In England, ale or bitter—as opposed to lager. *See* Ale and Lager.

Black and Tan—A mixture of stout and pale ale or lager.

Body—The weight and feel of a beer on the palate, from thin or watery to full-bodied.

Bottle-Conditioned—A secondary fermentation that occurs by adding yeast and sugars to the beer before it is bottled. Leaves a sediment that can be removed by decanting.

Brew on Premises (BOP)—Rental brewing operations that allow do-it-yourself brewers to come in and use their facilities for making their own recipes.

Brewpub—Bar and/or restaurant serving beer made on the premises.

CAMRA—The Campaign for Real Ale, the British-based consumer education and lobbying group that promotes craft brewing around the world, and traditional British brewing at home.

Cask-Conditioned—Unfiltered, unpasteurized beer that undergoes a secondary fermentation in the barrel.

Cold-Filtered—Beer that has been filtered to remove sediment and contaminants and make the beer clearer. All filtered beer is filtered at cold temperatures.

Contract Brewer—A brewing operation that does not own a brewery, and instead has another brewery make beer to its specifications.

Draft Beer—Beer drawn from kegs or barrels. Also called tap beer in America, and draught beer in Britain.

Draft Lines—The pipes or hoses connecting bar taps to barrels of beer that are often in the basement of the establishment.

Fermentation—The process by which yeast acts on the sugars in wort to create a number of by-products, including alcohol and carbon dioxide.

Flights—Samples of different beers in small tasting glasses, a feature of many brewpubs and good beer bars.

Guest Beer—A special beer on offer temporarily, usually by a brewpub, often in a style that does not compete locally with any of its own styles.

Hefe—The German word for yeast, often used as a prefix for bottle-conditioned beers.

Hops—Flowers from a vine, a member of the thistle family, related to cannabis, used for flavor and aroma in brewing, and in some beer styles as a preservative. Different varieties of hops produce different tastes in beer.

Lager—Beer fermented more slowly, at cooler temperatures than ale, with bottom-fermenting yeast, and then aged to smooth out rough flavors and aromas.

Lightstruck—*See* Skunked.

Malt—Barley that has been prepared for brewing: soaked in water, allowed to germinate and kiln-dried or roasted. Also called malted barley and barley malt.

Malt Liquor—American term for a stronger version of the typical mass-market lager, usually 6 or 7 percent ABV.

Mash—In the brewing process, the porridge-like blend of water and ground malt that releases sugars for brewing. *See* Wort.

Microbrewery—Currently, any brewery that produces fewer than fifteen thousand barrels of beer a year, but the definition has shifted upward several times.

Mouthfeel—Literally how beer feels in the mouth before swallowing, from light to heavy, thick to thin, watery to sticky.

Nose—The aroma or bouquet of beer.

Oktoberfest—The traditional autumn beer festival held in Munich over the sixteen days ending on the first Sunday in October; the term now refers to many local beer festivals around the world.

Original Gravity (OG)—A representation of the percentage of sugars in the wort before fermentation; the higher the OG, the stronger the beer.

Oxidation—The cardboard-like aftertaste that results from fresh beer being exposed to oxygen for too long before drinking.

Pasteurization—The process of heating beer after fermentation, which kills off any remaining live yeast and bacteria, reducing the risk of infection and spoilage. *See* Bottle-Conditioned.

Real Ale—The term used by CAMRA for traditional cask-conditioned ale.

Regional Brewery—Brewery producing 15,000 to 500,000 barrels of beer a year, irrespective of where it is distributed.

Reinheitsgebot—The Bavarian Purity Law, dating to 1516, which holds that beer can be made only with water, hops, malted barley (or wheat) and yeast—nothing else.

Shelf Life—The amount of time after bottling, three to four months for most American beers, before the beer begins to taste stale.

Skunked—Also called lightstruck, the "skunky" smell and/or taste that results from beer, particularly pale lagers and other light-colored beer in green or clear bottles, being exposed to too much light, particularly direct sunlight. Brown bottles help prevent skunking.

Trappist—The order of monks known for its six breweries and strong, flavorful ales.

Wort—Sweet liquid derived from the mash; it is boiled, with hops, and then fermented to become beer.

Yeast—Microscopic single-cell fungus that is used during brewing to consume sugars in the wort, producing alcohol, carbon dioxide, aromas and flavors. Thousands of strains are available to brewers, each with its own characteristics.

Zymurgy—The science of fermented beverages.

Index

About the Authors

GARRETT OLIVER, brewmaster at the Brooklyn Brewery, is one of America's most sought-after writers and lecturers on beer. He has judged both the Great American and Great British Beer Festivals, has spoken before CAMRA conferences on classic British beer styles, and has written on beer and brewing for many publications, including *Ale Street News, All About Beer, Malt Advocate* and *Cigar Aficionado*. An expert on matching food and beer, he has appeared on many network television programs about good beer and food, and has hosted hundreds of beer dinners and tastings. As a brewer, he is well known for his robust, flavorful interpretations of traditional beer styles.

TIMOTHY HARPER, one of the original partners in the Brooklyn Brewery, is a journalist, author and lawyer who writes and consults on many topics, including international politics, economics, law, business, travel and communications technology. A native of Peoria, Ill., and a former national correspondent for the Associated Press, he became interested in good beer during the nine years he lived and worked in Europe. He has written on beer and the brewing industry for a wide variety of American and international publications. His previous books include *The Good Beer Guide to New York, Cracking the New European Markets, The US-EC Trade Directory, Passport UK* and *Chicago: The Insight CityGuide*.